FREE COMPOSITION

Longman Music Series

Series Editor: Gerald Warfield

FREE COMPOSITION

(*Der freie Satz*)

Volume III of New Musical Theories and Fantasies

Heinrich Schenker

Semper idem
sed non
eodem modo

Translated and edited by Ernst Oster

LONGMAN   New York and London
Published in cooperation with the American Musicological Society

FREE COMPOSITION
(Der freie Satz)

Longman Inc., New York
Associated companies, branches, and representatives
throughout the world.

Developmental Editor: Gordon T. R. Anderson
Interior Design: Albert M. Cetta
Cover Design: Dan Serrano
Manufacturing and Production Supervisor: Louis Gaber
Composition: Kingsport Press
Printing: The Murray Printing Company
Binding: The Book Press

Library of Congress Cataloging in Publication Data

Schenker, Heinrich, 1868–1935.
  Free composition (Der freie Satz)

  (Longman music series)
  "Published in cooperation with the American Musi-
cological Society."
  "The text is based mainly on the second German edition
(ed. Oswald Jonas, Vienna, 1956), but the first edition
(Vienna, 1935) was also consulted."
  Includes bibliographical references.
  1. Music—Theory. 2. Counterpoint. I. Oster,
Ernst. II. Jonas, Oswald. III. Title.
IV. Title: Der freie Satz.
MT40.S29213   781   79–14797

Manufactured in the United States of America

9 8 7 6 5 4 3 2 1

HEINRICH SCHENKER was born in Podhyce (Podgajcy), Galicia, on June 19, 1868. (His birthplace lies in what is today the western region of the Ukraine, near L'vov.) As a youth he demonstrated great talent as a pianist and received encouragement from Carl Mikuli, a student of Chopin. He emigrated to Vienna where, in the late 1880s, he studied at the Conservatory and also earned the Dr. Jur. degree at the University.

Before the appearance in 1906 of his first major theoretical work, *Harmonielehre*, Schenker was active chiefly as a practical musician—as a pianist, a conductor, an editor, and a composer. He toured as accompanist to one of the greatest singers of the period, the Dutch baritone Johannes Messchaert. In connection with his activity as a conductor, he made continuo realizations and arrangements of music of earlier periods, including Bach cantatas, piano concerti by C.P.E. Bach, and organ concerti by Handel. His compositions gained the approval of Brahms, who recommended them to his publisher, Simrock. Busoni also took an interest in Schenker's music and programmed several of his works on a concert series in Berlin beginning around 1905.

During the 1890s Schenker wrote essays in musical criticism for various periodicals in Berlin, Leipzig, and Vienna. It was partly the desire to establish a more precise foundation for criticism, both of composition and of performance, that motivated Schenker to embark upon the path that led to the connected series of original theoretical works culminating with *Free Composition*. Dissatisfied with the prevalent approach to music theory with its abstract speculations (for example, the question of harmonic "dualism") and rigid formal schemata, Schenker set out to discover and formulate the principles of tonal art as they were manifested in the greatest products of that art. For Schenker, it was their intimate connection to the musical artwork that set his theories apart from all others then in vogue. Thus the cover of *Harmonielehre* attributes the work merely to *"einem Künstler,"* without further specification of the artist's identity.

v

From the writing of *Harmonielehre* until the end of his life, Schenker devoted himself primarily to his theoretical work, to editing masterworks, and to teaching musical interpretation to theorists and performers on an individual basis. Schenker died in Vienna on January 22, 1935.

For my beloved wife

Contents

PART III   THE FOREGROUND

Chapter 1   The Concepts of Strict Counterpoint

Chapter 2   The Later Structural Levels

Chapter 3   Specific Foreground Events

CONTENTS

Series Editor's Acknowledgment

Ernst Oster died before the initial stages of the publication of *Free Composition* had begun. As a result, many authorial responsibilities for the production of the book had to be assumed by friends and colleagues whom we would like to thank for their gracious and dedicated assistance.

Gail Rehman, who checked the entire translation, was meticulous in proofreading, checking data, translating and preparing copy for the example volume, and offering invaluable suggestions about all phases of production.

While Ernst Oster restored some deletions made by Oswald Jonas in the second German edition, he retained others and deleted some additional passages which he mentions in the Preface to the English Edition. However, for the sake of comprehensiveness it was decided to provide these passages in an appendix. John Rothgeb translated the deleted passages which appear in Appendix 4. He checked the entire translation, and several footnotes have been added which bear his initials. In addition, he provided the biographical sketch of Schenker and was a second proofreader for the entire text.

Gratitude is due the American Musicological Society for financial support; its president, James Haar, and the chairman of the editorial committee, Martin Picker, gave enthusiastic encouragement to the publication.

Gerald Warfield

Preface to the English Edition

Almost half a century has passed since the publication of this book shortly after Heinrich Schenker's death in 1935. The political events of the subsequent years naturally made it impossible for Schenker's ideas to become widely known in Europe;*1 to this day they find relatively little recognition there, even in German-speaking countries. In contrast to this, interest in Schenker has been growing at an ever-increasing pace in the United States. More and more colleges and universities are offering courses devoted to Schenker's theories, his name appears almost regularly in the programs of musical conventions, and, especially during the past decade, the number of "Schenker-oriented" or more or less "Schenker-influenced" books has increased to a remarkable degree.

In view of this situation, it is astonishing that of Schenker's major works only one has been available in English up to now: his *Harmonielehre*, originally published in 1906. (This book is actually volume one of a larger, three-volume work which

Schenker entitled *Neue musikalische Theorien und Phantasien*. The second volume of this comprehensive work was *Kontrapunkt*, whose two parts appeared in 1910 and 1922, and the third is the present volume, *Der freie Satz*.) In *Harmonielehre*,*2 Schenker laid the foundation for the *harmonic* aspect of his theory. But the specific *voice-leading* aspect of the theory was a considerably later development that begins rather suddenly in 1919. The first publication to reflect this was his analysis of Beethoven's Sonata op. 101,*3 which contains the first rudimentary examples of "graphic" notation, that is, of specifically *linear* reductions. During the ensuing 15 years of Schenker's life, the development of the concept of voice-leading progressed with astonishing rapidity and brilliance; the present volume forms the culmination of this process, for it is here that the idea of voice-leading receives its most detailed and precise formulation. Since voice-leading is the chief

---

*1. He was Jewish and his works were suppressed by the National-Socialist government. (Oster)

*2. *Harmony* (University of Chicago Press and M.I.T. Press). See Appendix 3: "Works of Heinrich Schenker." (Oster)

*3. See Appendix 3: "Works of Heinrich Schenker." (Oster)

subject of *Der freie Satz*, the reading of this volume requires at least a rudimentary understanding of Schenker's earlier ideas. The English-speaking reader has, as noted, the translation of *Harmony*. In addition, its editor, Oswald Jonas, has provided an excellent introduction and a profuse number of footnotes that relate the material of this book to Schenker's later works. But the unfortunate fact remains that, with the exception of a few isolated essays and analyses, none of these later works has been published in English or, for that matter, in any language other than German. The almost unavoidable result is that much that has been said and written about Schenker shows an incomplete understanding and, consequently, distortion of his original thoughts. It is to be hoped that the appearance of the present translation, by making Schenker's most important ideas accessible to a wider musical public, will at least partly remedy this situation.

Translating this important contribution to music theory has presented some rather special problems. The first of these arises from the sheer breadth of Schenker's thought, which ranged over all the aspects of music and attempted to elucidate them in the most detailed and penetrating way. The intellectual demands which Schenker makes of us come directly from the scope and depth of this achievement. To help the reader meet these demands, I would like to offer some remarks about the difficulties of language and style in the work and about the translation itself.

Schenker was concerned about making the book as concise as possible in order that it might not become unmanageably large. Therefore his comments on the musical examples and his definitions of terms are often quite brief—sometimes too brief to be understood. I could do little to remedy this other than to make occasional editorial insertions or a footnote.

The way in which the book was written down makes for another difficulty. Schenker dictated the greater part of his later works to his wife, who transcribed them from shorthand into ordinary script. Though Schenker then made corrections, im-provements, and additions, the general effect often remains that of spoken language with its inevitable omissions and poorly chosen words. On the other hand, this very same spoken quality produces a poetic, sometimes almost rhapsodic, quality in the German original. To make sure that the thought was always understandable, it became necessary for me to paraphrase in a few places, and in two instances (see "Reaching-over," at § 134, and "Sonata Form," at § 316) substantial editorial commentary seemed the best way to make the material clear.

The difficulties of style and language make the translator's task an arduous one, for he must follow the original as closely as possible lest the meaning be in the slightest degree modified. But faithfulness to Schenker's concise style results in an English that the reader will occasionally find awkward. In these instances I must ask the reader's indulgence and direct his attention to the thought rather than to its elegant expression.

The most conspicuous problem which the book presents to the translator is its title: there is no English equivalent for *Der freie Satz*. The literal translation "Free Composition" might give the misleading impression that the book is a treatise on free-style compositions such as fantasies. In order to preclude such misunderstanding, I decided to retain the original German as a subtitle; it is necessary, however, to indicate what Schenker meant by "freier Satz." As Oswald Jonas points out in the preface to the second German edition (p. xvi of this book), Schenker originally meant to publish the first version of *Der freie Satz* as the third volume (part VII) of his *Kontrapunkt*. He intended to demonstrate that the voice-leading principles of strict counterpoint *(der strenge Satz)* also underlie the voice-leading events of actual "free" compositions, that is, of music written in *freier Satz*. (The emphasis is on *Satz*, meaning contrapuntal, or voice-leading, structure.) In *freier Satz*, the original "strict" laws of counterpoint are extended and prolonged, not just through freer treatment, but particularly through the composing-out process *(Auskomponierung)* and the inclusion of other aspects of music, notably harmony. So, too, the present, final version of *Der freie Satz* deals essentially with voice-leading: this remains the primary viewpoint even in chapters that concern themselves with other aspects of music such as diminution, rhythm, and, most remarkably, form.

The least of the difficulties encountered was to decide on English equivalents for Schenker's *terms*. Thanks to the work of Allen Forte and Felix Salzer, most of these terms have already found generally accepted English equivalents. My bilingual list, which appears in Appendix 5, includes these equivalents and supplies yet a few new ones.

It remains for me to say a few words about my editorial procedures. The text is based mainly on the second German edition (ed. Oswald Jonas, Vienna, 1956), but the first edition (Vienna, 1935) was also consulted. From the first edition I have reinstated a few short passages and, above all, the headings of the individual smaller sections. I have also corrected the many important misprints, such as wrong pitch-names and other musical symbols, and errors in references. Finally, I have corrected a few misengravings which I overlooked when helping to prepare the example volume in 1956.

In his editorial preface Oswald Jonas mentions briefly that he omitted a number of passages that have no bearing on the musical content of the work. These passages were almost exclusively taken from Schenker's introduction and the first chapter, "The Background." (The introduction and first chapter in the original edition give the impression of being a collection of more or less unrelated remarks and aphorisms; it is impossible to determine whether this material was given its final, published form by Schenker himself or by an editor.) I felt it best to omit several additional passages of a very general, sometimes semiphilosophical nature here; these omissions are not expressly indicated. The few deletions in later parts of the book, made either by Jonas or by me, are mentioned in footnotes.[*4]

Schenker's cross-references to other parts of the text and to figures are differentiated from those of the editors by the following system of brackets: (Schenker), [Jonas], ⟨Oster⟩. My own editorial insertions are also set off by ⟨ ⟩'s.

In closing, I would like to turn from matters of text and translation in order to share some of my experiences of this work with its future readers. A very practical suggestion to the uninitiated reader might be that he adopt a somewhat unusual procedure and not begin at the beginning. The opening part, "The Background," assumes a more than superficial knowledge of the whole of Schenker's system; without this knowledge this part would probably remain largely meaningless. The reader should instead begin with the section on diminution (§§ 251 ff.), a very good introduction to Schenker's way of thinking, and continue through the next three sections (up to § 275). Next, he should study part III, "The Foreground," in its entirety, skipping, however, the difficult section on linear progressions (§§ 203 to 229). At this point, he will be ready to tackle the opening part—"The Background." Of course, rereadings and continued use of the example volume in reference to particular compositions will lead to an ever greater understanding of the work.

As an aid to studying this book I would strongly advise the reader to have at hand Schenker's *Five Graphic Music Analyses*.[*5] This publication shows, as no other work from Schenker's late period does, the complete picture of all the structural levels. (This was, unfortunately, not possible for Schenker in the present work, for reasons of space limitation.) *Der freie Satz* makes frequent reference to the *Five Graphic Analyses* and the five compositions it contains.

In conclusion I would very much like to extend my thanks to several friends and associates for their helpful efforts: Allen Forte helped the work move forward in many ways; Charles Burkhart made several helpful suggestions; Carl Schachter

---

[*4.] All deletions have, in fact, been reinstated in Appendix 4. For an explanation, see "Series Editor's Acknowledgment," p. vii.

[*5.] See Appendix 3: "Works of Heinrich Schenker." (Oster).

showed unflagging interest in the work and gave it his critical attention; Oswald Jonas made necessary diplomatic overtures on behalf of the work; Gail Rehman spent many hours in the huge undertaking of preparing the final typescript; finally I must thank the Robert Owen Lehman Foundation for a grant of funds which enabled me to undertake this translation.

New York, 1977   Ernst Oster

Preface to the Second German Edition

My concepts present, for the first time, a genuine theory of tonal language.

Free Composition

This book, here published in a new form, first appeared in 1935, only a few months after the death of its author. It is deeply to be regretted that Heinrich Schenker was not granted to see this crowning achievement of his most productive life in print. We can take comfort only in the fact that his death spared him from what might well have been a dire fate in the storm of the years that followed. The controversy surrounding Schenker's work is not at an end, but the number of those who are convinced of the truth of his teaching steadily increases. The time of indifference—when one might merely have overlooked his work without saying yes or no to it—is over.

If I speak of this book as the crowning achievement of Schenker's work, this phrase must also describe the book's conception and the attainment of its final form. For twenty years it occupied Schenker's mind and musical thought, from initial ideas to several attempts to write down the entire work in a more or less definitive form. Even the final manuscript is full of numerous changes, revisions, and significant improvements.[1] This slow process toward final formulation can also be seen in several other of Schenker's major writings. For example, the germinal thoughts of his *Harmonielehre*, published in 1906, had already appeared in 1895 in the brochure "Der Geist der musikalischen Technik" ("The Spirit of Musical Technique"), and important ideas for his monograph *Beethovens Neunte Sinfonie* (1912) can be found in a 1901 newspaper article *(Wiener Abendpost)* entitled "Beethoven-Retouche" ("Retouching Beethoven").

A complete history of *Der freie Satz* cannot, of course, be presented here. This belongs to the biography of Schenker, which sooner or later must be written.[2] Sketches, thoughts quickly jotted down on thousands of little pieces of paper, as well as more or less integrated discussions, even in fair copy, are lying in the folders which were left after his death.[3] The earliest version of the book was begun in 1915. It gives us

---

[1]. The editor had opportunity to examine the manuscript through the kindness of Mr. Anthony van Hoboken, who did so much to make the first edition possible. (Jonas)

[2]. A brief survey by this editor of the development of Schenker's theories can be found in the Introduction to the English edition of *Harmony*. (Jonas)

[3]. These folders, along with a great deal of other unpublished material, including a "Lehre des Vortrags" (an essay on "Performance"), are in the possession of Mr. Ernst Oster, to whom the editor is especially indebted for his careful revision of the example volume. (Jonas) ⟨They are now known as the Oster Collection, and are housed in the Music Division of the New York Public Library, Special Collections. (Rothgeb)⟩

evidence that Schenker first thought of the book as a continuation of his work on counterpoint: "free composition," section VII of the theory of counterpoint. Here he meant to show how the laws of strict counterpoint continued to operate in free composition. Even at this point, Schenker speaks of the "composing-out" of the scale degree and of "horizontalization." The concept of the "fundamental line" already appears, first as "melodic line," then as "line," graphically indicated by vertical arrows over the relevant notes of the example. In a later version there is a special section on "piano style" *(Klaviersatz)*, and also a section devoted to thoroughbass.

The various later stages in the development of his theories found their expression in a series of publications—*Der Tonwille* and *Jahrbücher*—which appeared in the nineteen-twenties. In them Schenker refers to his definitive, concluding work, even though it was yet to appear. Thus, one must regard *Der freie Satz* as the definitive form, indeed the codification of Schenker's concepts. The clarification and formulation of the theory pursued and possessed its creator like a demon. He felt that it was his mission to present this concept of the masterworks to the world, to reveal the laws of art which he saw fulfilled in the works of the great masters—and in them alone—according to his motto *semper idem sed non eodem modo* ("always the same, but not in the same way").

In 1921, on his departure for a vacation in the Tyrolean Alps, Schenker wrote to his beloved friend and helper, Moritz Violin, "Now, as I said, to the Tyrol, and then further climbing, climbing to the peaks of II^3 *(Freier Satz)!*" And later (July 1928), again to Violin, documenting the practical purpose of the work: *"Der freie Satz,* which I am busy putting into final form, will include, in addition to the text, a great many examples in a separate volume. These are intended expressly for the teacher, as instructional material."

May the work now fulfill the wish of its author in this new edition!

Because Schenker himself could not supervise the printing of his work and because publication was brought about as quickly as possible (perhaps out of false piety), the form of the first edition, unfortunately, left something to be desired. Aside from an unusually large number of misprints, both in the text and the example volume, the layout itself was highly questionable. Its failure to present an organized picture to the eye only served to make a difficult work even more difficult. Here, then, lay the editor's task: to present the text in a fashion that is, above all, clearer to the eye. In the course of this endeavor some stylistic changes proved necessary. An additional number of references and cross-references were also provided, which should aid the reader in comprehending the work. The references added by the editor are enclosed in brackets. The editor also felt himself justified in omitting certain passages which have no bearing on the musical content.

Finally, the editor would like to express his gratitude both to the Austrian Ministry of Education and to the president of the Academy for Music and the Performing Arts, Professor Dr. Hans Sittner. Their active support made it possible for the editor to carry out his tasks in Vienna and for him to arouse and maintain an interest in Schenker's teachings during this time by giving a course at the Academy in the work of Heinrich Schenker.

Vienna, 1955   Oswald Jonas

Introduction to the English Edition

It is entirely appropriate that the English translation of Heinrich Schenker's *Der freie Satz* be published in the United States, since it is here that Schenker's ideas have gained widest acceptance and have been broadly disseminated.

The tradition of instruction in Schenker's theory in the United States began with Hans Weisse (1892–1940), who initiated courses at the Mannes School of Music in New York after his arrival from Vienna in 1931. In Vienna he had taught several young Americans, notably William J. Mitchell (1906–1971), who later became an eminent scholar and professor at Columbia University. The tradition continued with Felix Salzer (b. 1904) at the Mannes School, a student of Schenker and Weisse, with Oswald Jonas (1897–1978), a student of Schenker, at Roosevelt College in Chicago, and with Ernst Oster (1909–1977), a student of Jonas, who taught in his private studio in New York for a number of years before being appointed to the faculties of the New England Conservatory of Music and the Mannes College of Music. In a growing number of institutions of higher learning in the United States the tradition continues today.

No one was better qualified to undertake the definitive translation of *Der freie Satz* than Ernst Oster. His entire life was devoted to Schenker, to understanding his writings in as much depth as possible, to applying the analytical procedures to a large number of compositions, and to teaching.*1

From 1938 Oster was the sole custodian of most of the Schenker *Nachlass*, a large collection of unpublished analytical and other material, including the manuscript of an earlier version of *Der freie Satz*, which had been given to him by Mrs. Schenker in Vienna in order to save it from destruction by the invading German forces. Access to these documents enabled Oster to understand Schenker's work methods and creative

*1. Some of Oster's own excellent contributions include "The Dramatic Character of the Egmont Overture," *Musicology*, vol. 2, no. 3, 1949; "Chopin's Fantasie-Impromptu; op. 66: A Tribute to Beethoven," *Musicology*, vol. 1, no. 4, 1947; "Register and the Large-Scale Connection" and "An Analysis of Mozart's Menuetto, K.355" republished in Yeston, Maury, ed., *Readings in Schenker Analysis and Other Approaches*, Yale University Press, New Haven, 1977.

processes in a special way not available to anyone else. Thus, it is not surprising that the English language translation of *Der freie Satz* is more lucid than the original German in a number of instances. Moreover, a number of mistakes that persisted through the second German edition were corrected, as well as errors in the volume of musical examples.

The publication history of *Der freie Satz* is rather unusual. It was brought out posthumously (as indicated in Oswald Jonas's Preface to the Second German Edition), so that Schenker did not have the opportunity to correct proofs and to make changes in the manner ordinarily available to an author. Responsibility for the first edition was assumed by Schenker's students, Oswald Jonas and Moritz Violin. The volume was hastily prepared for publication, with the unfortunate consequences described by Jonas in his Preface. Again, the English translation will prove to be superior to both German editions in clarity as well as in format.

The modern-day English language reader may be somewhat puzzled, or perhaps even offended, by the polemical and quasi-philosophical material in Schenker's introduction and elsewhere, most of which was deleted from the second edition, but restored to the English translation in an appendix. In part, this material is typical of many other German language authors of an older period; in part, it is characteristic of Schenker, and must be placed in proper perspective. Almost none of the material bears substantive relation to the musical concepts that he developed during his lifetime and, from that standpoint, can be disregarded; it is, however, part of the man and his work. The extreme German nationalism which is evident in other portions of Schenker's published writings is not very apparent in *Der freie Satz*. Schenker's political views would certainly have changed radically had he lived to witness the 1938 *Anschluss* of Austria and its aftermath.

Schenker's polemics against the musical establishment must also be understood in the context of the time and with respect to the way in which his work was received. During Schenker's lifetime, instruction in music theory almost completely disregarded the traditional disciplines of species counterpoint (after Fux) and figured bass (for which Schenker cites C.P.E. Bach). "This false theory" to which he refers in his introduction is not specifically identified. However, he probably had in mind the German theorists of the early part of the 19th century, A.B. Marx (1795–1866) and Gottfried Weber (1779–1839) among them, and the most influential theorist in Vienna, Simon Sechter (1788–1867). And surely he would have included Hugo Riemann (1849–1919), whose Rameau-influenced theory of harmony dominated instruction in German music institutions at the time Schenker completed *Der freie Satz* (and beyond). Schenker felt, justifiably so, that the traditional disciplines of species counterpoint and figured bass had demonstrated their worth in that they had been studied seriously by composers who had produced a large repertory of culturally significant and highly valued musical works. Brahms was the last of these, and, typically, Schenker dedicated his 1912 study of Beethoven's Ninth Symphony to the memory of that composer, "the last master of German composition." Thus, Schenker's view of the musical situation from the time he reached manhood to his death in 1935 was very pessimistic.

The other factor involved in Schenker's view of the musical situation was the reception accorded his writings. With the exception of the Ninth Symphony study mentioned above, his work was ignored by all but a few musicians—what Jonas has called "a conspiracy of silence." He was able to make a living as a pianist—and a very highly regarded one—in Vienna, accompanying well-known singers and participating in chamber music concerts. He also wrote newspaper critiques and, most important, gave lessons in piano, counterpoint, thorough-bass, and analysis in his private studio. However, he was excluded from the higher academic circles to which he should have had access. Hence, his bitterness against the musical establishment can be seen to have had a personal as well as a purely musical-intellectual basis.

A thorough understanding of Schenker's work requires many years of serious study, not only because of the extent and complexity of his writings, although that is, of course, an important factor, but also because of the time required to learn to construct analytical graphs. It is therefore important to bear in mind that although *Der freie Satz* is Schenker's final and summational work, it is not a textbook on analysis, but is organized as a presentation of this theory in accord with the major concept that governed his approach to the study of tonal music, the concept of structural levels.*2 It begins with the background level (the fundamental structure), proceeds to the middleground level with its prolongations of the fundamental structure, and finally deals with the complexities of the foreground, or what Schenker characterizes as the later levels. Something like sixty percent of the book is devoted to the foreground, a fact at variance with the opinion one has sometimes heard to the effect that Schenker was concerned only with background and middleground.

The traditional way of learning how to do Schenkerian analysis has been to study with someone who studied with Schenker or with a student of such a person. Only after much practical experience in constructing analytical graphs was reading of Schenker's work undertaken. For the reader of *Der freie Satz* who does not have a background of direct instruction in Schenkerian analysis, the advice given by Ernst Oster to begin with the later sections of the book—for example, with the section on diminution—is certainly excellent. To that should be added the exhortation to study the graphs in the example volume very carefully while reading the text.

The graphic methods that Schenker developed concurrently with his powerful concepts of musical structure are unique in the history of music theory and analysis. And he invested them with singular importance. He tells us that ". . . the graphic representation is part of the actual composition, not merely

*2. Only one of his writings, the first volume of *Kontrapunkt (Cantus Firmus und Zweistimmiger Satz)*, 1910, can be regarded as a textbook.

an educational means." (p. xxiii) In this remarkable statement, which at first seems puzzling, Schenker dramatizes the significance of the graphs: They are not to be regarded merely as pedagogical devices but rather as accurate representations of the musical structures.

It is valuable, if not absolutely necessary, to learn to read the graphs. This is because a particular example almost always contains information in graphic form that is not discussed in the text. With experience the serious reader will learn to read and understand the graphs. A survey of the graphic symbols may be of assistance, however, and the reader may wish to return to this part of the introduction as he begins to study the graphs. (Schenker, unfortunately, does not supply any explanations.)

Before undertaking this survey of Schenker's graphic notation it is essential to warn the reader that Schenker's use of the various symbols is flexible. The normative usage is discussed below; a completely systematic interpretation, however, is not possible, and any effort to do so would certainly be subject to serious errors. It is also necessary to point out that there are two basic kinds of graphs presented in the volume of examples, in addition to the examples which reproduce the composer's notation with few or no symbols added. The first of these may be characterized as "rhythmic." In a graph of this kind Schenker retains the basic durational values of the music, but enlarges them now and then to eliminate decorating notes (diminutions) which do not affect the basic voice-leading. An instance is figure 54, 15. Comparing the second measure of Schenker's example with the Bach score one finds that Schenker has omitted a turn, an anticipation, a trill, and a lower neighbor-note figure, thus reducing a complicated rhythmic succession to quarter note followed by half note. The second type of graph is the "structural" graph, in which some of the traditional durational note values are used to represent structural relations among the musical components. It is the structural graph that is the subject of the following exposition.

In general, the larger note values, half and whole notes, belong to the deeper structural levels, that is, to middleground and background. Beams and stems are used to connect components of the fundamental line and components of linear progressions at the middleground level. They are also used to connect the main bass notes of a span of music. Slurs delineate structurally cohesive motions involving two or more components (and thus are similar to performance slurs in ordinary notation). The doubly curved slur is used in the bass to show a motion from tonic to dominant via a secondary harmony such as supertonic or subdominant. Large parentheses are sometimes used (as in figure 12) to delimit passages that are in some way preparatory to the initial structural statement.

Usually, the half note with eighth-note flag indicates a bass note with special function, such as a third-divider. The large V marks a hiatus of some kind, such as a discontinuity in a linear progression or a break in an otherwise stepwise bass motion. The diagonal line serves a number of purposes, the most important of which are to show that a particular bass note and a particular soprano note belong together even though they do not coincide temporally, and to indicate an octave displacement of a note.

To designate components of the fundamental line, carets above scale-degree numbers are used. If a succession of such numbers is enclosed in parentheses, it means that the succession replicates the fundamental line but is not equivalent to it. The short double thin barline above the upper staff is the symbol for interruption of the progression of the fundamental line. A long-range connection of some kind between unison-related or octave-related notes (for example, an octave coupling) is indicated by a dotted line, and dotted lines are rarely used for any other purpose. Right brackets above the staff point to parallel fifths or octaves.

One frequently used graphic device requires special explanation: the beam connecting the down stem of the first note of a pair with the up stem of the other, or vice versa. One or both of the notes may have an additional stem (and flag). This is the symbol for an unfolding, one of the most important types of prolongations in free composition.

In addition to these symbols, which belong to Schenker's special graphic system, he employs conventional symbols, such as figured bass, Roman numerals to specify scale degrees upon which harmonies are based (often at more than one level), numerals to show contrapuntal patterns, such as 10–10, and letters designating form. Labels are frequently given to show the type of prolongation in operation at a particular point, such as initial ascent, or to indicate contrapuntal function, such as neighbor or passing note.

Finally, a symbol of which Schenker was very fond: the exclamation point. This graphic always marks an event that is unusual in some very striking respect, one to which Schenker wished to draw special attention.

Schenker's work has been very influential, especially during the past twenty years in the United States, as indicated at the beginning of this introduction. The general concept of structural levels, which Schenker began to develop as early as the 1906 *Harmonielehre*, has attracted the serious attention not only of scholars in music but also of scholars in other fields. Of these, structural linguistics is perhaps most prominently represented, for it is clear that the modern notion of leveled structures in language corresponds in a remarkable way to Schenker's concept of musical organization.

With the publication of the present volume, Schenker will be able to address the English-speaking portion of the musical world directly, thus permitting serious composers, performers, and scholars to judge for themselves the value of his work. It is hoped that the publication of the English translation of *Der freie Satz* will be followed by English translations of similarly high quality of Schenker's other important writings.

Hamden, Ct., 1978   Allen Forte

Introduction

But those who are like the master go forth,
And beauty and sense appear in all they see.

Hugo von Hofmannsthal:
"The Death of Titian"

To every thing there is a season, and a time to every purpose
under the heaven.

Ecclesiastes 3:1

The hearing ear, and the seeing eye,
The Lord hath made even both of them.

Proverbs 20:12

For more than a century, a theory has been taught which claims to provide access to the art of music, but in fact does quite the opposite. This false theory has obscured the musical discipline of previous centuries—that is, strict counterpoint and true thoroughbass. One might explain this break by looking to the impatience of the generation which lived during the third decade of the nineteenth century: dazzled by the tremendous outburst of genius which had come before them, they sought, as mediocrity usually does, to cut the shortest possible path to genius. This shortcut, a "practical" one, proved to be a failure, since it was essentially contrary to the historical background and artistic development of the great composers. It did not lead to the masters; indeed, it ultimately led away from them.

In our day it seems that this betrayal is no longer acceptable. The flight from music which characterizes our time is in truth a flight from an erroneous method of instruction, one which renders impossible an effective approach to art.

In opposition to this theory, I here present a new concept, one inherent in the works of the great masters; indeed, it is the very secret and source of their being: the concept of organic coherence. The following instructional plan provides a truly practical understanding of this concept. It is the only plan which corresponds exactly to the history and development of the masterworks, and so is the only feasible sequence: instruction in strict counterpoint (according to Fux-Schenker), in thoroughbass (according to J. S. and C. P. E. Bach), and in free composition

(Schenker). Free composition, finally, combines all the others, placing them in the service of the law of organic coherence as it is revealed in the fundamental structure (fundamental line and bass arpeggiation) in the background, the voice-leading transformations in the middleground, and ultimately in the appearance of the foreground.

C. P. E. Bach wrote his treatise on thoroughbass when he realized, to his grief, that the discipline of thoroughbass might disappear both in theory and in practice, because it was not really understood. His incomparably great work was motivated by a desire to do his utmost to save and clarify that discipline. Now the time has come for me—"To every thing there is a season," says the writer of Ecclesiastes—to proclaim the new concept of organic coherence and thereby to give the fullest possible expression to what the music of the masters was and must continue to be if we wish to keep it alive.

After the publication of some of my earlier works (those which already reached toward a clearer presentation of the new concept, especially the volumes of *Der Tonwille* and the three year-books, *Das Meisterwerk in der Musik*), the objection was often raised, "But did the masters also know about all this?" This objection, intended to be a trap, only betrays a lack of education. Those who raised the question were unaware that the masters in fact knew nothing of that false theory which for more than a century has been taught and learned as the only practical one. Neither J.S. Bach, C.P.E. Bach, Haydn, Mozart, Beethoven, Schubert, nor Mendelssohn knew any such concepts of harmony, thoroughbass, or form. And Brahms would have none of it! The objection can be answered very simply: the great composers in their works have shown a mastery which evinces, both in preconception and in total recall, such a clear overall comprehension of the laws of art that they need say no more to us; of necessity, every artistic act—indeed any action at all—requires a preconception of inner relationships. Consequently, should the reader find that what I say about a composition is verified in the work itself, he must surely concede that the masters did have a keen awareness of such relationships.

Those who advocate the present courses of instruction explain that their teaching is an expedient, that it is designed especially to lead the young and the moderately gifted to music. Even if this were true, we would still have to ask where, in what books, in which institutions can we find a way to the true art of music, and not merely an expedient? Where does the student or the serious music-lover learn what is essential to a true fugue, sonata, or symphony, what makes a true orchestration, what produces a truly great performance, true in the sense of the truth of the great masters? Expediency can give us no answer. This explanation is simply too weak. There is yet a further disgrace, for the so-called expedient could only have arisen through ignorance of the true nature of strict counterpoint and thoroughbass.

But the advocates of these erroneous teachings withhold the most important excuse: these theories have enabled many generations of teachers and musicians to earn their livelihood. Art in its truth and beauty has been ignored, but the practicalities of life have been assured, which made it easier to ascribe practicality to the teaching, whether honestly or dishonestly. These persons now fear lest my new teaching undermine their existence; they allege that its inherent difficulties make it unsuitable for large-scale exploitation in the schools. No such danger would exist, however, if teachers would devote themselves solely to one task, to training their students to hear music as the masters conceived it. The schools cannot pretend to breed composers (much less geniuses), though certain vain and arrogant young people would like them to do precisely that. Such sowing and reaping must be left to God. Only by the patient development of a truly perceptive ear can one grow to understand the meaning of what the masters learned and experienced. If a student, under firm discipline, is brought to recognize and experience the laws of music, he will also grow to love them. He will perceive that the goal toward which he strives is so meaningful and noble that it will compensate for the fact that he himself may lack a genuine talent for composition. Thus my teaching, in contrast to more rapid methods, slows the tempo of the educational process. This not only leads the student to genuine knowledge, but also improves the morale of artistic activities in general. Surely it is time to put a stop to the teaching of music in condensed courses, as languages are taught for use in commerce. It is also time that educational authorities cease to employ textbooks which are designed only for the less capable student. In spite of all this, I would hope for a great increase in educational activity, for a multiplicity of geniuses by nature demands also a multiplicity of nongeniuses. Even though it is fundamentally only vanity which causes the average musician to compose, we must be grateful that, through vanity itself, people are brought to dedicate themselves to art.

APHORISMS

All that is organic, every relatedness belongs to God and remains His gift, even when man creates the work and perceives that it is organic.

The whole of foreground, which men call chaos, God derives from His cosmos, the background. The eternal harmony of His eternal Being is grounded in this relationship.

The astronomer knows that every system is part of a higher system; the highest system of all is God himself, God the creator.

My concepts show that the art of music is much simpler than present-day teachings would have it appear. However, the fact that the simplicity does not lie on the surface makes it no less simple. Every surface, seen for itself alone, is of necessity confusing and always complex.

Specifically, my concepts demonstrate the following:

A firmly established linear progression can withstand even the most discordant friction of voices as they move contrapuntally.

A firmly established tonality can guide even a large number of chromatic phenomena securely back into the basic triad.

A performance, in serving background, middleground, and foreground, can employ the greatest variety of color. Even the richest and most varied resources of performance can be taught—and learned—with great exactness. On the other hand, commitment to background, middleground, and foreground excludes all arbitrary personal interpretation.

The musical examples which accompany this volume are not merely practical aids; they have the same power and conviction as the visual aspect of the printed composition itself (the foreground). That is, the graphic representation is part of the actual composition, not merely an educational means. Therefore the presentation of the examples required extreme care.[*1]

There is no doubt that the great composers—in contrast to performers and listeners—experienced even their most extended works not as a sum total of measures or pages, but as entities which could be heard and perceived as a whole.

Music is always an art—in its composition, in its performance, even in its history. Under no circumstances is it a science.

Since the linear progression, as I have described it, is one of the main elements of voice-leading, music is accessible to all races and creeds alike. He who masters such progressions in a creative sense, or learns to master them, produces art which is genuine and great.

In its linear progressions and other comparable tonal events, music mirrors the human soul in all its metamorphoses and moods—"alles Vergängliche ist nur ein Gleichnis" ("what is passing is only resemblance," Goethe). How different is today's idol, the machine! It simulates the organic, yet since its parts

---

*1. Since the task of revealing the world of the background in music fell to me, I was not spared the difficulty of finding symbols for it. This required many years. Furthermore, the engravers did not always demonstrate the necessary degree of understanding. For these reasons the illustrations in *Der Tonwille* and in the *Jahrbücher* do not always represent the definitive form. (Schenker)

are directed toward only a partial goal, a partial achievement, its totality is only an aggregate which has nothing in common with the human soul.

Every organic being yearns for another organic being. And art, which is organic, drives toward the organic human soul. However, in these times when man himself destroys his organic nature, how is he to respond to organically developed art?

It is certain that almost half of mankind is unmusical, even incapable of singing a folk tune—a sorry ratio, one which would be unthinkable in the case of language. How then can the ear be expected to hear polyphony, which is fundamental to the linear progression? The musical person, however, is certainly capable of recognizing linear progressions and of learning to use them. Therefore, let him apply himself to this task and refrain from the "experiments" so popular today and, alas, so costly. It follows that he must also be taught the theory of organic coherence; but this does not mean that the drafting of extensive analytical sketches *(Urlinie-Tafeln)* is necessary, since this would be tantamount to a demand for creative powers.*²

Philosophers and aestheticians will be able to establish a general theory of music as an art only after they have absorbed my concepts.*³ Ultimately it will be possible to set forth the highest principle which is common to all arts: the principle of inner tension and its corresponding outward fulfillment, a princi-

*2. Passage (A), omitted here, is supplied in Appendix 4: "Omissions from the Original German Edition."   (Rothgeb)

*3. Nietzsche complains ("The Will to Power," 838):

"What we lack in music is an aesthetic which would impose laws upon musicians and give them a conscience; and as a result of this we lack a real contest concerning 'principles.' For as musicians we laugh at Herbart's velleities just as heartily as we laugh at Schopenhauer's. As a matter of fact, great difficulties present themselves here. We no longer know on what basis to found our concepts of what is 'exemplary,' 'masterly,' 'perfect.' With the instincts of old loves and old admiration we grope about in a realm of values, and we almost believe, 'that is good which pleases us.' "   (Schenker)

ple which manifests itself differently in different material.

Man lives his whole life in a state of tension. Rarely does he experience fulfillment; art alone bestows on him fulfillment, but only through selection and condensation.

If a differentiation is to be made between "classic" and "romantic," only the degree of tension and fulfillment should be considered. A classical work will exceed a romantic one in the height and extent of its tension and in the profundity of its fulfillment, even if it may be a short work. Thus Schubert's *Wanderers Nachtlied ("Der du von dem Himmel bist")*⁴ is classical in every way by virtue of the power and tension of its few scale-degrees which unify the entire text.

The phenomenon of genius signifies a breath drawn from the unconscious, a breath which keeps the spirit ever young.*⁵

The cultivation of genius is neither romantic nor "living in the past." Rather it is the cultivation of a contemporaneity that bridges time; it is a strong belief in the absoluteness of art and its masters. If, after centuries have passed, only one person is once more capable of hearing music in the spirit of its coherence, then even in this one person music will again be resurrected in its absoluteness.

"And the Spirit of God moved upon the face of the waters." But the Creative Will has not yet been extinguished. Its fire continues in the ideas which men of genius bring to fruition for the inspiration and elevation of mankind. In the hour when an idea is born, mankind is graced with delight. That rapturous first hour in which the idea came to bless the world shall be hailed as ever young! Fortunate indeed are those who shared their young days with the birth and youth of that idea. They may justly proclaim the praise of their youth to their descendants!

Heinrich Schenker

*4. Fig. 37a in the example volume.   (Schenker)

*5. Passage (B), omitted here, is supplied in Appendix 4.   (Rothgeb)

Part I

The Background

Sometimes a most curious demand is made: that one should present experiences and perceptions without recourse to any kind of theoretical framework, leaving the student to establish his conviction as he will. But this demand cannot be fulfilled even by those who make it. For we never benefit from merely looking at an object. Looking becomes considering, considering becomes reflecting, reflecting becomes connecting. Thus, one can say that with every intent glance at the world we theorize. To execute this, to plan it consciously, with self-knowledge, with freedom, and, to use a daring word—with irony—requires a considerable degree of skill, particularly if the abstraction which we fear is to be harmless and if the empirical result which we hope to achieve is to be alive and useful.

Goethe, *Farbenlehre*

Chapter 1

The Background

Section 1:   The Concept of Background in General

The origin of every life, whether of nation, clan, or individual, becomes its destiny. Hegel defines destiny as "the manifestation of the inborn, original predisposition of each individual."

The inner law of origin accompanies all development and is ultimately part of the present.

Origin, development, and present I call background, middleground, and foreground; their union expresses the oneness of an individual, self-contained life.

In the secret perception of the interaction of origin, development, and present, as well as in the cultivation of this awareness until it becomes definite knowledge, lies what we call tradition: the conscious handing down, passing on of all relatedness which flows together into the wholeness of life.

To the person who is vitally aware of such relatedness, an idea is also part of real life, be that idea religion, art, science, law, the state. Therefore the principle of origin, development, and present as background, middleground, and foreground applies also to the life of the idea within us.*1

In order to comprehend what lives and moves behind the phenomena of life, behind ideas in general and art in particular, we ourselves require a definite background, a soul predisposed to accept the background. Such a soul, which constitutes a peculiar enhancement of nature in man—being almost more art than nature—is given only to genius.

The masses, however, lack the soul of genius. They are not aware of background, they have no feeling for the future. Their lives are merely an eternally disordered foreground, a continuous present without connection, unwinding chaotically in empty, animal fashion. It is always the individual who creates and transmits connection and coherence.*2

Until now it was unknown that a background and middle-

*1. Passage (C), omitted here, is supplied in Appendix 4: "Omissions from the Second German Edition."   (Rothgeb)

*2. Passage (D), omitted here, is supplied in Appendix 4.   (Rothgeb)

ground were also indispensable prerequisites to a musical work of art. My work is the first to introduce that concept.

Section 2: The Background in Music

The history of music reveals that music really began and flourished in ecclesiastical, royal, and aristocratic circles. This is confirmed by the fact that music developed polyphony, which must forever remain alien to the masses. For them music has always been and remains only an accompaniment to dance, march, or song: at best, a kind of utilitarian art, if one can accept the inherent contradiction. A feeling for such music fills head and heart, even those of the masses, but this feeling is not adequate to comprehend the true and lofty art of Bach, Handel, Haydn, Mozart, Beethoven. Indeed, it tends to lead away from those concepts and responses which are essential to music as an art. Although J.S. Bach in his *Passions* provides the aurally "visible," the greater portion of his art remains incomprehensible to the masses. Although Haydn offers them his oratorios, the absolute music of his chamber works and symphonies can never assume real importance in their lives. Mozart lets them view his operas, yet they will never comprehend the distance which separates his great operatic art from the operatic music of other composers. Beethoven jubilantly sings the praise of womanly fidelity in the visible *Fidelio*, and in the Ninth Symphony, together with Schiller, he sings the "Hymn to Joy"—nevertheless, the masses will never have access to the rest of his art.

But who can make the masses realize that, contrary to their impression, the highest art of the genius takes part in human life as they themselves live it, and that this high art furthers life and health just as milk and bread do, and can lead to Eros in the way any sacrament does? It is useless, therefore, to look to the masses for the support of art—an effort which is being made everywhere today. Indeed, it is highly probable that this effort will prevent our time from developing into a background

for the music of the future, into one as valid as was the period a thousand years ago when men believed in gods and heroes and patiently created polyphony.

The fate of the art of music is especially bound to the law of its origin. Polyphony, once discovered, has become indispensable for music. So the art irrevocably belongs only to those who have ears capable of perceiving polyphony. This the historical background of music reveals.

Section 3: The Fundamental Structure as the Content of the Background in Music

The *background* in music is represented by a contrapuntal structure which I have designated the *fundamental structure:*[3]

Fig. 1

Fundamental line is the name which I have given to the upper voice of the fundamental structure. It unfolds a chord horizontally while the counterpointing lower voice effects an *arpeggiation* of this chord through the upper fifth.

Since it is a melodic succession of definite steps of a second, the fundamental line signifies motion, striving toward a goal, and ultimately the completion of this course. In this sense we perceive our own life-impulse in the motion of the fundamental line, a full analogy to our inner life. Similarly, the arpeggiation of the bass signifies movement toward a specific goal, the upper fifth, and the completion of the course with the return to the fundamental tone.

The life of the fundamental line and the bass arpeggiation manifests itself not only in the first horizontal succession and in the first arpeggiation; it also expands through the *mid-*

[3]. Fig. 1 shows a third-progression in the upper voice. The fundamental line may also show a fifth-progression or an octave-progression (Figs. 10 and 11). (Oster)

dleground, through what I have called the voice-leading and transformation levels, prolongations, elaborations, and similar means, into the *foreground.*

Whatever the manner in which the foreground unfolds, the fundamental structure of the background and the transformation levels of the middleground guarantee its organic life.

The fundamental structure represents the totality. It is the mark of unity and, since it is the only vantage point from which to view that unity, prevents all false and distorted conceptions. In it resides the comprehensive perception, the resolution of all diversity into ultimate wholeness.

Even a bouquet of flowers requires an ordering of some kind, lines which lead the eye to comprehend the whole in a brief glance. The ear requires guiding lines all the more, since it is, in a sense, a younger organ than the eye.

I call the content of the fundamental line, counterpointed by the bass arpeggiation, *diatony (Diatonie)* ⟨§ 4⟩. This is the fundamental, determinate melodic succession, the primal design of melodic content. In contrast, *tonality*, in the foreground, represents the sum of all occurrences, from the smallest to the most comprehensive—including illusory keys and all the various musical forms.

Within the poles of fundamental line and foreground, of diatony and tonality, the spatial depth of a musical work is expressed—its distant origin in the simplest element, its transformation through subsequent stages, and, finally, the diversity of its foreground.*4

The *goal* and the course to the goal are primary. Content comes afterward: without a goal there can be no content.

In the art of music, as in life, motion toward the goal encounters obstacles, reverses, disappointments, and involves great distances, detours, expansions, interpolations, and, in short, retardations of all kinds. Therein lies the source of all artistic delaying, from which the creative mind can derive content that is ever new. Thus we hear in the middleground and foreground an almost dramatic course of events.

As the image of our life-motion, music can approach a state of objectivity, never, of course, to the extent that it need abandon its own specific nature as an art. Thus, it may almost evoke pictures or seem to be endowed with speech; it may pursue its course by means of associations, references, and connectives; it may use repetitions of the same tonal succession to express different meanings; it may simulate expectation, preparation, surprise, disappointment, patience, impatience, and humor. Because these comparisons are of a biological nature, and are generated organically, music is never comparable to mathematics or to architecture, but only to language, a kind of tonal language.*5

The fact that the fundamental line itself *traverses* a third, a fifth, or an octave in linear fashion is of great significance to horizontal motion in general. Since the smallest compass of the fundamental line is the third, neither a tone which is simply stationary in the foreground nor a tone which, by virtue of octave coupling or register transfer is understood to be stationary, is relevant to diminution or to the so-called melody.

A person stretches forth his hand and indicates a direction with his finger. Immediately another person understands this sign. The same gesture-language exists in music: every linear progression is comparable to a pointing of the finger—its direction and goal are clearly indicated to the ear.

In the linear progressions the composer lives his own life as well as that of the linear progressions. And, conversely, their life must be his, if they are to signify life to us.

The principles of *voice-leading*, organically anchored, remain the same in background, middleground, and foreground, even

---

*4. Passage (E), omitted here, is supplied in Appendix 4. (Rothgeb)

*5. See Figs. 62,2; 119,7; 119,10; 121,1–3; 148,3, and Schenker's comments on these examples. (Oster)

when they undergo transformations. In them the motto of my work is embodied, *semper idem sed non eodem modo* ("always the same, but not in the same way"). Nothing new is to be expected, yet this need not surprise us when we see that even in technology, which today stands in the forefront of all thought and activity, nothing truly new appears: we witness only further transformations.*6

The power of will and imagination which lives through the transformations of a masterwork reaches us in our spirit as a power of imagination—whether we have specific knowledge of the fundamental structure and the transformations or not. The life of the transformations conveys its own nature to us. We receive not only profound pleasure from a masterwork, but we also derive benefits in the form of a strengthening of our lives, an uplifting, and a vital exercise of the spirit—and thus achieve a heightening of our moral worth in general.

Section 4: The Significance of the Fundamental Structure for Composition, Instruction, and Performance *7

Musical coherence can be achieved only through the fundamental structure in the background and its transformations in the middleground and foreground.

It should have been evident long ago that the same principle applies both to a musical organism and to the human body: it grows outward from within. Therefore it would be fruitless as well as incorrect to attempt to draw conclusions about the organism from its epidermis.

The hands, legs, and ears of the human body do not begin to grow after birth; they are present at the time of birth. Similarly, in a composition, a limb which was not somehow born with the middle and background cannot grow to be a diminution. Hugo von Hofmannsthal has found ingenious words for this: "One must conceal the depths. Where? On the surface." And:

"No part of the surface of a figure can be formed except from the innermost core outward."

Thus, in the foreground, coherence lies behind the tones, as, in speech, the coherence of thought lies behind the words. Consequently, one can understand that the layman is unable to hear such coherence in music; but this unfortunate situation obtains also at higher levels, among musicians of talent. Even they have not yet learned to hear true coherent relationships. Since most people today lack coherence themselves, they are quite unable to bear the tension of musical coherence.

As a motion through several levels, as a connection between two mentally and spatially separated points, every relationship represents a path which is as real as any we "traverse" with our feet. Therefore, a relationship actually is to be "traversed" in thought—but this must involve actual time. Even the remarkable improvisatory long-range vision of our great composers, which I once referred to as "aural flight," presupposes, indeed, includes time.*8 And what has become of the concept of time at the present? Technology enables distant parts of the world to be connected at a rate of speed which is approaching the point of frenzy. This has also conditioned our attitude to art. Today one flies over the work of art in the same manner as one flies over villages, cities, palaces, castles, fields, woods, rivers, and lakes. This contradicts not only the historical bases of the work of art but also—more significantly—its coherence, its inner relationships, which demand to be "traversed." *9

The ability in which all creativity begins—the ability to compose extempore, to improvise fantasies and preludes—lies only in a feeling for the background, middleground, and foreground. Formerly such an ability was regarded as the hallmark of one truly gifted in composition, that which distinguished him from the amateur or the ungifted. Subsequently the rise of the masses made it necessary for the composer to give consideration

---

*6. Passage (F), omitted here, is supplied in Appendix 4.   (Rothgeb)

*7. Passage (G), omitted here, is supplied in Appendix 4.   (Rothgeb)

*8. *Der Tonwille 5*, p. 55.   (Schenker)

*9. Passage (H), omitted here, is supplied in Appendix 4.   (Rothgeb)

to the incapabilities of an ever-growing number of musicians. So it would be of greatest importance today to study thoroughly the fantasies, preludes, cadenzas, and similar embellishment which the great composers have left to us. All music instruction, be it public or private, should assign high priority to such study.

Anyone who has seen *sketches* by the great composers must have encountered voice-leading progressions which are far more than brief ideas or mere suggestions. These voice-leading progressions really present structural goals and the paths to them in a manner which could only stem from the far-flung inspiration of a genius. Such a vision, which is based upon the relationship of background, middleground, and foreground, can create a purely musical coherence even, as it were, in flight.*10 Therefore, a thoroughgoing study of the extant sketches of the masters is most necessary. These sketches reveal musical coherence in the process of evolution.

What a deplorably low value is generally placed on music is reflected in the fact that sketches by the masters, although long a commercially viable commodity, have been little understood by musicians. The exigencies which the composer encounters as he creates are foreign to these persons; therefore the written records of the composers' successful struggle with such exigencies must necessarily also have a foreign look about them. Under these circumstances Nottebohm's *Beethoveniana*, which Brahms so strongly recommended for publication, had to wait almost a half-century for the printing of its second edition. It is the musicians themselves who abandon their art! How different is the case of the first drafts, fragments, or sketches of great poets and painters—they have always met with a more general and lively appreciation!

Since the musicians up to the present have been unable to perceive the musical coherence in the masterworks, they have been even less able to read the *autographs* of the great compos-

ers. These last present the additional difficulty of problems of notation which are highly individual, ever new, and never schematic, but which always correspond to the musical content. *Autograph-study*, a completely new and special field of knowledge, thus goes hand in hand with the theory of musical coherence. The extent to which I have surpassed my few predecessors in this subject—editors, analysts, and the like—is indicated by those works of mine which secure for me the honor of being the true founder of the discipline of autograph-study.*11

Organic coherence also underlies the art of *orchestration* and the treatment of the instruments in *chamber music*. In the masterworks, orchestral colors are not mixed according to whim and applied at random; they are subject to the laws of

*11. In my edition of the Beethoven piano sonatas, the following texts are based upon the autographs: op. 27 no. 2, op. 28, 57, 78, 81a (first movement), 90 (after the manuscript copy by Archduke Rudolph), 101, 109, 110, and 111 (cf. also the *Erläuterungsausgabe*).

In addition, I revised the "Philharmonia" edition of Schubert's Symphony in *B* Minor according to its autograph.

The analytic presentations of Beethoven's Fifth Symphony (Universal Edition), Mozart's Symphony in *G* Minor *(Jahrb. II)*, Chopin's Études op. 10 nos. 5 and 6 *(Jahrb. I)*, and Schubert's Menuetto in *B* Minor (*Kunstwart*, March 1929) are based upon autographs. In the *Five Graphic Analyses*, the autographs of J.S. Bach's Prelude in *C (WTC I)*, Haydn's Sonata in *E♭* (Hob. 49), and Chopin's Étude op. 10 no. 12 were of the utmost value.

The presentation of the *Eroica* in *Jahrbuch III* relies upon a copy of the manuscript revised by Beethoven.

As a result of a suggestion I made in the preface to my *Erläuterungsausgabe*, which was later orally reinforced in private instruction, Mr. Anthony van Hoboken, a Dutch music enthusiast equipped with the finest musical intelligence, established an archive for *Photogramme von Meisterwerken* and presented it to the *Nationalbibliothek* in Vienna in 1927. This collection has already increased in size to more than 30,000 prints. However, this invaluable treasure is appreciated least of all by the musicians. They gaze at the prints as they would at locks of hair, watches, writing desks and the like, which are shown at exhibits that honor the memory of the great dead. I have often stressed that information of the greatest significance regarding the principles of art, the creation of musical coherence, the individual style of notation, etc., is to be derived from autographs as well as from sketches. (Schenker)

*10. In my work, particularly in the annotated editions *(Erläuterungsausgabe)* of op. 101, 109, 110, and 111, I have often referred to this quality in Beethoven's sketches. (Schenker)

the whole (cf. *Jahrb. III*, Scherzo of the *Eroica* Symphony). [§ 269]

The *performance* of a musical work of art can be based only upon a perception of that work's organic coherence. Interpretation cannot be acquired through gymnastics or dancing; one can transcend "motive," "theme," "phrase," and "bar line" and achieve true musical punctuation only by comprehending the background, middleground, and foreground. As punctuation in speech transcends syllables and words, so true punctuation in music strives toward more distant goals. This, of course, does not mean that the tones of the fundamental line need be overemphasized, as are the entrances in a poor performance of a fugue. The player who is aware of the coherence of a work will find interpretative means which allow the coherence to be heard. He who performs in this way will take care not to destroy the linear progressions; such destruction would paralyze our participation. Nor will he overestimate the value of the bar line, which indicates neither linear progression nor direction. Consequently, the concept of background, middleground, and foreground is of decisive and practical importance for performance *12 [§§ 252–54, 265, 299].*13

All previous theory has succeeded in blighting the art of music; it has instilled its own chaos into what is yet an unshakeable organism. It is not the province of theory to provide anything that is totally new or truly its own—yet theory seeks for one new solution after the other, with the emphasis usually upon the "new" and not upon "solution."

Since conventional theory is not able to measure all musical

motion in relation to the filling-in of the space of a third, fifth, or octave, it postulates the overtone series and, further, a series of subharmonics as the origin of the major-minor system.*14 But the subdominant, which most definitely forms part of the diatonic system, cannot have its origin in the overtone series. Theory has never departed from this contradictory teaching.

Even up to the present day, theory has not always been able to read foreground *intervals* correctly; one can only recognize them by examining their relation to background and middleground. All too frequently theory has failed to recognize many events in the foreground, simply because it has not understood their origin in the more elemental. Since thoroughbass figures can be understood only in terms of such relations, theory also fails when treating *thoroughbass*. To theory, the figures represent empty, frozen concepts; consequently, musicians of today cannot intelligently realize a continuo part.

But the most baleful error of conventional theory is its recourse to *"keys"* when, in its lack of acquaintance with foreground and middleground, it finds no other means of explanation. Often its helplessness is so great that it abandons even this most comfortable means of avoiding difficulties. Nothing is as indicative of the state of theory and analysis as this absurd abundance of "keys." The concept of the "key" as a higher unity in the foreground is completely foreign to theory: it is even capable of designating a single unprolonged chord as a key. To be sure, the great composers spoke of keys in the incorrect sense in their letters and notes. However, when we consider the singularly profound and masterly character of their works, we can certainly disregard their theoretical nomenclature. But we, incapable of such mastery, dare not permit ourselves the luxury of erroneous theories.

It is no wonder, then, that the masterwork remains inaccessi-

---

*12. Passage (I), omitted here, is supplied in Appendix 4. (Rothgeb)

*13. Many of Schenker's publications contain beautiful and deeply considered suggestions for performers. See especially the *Erläuterungsausgabe* of the late Beethoven sonatas; also Beethoven's op. 57 in *Der Tonwille 7*, Brahms's Handel Variations in *Der Tonwille 8*, Mozart's *G*-Minor Symphony in *Jahrbuch II*. (Oster)

*14. Bruckner used to teach (following Sechter) that even the sixth tone of the diatonic scale was dissonant and therefore had to be resolved downward. (Schenker)

ble to theory, and that its analyses resemble unsuccessful decipherings of papyrus rolls.

From such theory, who could expect to learn how to improvise, or to develop all the capabilities which lead to the secrets of truly organic and artistic activity? *15

Music is not only an *object* of theoretical consideration. It is *subject,* just as we ourselves are subject. Even the octave, fifth, and third of the harmonic series are a product of the organic activity of the tone as subject, just as the urges of the human being are organic. Accordingly, the quest for a new form of music is a quest for a homunculus. But nature will endure, indeed, will conquer, in music also; she has revealed herself in the works of the masters and, in this form, she will prevail.

My concepts present, for the first time, a genuine *theory of tonal language.*

Instruction at least in the *linear progressions,* the *primary means of coherence,* is indispensable. Because these progressions are anchored in polyphony, we must first learn to think *contrapuntally.* Even though counterpoint has long existed in the West, it is not yet at home in the mind of Western man. His ear is more apt to disregard counterpoint, to follow the upper voice which is the bearer of the melodic element, just as children rely on the right hand at their first piano lesson. At best, one hears a bass which is inactive; but when the bass goes beyond mere support and undertakes contrapuntal motion, the ear immediately turns back toward the upper voice.

*15. Passage (J), omitted here, is supplied in Appendix 4. (Rothgeb)

My theory shows that music is a self-contained unity in every respect that gives it its particular life among the arts. I would not presume to say how inspiration comes upon the genius, to declare with any certainty which part of the middleground or foreground first presents itself to his imagination: the ultimate secrets will always remain inaccessible to us [§§ 29, 85].

The greatest disaster for music is the so-called composition school. At best, one might allow music schools to serve as centers where the construction and performance of the instruments would be taught. Without any right, the schools attempt to justify their existence by providing instruction in composition: they even dispense legally binding documents testifying to the results of their instruction. Is not learning to hear the first task, during which time the student might well dispense with composition? Admittedly, to hear correctly and to compose correctly are equally difficult; but no music school can be released from the obligation of teaching to hear correctly. We cannot indulge the student in his favorite objection that he will never be able to reach such a high goal. Do not people devote themselves to many ends, even though they are conscious that they can never attain complete mastery? Are not the masses in the public schools instructed in matters which have no place in everyday life? Therefore, why should they not learn that strange mysteries also lie behind tones? [§ 316] Goethe's words are true: "That which the masses believe is easy to believe"; and, "What the intelligent person knows is difficult to know." It is also true that the fundamental structure amounts to a sort of secret, hidden and unsuspected, a secret which, incidentally, provides music with a kind of natural preservation from destruction by the masses. But, despite all difficulties, the schools ought definitely to give some suggestion of this secret!

Chapter 2

The Fundamental Structure

Section 1: The Fundamental Structure in General

§ 1. Arpeggiation as an outgrowth of the harmonic series

In nature sound is a vertical phenomenon:

Fig. 2

In this form, however, it cannot be transferred to the human larynx; nor is such a transfer desirable, for the mere duplication of nature cannot be the object of human endeavor. Therefore art manifests the principle of the harmonic series in a special way, one which still lets the chord of nature shine through. The overtone series, this vertical sound of nature, this chord in which all the tones sound at once, is transformed into a succession, a horizontal arpeggiation, which has the added advantage of lying within the range of the human voice. Thus the harmonic series is condensed, abbreviated for the purposes of art (*Harm.* § 13).

This basic transformation of the chord of nature into an arpeggiation must not be confused with the voice-leading transformations of the fundamental structure which occur in the middleground.

§ 2. The fundamental structure as transmitter of the primary arpeggiation

In the service of art, the arpeggiation throws off the restrictions of nature and claims the right to assert itself in either an upward or a downward direction. The following two forms represent the briefest and most direct ways for the harmonic series to be realized by human vocal organs:

Fig. 3

The upper voice ⟨of a fundamental structure⟩, which is the fundamental line, utilizes the descending direction; the lower voice, which is the bass arpeggiation through the fifth, takes the ascending direction ⟨Fig. 1⟩. As in the natural development of the arpeggiation, the ascending direction is the original one; indeed, in the fundamental structure it serves as a constant reminder of the presence of the chord of nature ⟨Fig. 1⟩ [§§ 10, 12].

§ 3. The fundamental structure as a unity

The combination of fundamental line and bass arpeggiation constitutes a *unity*. This unity alone makes it possible for voice-leading transformations to take place in the middleground and enables the forms of the fundamental structure to be transferred to individual harmonies (§§ 242 ff.).

Neither the fundamental line nor the bass arpeggiation can stand alone. Only when acting together, when unified in a contrapuntal structure, do they produce art.*1

Section 2: The Fundamental Line in General

§ 4. The path toward diatonic organization

After centuries of striving, when creative ears had finally learned to mold several voices successfully into a *contrapuntal complex*, it became possible to fill in the spaces in the arpeggiation in the upper voice of the fundamental structure with passing tones in a manner which did justice to both nature and art. In the process musicians also gradually learned to conform to nature by adjusting the horizontal and vertical aspects simultaneously: they adopted the octave, fifth, and third, which dominate the fundamental arpeggiation of the chord of nature. In addition they learned how to treat the passing tone as consonant

or dissonant according to what the practice of strict counterpoint ⟨in composition⟩ revealed.

Within the octave, this first adjustment resulted in a relatedness of the whole structure to a single tone, the fundamental of the chord. The series of tones thus created in the upper voice, the fundamental line, represents diatony *(Diatonie)*. In the narrowest sense, diatony belongs only to the upper voice. But, in accord with its origin, it simultaneously governs the whole contrapuntal structure, including the bass arpeggiation and the passing tones.

The same relationship to a fundamental tone prevails also in the foreground: all the foreground diminutions, including the apparent "keys" arising out of the voice-leading transformations, ultimately emanate from the diatony in the background. I have used the term *tonality* to include the various illusory effects in the foreground; yet the tonal sparseness of diatony in the background and the fullness of tonality in the foreground are one and the same.

Thus, so-called exotic music necessarily lacks diatony, because the absence of a contrapuntal structure makes the adjustment and selection of intervals impossible. One can clearly hear how it senses and strives for octaves, fifths, thirds, and other intervals in its horizontal projections, but one can also hear how it falls short of attaining them with the definiteness that nature demands; there is nothing against which these intervals can be tested contrapuntally. Conversely, the present decline of counterpoint has brought about the decline of diatony. This is the fault of the musicians, who still have not grasped the fact that as long as the fifth determines the natural sonority—and that will always be so—a voice-leading technique based upon the fifth, as nature requires, cannot lead to any diatony other than the diatony which our art has exhibited up to the present day. All attempts to deprive nature of her rights will shatter against the wall of her resistance.

Diatony therefore does not stem from the so-called Greek or Gregorian modes, but rather from the composing-out process,

---

*1. Those new to the concept of musical background tend to turn their attention exclusively to the fundamental line, because it is the upper voice. They all too hastily accept any tone series as the fundamental line, without determining whether it rests securely upon the counterpoint of the lower voice. Thus they often meet with disappointment (§§ 210, 257). (Schenker)

which is governed by the principle of the fifth. Tone series such as those of the Credo or Confiteor do not begin to evoke a sense of diatony; not even the fugal settings of a J.S. Bach (as in the *B*-Minor Mass) can bestow on them the credibility of true diatony.*[2]

§ 5.   The space occupied by the fundamental line; the primary passing-motion

In accordance with the arpeggiation from which it stems, the fundamental line exhibits the space of a third, fifth, or octave. These spaces are filled by passing tones.

The space of a fundamental line must contain the linear progression of at least a third; the step of a second as fundamental line is unthinkable (§ 13).

The traversal of the fundamental line is *the most basic of all passing-motions;* it is the necessity (derived from strict counterpoint) of continuing in the same direction which creates coherence, and, indeed, makes this traversal the beginning of all coherence in a musical composition.

§ 6.   The indivisibility of the fundamental line

Of necessity, the passing-motion through the fundamental line implies its indivisibility [§ 38].

No matter what upper voices, structural divisions, form, and the like the middleground or foreground may bring, nothing can contradict the basic indivisibility of the fundamental line. This is the greatest possible triumph of coherence in music.

§ 7.   The segment of the fundamental line $\hat{8}$—$\hat{5}$ (a fourth) derives from diatony, not from nature

In the overtone series the fourth is not represented; for, even though we may think we perceive a fourth between the fifth

*2. Passage (K), omitted here, is supplied in Appendix 4.   (Rothgeb)

and the double octave (when we reinterpret the series in horizontal terms, as art necessitates), the series in its vertical aspect reveals only a double octave. Since the interval between the fifth and the double octave is not equivalent to the horizontal fourth, the span $\hat{8}$—$\hat{5}$ cannot have validity as an independent segment of the fundamental line (not even as the inversion of $\hat{5}$—$\hat{1}$). It is only a part of the span $\hat{8}$—$\hat{1}$, where we encounter the $\hat{8}$ once again, in accordance with nature, as an octave, not a fourth [§§ 76, 96, 102, 212].

Fig. 4

§ 8.   The register of the fundamental line

The succession of tones of the fundamental line must be understood to lie within one octave, which I term the *obligatory register* of the fundamental line (§§ 268–70).

This, however, does not exclude the possibility that a change of register can occur in the foreground or middleground. The change is both possible and understandable precisely because it refers back to the obligatory register; thus, any change in register of the tones of the fundamental line creates only an illusion of independence from this register.

§ 9.   The tones of the fundamental line are not overtones

Even in the artistic realization of sound, every individual tone of the fundamental line, like any tone, arises as an independent bearer of its own overtones. If, when we hear the tones of the fundamental line in succession, we nevertheless understand ⟨some of⟩ them as fifth or third of a particular bass tone, it is only because we recognize in them the same relationships which establish the octave, fifth, and third of the harmonic series. But these notes are no longer actual overtones: they are only images of the overtones.

Still less should the passing tones in the spaces of the arpeggiation be taken for overtones; they are not contained in the harmonic series at all. It is therefore not permissible to ascribe the same significance to passing tones as to the main bass tone; by definition, a passing tone is dependent upon the consonant tones which surround it.*3

§ 10. The fundamental line begins with $\hat{8}$, $\hat{5}$, or $\hat{3}$ and moves to $\hat{1}$ via the descending leading tone $\hat{2}$ *4

To man is given the experience of ending, the cessation of all tensions and efforts. In this sense, we feel by nature that the fundamental line must lead downward until it reaches $\hat{1}$, and that the bass must fall back to the fundamental. With $\frac{\hat{1}}{I}$ all tensions in a musical work cease. Thus a fundamental line can never end, for example, with $\hat{3}$—$\hat{2}$.*5

*3. It is therefore a contradiction to maintain, for example, that all scale tones between *C* and *c* have real independence or, to use a current but certainly musically unsuitable expression, "equal rights." No matter how one would divide this tone series, any division compels recognition of diatony in the sense of a relationship of all tones of the series to the fundamental, *C*. In compositional practice, the error of this point of view results in a constant violation of the tonality in the foreground. One feels justified in setting down any key whatsoever, claiming for it independence, without any relation to the fundamental key. The effect may well be imagined . . . . (Schenker)

*4. In German theoretical writings the second step of the scale is sometimes referred to as *der abwärtssteigende Leitton*, literally "the descending leading tone." Schenker's reference in § 17 to "both leading tones" designates the second and seventh scale degrees. (Rothgeb)

*5. The question often arises why the fundamental line always descends to $\hat{1}$ but never ascends, for example, from $\hat{5}$ to $\hat{8}$. Since Schenker nowhere explained this phenomenon, the following may serve as an answer.—As Schenker said in § 9, the $\hat{8}$, $\hat{5}$, and $\hat{3}$ are only images of overtones. But, like true overtones, they too seem to be generated by a fundamental tone, which in the fundamental structure is the I. And the "tensions" come to rest only when the $\hat{8}$, $\hat{5}$, or $\hat{3}$ have "gone home"—when they have returned to where they came from, that is, to the fundamental which created them. Accordingly, they have to move in the direction of the fundamental, and this means downward. But the fundamental line does not have to descend to the I in the bass register in order to

A sequence of tones cannot live in the foreground unless the total tension of the fundamental linear progression provides it with breath; no life can be breathed into it from the foreground. How preposterous therefore to try to fashion an organic, living work by assembling various tone series without background!

§ 11. The ascending leading tone is not contained in the fundamental line

Since the fundamental line can descend to $\hat{1}$ only through $\hat{2}$, the ascending leading tone is excluded; in all cases it appears as an inner-voice tone ⟨§ 118⟩.

§ 12. $\hat{8}$, $\hat{5}$, $\hat{3}$ anticipated chordally

Since the fundamental line rests on the counterpoint of the bass, its first pitch-level, $\frac{\hat{8}}{I}$ or $\frac{\hat{5}}{I}$ or $\frac{\hat{3}}{I}$, is anticipated, all at once, in chordal fashion [§ 122].*6

The acknowledgment of the principle of nature is reiterated in the opening interval, a vertical event. From that point on, the fundamental line descends according to the principles of art and of diatony.

In the middleground and foreground, however, the first actual interval of the fundamental structure can be altered by means of a prolongation (§§ 120 ff., 125 ff., 129 ff.). For this reason caution is advised when regarding a foreground-beginning: are we hearing the actual opening interval of the fundamental-line progression or merely a prolongational interval which precedes it?

———

come to rest. For exactly as the $\hat{5}$ or the $\hat{3}$ are only images of the third or fifth overtones, so the final $\hat{1}$ is an image of the fundamental bass tone and represents the return to it. (Oster)

*6. That is, instead of reaching this pitch-level by means of arpeggiation (§ 2). (Oster)

§ 13. The horizontal fulfillment of the fundamental line as tone-space

By the concept *tone-space* I understand the space of the horizontal fulfillment of the fundamental line. Thus, only the fundamental-line progression of the third $\hat{3}$—$\hat{2}$—$\hat{1}$ represents the tone-space $\hat{3}$—$\hat{1}$; only the fundamental line of a fifth or an octave represents the tone-space of a fifth or an octave. A vertical third (tenth), fifth, or octave as the first interval of the composition cannot represent a tone-space; misunderstandings easily arise in connection with these beginning intervals.*7

Therefore, I repeat: tone-space is only to be understood horizontally ⟨see the brackets⟩:

Fig. 5

§ 14. $\hat{5}$—$\hat{1}$ and $\hat{3}$—$\hat{1}$ represent the entire triad

The choice of a beginning interval follows the principles of counterpoint. The interval must be in accord with middleground and foreground, and its specific identity is determined by the needs of the piece—just as in a *cantus firmus* exercise the best possible continuation is determinant.

In any case $\hat{5}$—$\hat{1}$ or $\hat{3}$—$\hat{1}$ represents the whole triad, exactly as does $\hat{8}$—$\hat{1}$; the bass comes to the aid of the incomplete lines with the same arpeggiation.

Section 3: The Bass Arpeggiation in General

§ 15. In the bass arpeggiation through the fifth, the ascending direction precedes ⟨the descending⟩

*7. Such intervals might belong to a later prolongational level—see Figs. 7a and 20,4. (Oster)

As in the overtone series, in the bass arpeggiation the ascending direction takes priority.

Fig. 6

Therefore forms such as those shown in 2) through 5) are out of the question:

at 2) the arpeggiation is completely lacking;

at 3) the descending arpeggiation is missing;

at 4) the arpeggiation moves through the IV instead of the V;

at 5) the descending direction comes first, in opposition to nature. The two forms shown at 2) and 4), as they stand, express no motion whatsoever and thus do not signify an artistic realization of a chord.

§ 16. The fifth in nature and in art

From music history we know that in the beginning the influence of science upon music was so strong that music allowed itself to be forced to use the fifth as the only interval for polyphonic settings. Nature, of course, knows only the fifth that appears in the overtone series, and no other kind of fifth. Man, however, who within his own capacities can experience sound only in a succession and must advance to diatony, is led to the fifth (as well as other intervals) in various applied ways.

§ 17. V—I

Contrapuntal practice provides an additional reason for the descending arpeggiation V—I, specifically in the setting-up of the close in three-part strict counterpoint. When both leading tones appear in the upper and inner voices there is only one tone, the root of the dominant, which permits the complete triad to occur in the penultimate measure (*Kpt. II*, III/1, § 27) [§ 23].

§ 18.   The division of the bass arpeggiation

Just as the concept of an interval presupposes two tones, so three tones divide the bass arpeggiation into two parts:

Fig. 7

All musical content arises from the confrontation and adjustment of the indivisible fundamental line with the two-part bass arpeggiation. The paths to prolongation, and ultimately to form, open here ⟨§§ 25, 33⟩.

§ 19.   The sacred triangle

May the musician always carry in his heart the image of the bass arpeggiation (Fig. 7)! Let this triangle be sacred to him! Creating, interpreting—may he bear it always in ear and eye!

By extension, every triad, whether it belongs to middleground or foreground, strives for its own triangle (§§ 242 ff.).

Section 4:   Specific Characteristics of the Fundamental Structure

§ 20.   Significance of high and low register with respect to fundamental line and bass

Even in the fundamental structure, the fundamental line presents its arpeggiation filled in with seconds, whereas the bass presents its arpeggiation bare. This is because of the general difference between high and low register [§ 53].

The difference between fundamental line and bass arpeggiation makes itself felt in all levels, including the foreground. Because of its low register, the bass diminution always remains

more restrained than that of the upper voice [§§ 64, 185, 210, 257].

§ 21.   The fundamental structure is arrhythmic

Rhythm can no more exist in the fundamental structure than it can in a strict-counterpoint *cantus firmus* exercise.

Only when, through voice-leading transformations, linear progressions arise in the upper and lower voices of the middleground, does a rhythmic ordering issue from the necessity of counterpointing the voices against each other. All rhythm in music comes from counterpoint and only from counterpoint (§§ 284 ff.) [§ 67].

In the middleground every individual level has its own specific rhythm, according to the extent of its contrapuntal content. Thus rhythm, too, progresses through various transformational stages until it reaches the foreground, just as do meter and form, which also represent end-results of a progressive contrapuntal differentiation (§ 290) ⟨Figs. 138,1 and 148,3⟩.

§ 22.   The fundamental structure in no way renders the discipline of strict counterpoint superfluous

It will not do to make the fundamental structure the first and only source of strict counterpoint and curtail, therefore, instruction in strict counterpoint, which is presumed to be lengthy and tedious. The fundamental structure represents only one special application of strict counterpoint and by no means exhausts all the problems and possibilities of voice-leading discipline. The upper and lower voices of the fundamental structure are presented only in contrary motion and in a version which has nothing to do with a *cantus firmus*. Where, then, can one learn how voices in other circumstances are to be led against each other, if not in strict-counterpoint instruction? At what intervals are the voices to be placed; what is the significance of these intervals; what errors are to be avoided? Is it not strict counterpoint alone which permits us to recognize the real intervals behind those on the surface, which makes clear to us that voice-leading must always and everywhere be regarded as the actual foundation of music, and that the true meaning of voice-leading must nevertheless still be probed and ascertained?

§ 23.   The cadential formula $\dfrac{\hat{2}—\hat{1}}{\text{V}—\text{I}}$

In $\dfrac{\hat{2}}{\text{V}}$ both leading tones in the upper and inner voices are united, and the bass brings in the root of the V. In this way alone is the complete triad achieved, as required by the arrangement for closing in three-part strict counterpoint [§ 17].

§ 24.   The meaning of a fifth or third at the close of a piece

A fifth or third occasionally found at the end of a composition occurs only in the service of a coda or some poetic idea unconnected with the fundamental line, which must certainly have come to an end earlier (§ 304) [§ 267].

§ 25.   Tone-space is anterior to form

One might ask: If all fundamental lines are similar, what accounts for the dissimilarity of form in the foreground? Must we not have a special concept of form to explain this? The answer is that since the fundamental line is identical with the concept of tone-space, this in itself provides a fountainhead for all form. Be they two-, three-, four-, or five-part forms, all receive their coherence only from the fundamental structure, from the fundamental line in tone-space. Thus is the anterior nature of tone-space explained (§ 13) [§ 306].

§ 26.   The fundamental structure can even be the content of a foreground

Slight as the content of a fundamental structure may appear, it is occasionally sufficient to be foreground. Such a foreground is usually carried out with the aid of the simplest of figurations, which do not yet signify prolongations: *8

Fig. 7a,b

*8. There is a difficulty here: Schenker seems to be speaking not so much of the fundamental structure in the strictest sense; rather he is representing the middleground of the two compositions, as the examples show.

In addition he seems to indicate that the background of these pieces, and certain features of the middleground, really form the content of their opening measures, even though the resemblance between foreground and background may not be exact.

In the Beethoven, measures 1–5 represent a preview of the fundamental structure of the entire movement (Fig. 149, 4). The triplet $g\sharp—c\sharp^1—e^1$ of measure 1 becomes the arpeggiation $g\sharp^1—c\sharp^2—e^2$ (mm. 5–27) which leads to the $\hat{3}$. (In mm. 42–49 this arpeggiation becomes, simplified, the sixth $g\sharp^1—e^2$.) Compare also the arpeggiation $ab^1—db^2—f^2$ in the second movement (Fig. 110, b3) and $g\sharp^2—c\sharp^3—e^3$ in the Finale (Fig. 40, 4). It is the unifying motive of this "Sonata quasi una Fantasia." For the middle section of the first movement compare § 310, b 1.

In the Chopin, compare especially the neighboring-note motion $a^3—bb^3—a^3$ in measures 1, 55, 61 to that of measures 1–8 (see Fig. 148, 5), and the final descent of measures 61–75 (95) to the third-progression $a—g—f$ in measures 8–9 (which also spans the first section mm. 1–28). The foreground arpeggiations of measures 1–2 and 5–6 express $a—f$ and $bb—g$ in whole notes; besides, they contain the sixteenth-note motives $a—g—f$ and $bb—a—g$, which in measures 8–9 give rise to $a—g—f$ in enlargement. $a^3—g^3—f^3$ and bb^3, a^3, g^3 are also the essential tones of the fundamental line as shown in Fig. 7b. Note further the third-progression $A—G—F$ in the bass of the middle section, measures 40–61.   (Oster)

Chapter 3

The Forms of the Fundamental Structure

Section 1: The Forms of the Fundamental Structure: General Remarks

§ 27.   Opening remarks

The forms of the fundamental structure represent a primordial state which exists beneath all voice-leading transformations.

§ 28.   The difference between the forms of the fundamental structure and cadences of conventional harmony

The forms of the fundamental structure must not be confused with the cadences of the conventional theory of harmony.

In the case of such cadences as shown in

Fig. 8

the greatest importance is attached to the harmonic progression of the bass; the upper voice can have various forms, such as those shown in Exx. 2 to 7. This contrasts most significantly with the fundamental structure, whose upper voice, the fundamental line, knows only the descending direction. Therefore, at 1, the similarity of the illustrated cadence with the form of the fundamental structure $\begin{smallmatrix} \hat{3} & \hat{2} & \hat{1} \\ I & V & I \end{smallmatrix}$ is merely external.

Furthermore, in the fundamental structure, the upper voice (the fundamental line) is the source of all the voice-leading transformations, a role that the upper voice in the cadences of customary harmonic theory never plays [§ 32].

Finally, in the cadences of harmonic theory the voices are led mechanically, according to the rule that common tones are to be retained. Since this rule is no longer valid even in thorough-bass, how much less must it apply to a fundamental structure where the inner voices are subordinate to the outer voices, that is, to the fundamental line and the bass arpeggiation.

The musician must master the forms of the fundamental structure in their complete conceptual as well as substantive opposition to the cadences of the customary theory of harmony.

Only then can he reach out into the horizontal dimension and create relationships which extend from the background through the middleground to the foreground.

§ 29.   The true meaning of the forms of the fundamental structure

The forms of the fundamental structure, derived from the masterworks, might give cause for misunderstanding to young artists, who are mainly dependent upon imitation. Specifically, the following question could arise: need one only vary some fundamental structure in order to arrive at the foreground of, say, a symphony? Whoever asks this introduces the notion of a time sequence, a "chronology of creation" into the idea of the fundamental structure ⟨and the transformation levels⟩. This notion is not correct. The concept of the fundamental structure by no means claims to provide specific information about the chronology of creation; it presents only the *strictly logical precision in the relationship* between simple tone-successions and more complex ones. Indeed, it shows this precision of relationship not only from the simple to the more complex, but also in reverse, from the complex to the simple. It is an inevitable principle that all complexity and diversity arise from a single simple element rooted in the consciousness or the intuition. (Even instruction in the beginning classes of music schools rests upon this principle.) Thus, a simple element lies at the back of every foreground. The secret of balance in music ultimately lies in the constant awareness of the transformation levels and the motion from foreground to background or the reverse. This awareness accompanies the composer constantly; without it, every foreground would degenerate into chaos [§ 301].

Creation may have its origin anywhere, in any suitable voice-leading level or tone-succession; the seed, by the grace of God, remains inaccessible even to metaphysics. Yet we must remember that all growth (every continuation, direction, or improve-

ment) finds its fulfillment only through the control of the fundamental structure and its transformations, through constant contact with background, middleground, and foreground. Thus in the creative act the fundamental structure is ever present. It accompanies each transformation in the middleground and foreground, as a guardian angel watches over a child [§§ 50, 85, 183].

Even the most successful graphic representation of the logical relationships between background and foreground must fail to portray this ultimate reality:

The fundamental structure is always creating, always present and active; this "continual present" in the vision of the composer is certainly not a greater wonder than that which issues from the true experiencing of a moment of time: in this most brief space we feel something very like the composer's perception, that is, the meeting of past, present, and future.

§ 30.   The transformation levels are repetitions or parallelisms and also constitute a delaying

As they move toward the foreground, the transformation levels are actually bearers of developments and are, at the same time, repetitions or parallelisms in the most elevated sense— if we permit ourselves to use the word "repetition" to describe the movement from transformation level to transformation level. The mysterious concealment of such repetitions is an almost biological means of protection: repetitions thrive better in secret than in the full light of consciousness [§ 46, 254].

But genius, the gift of improvisation and long-range hearing, is requisite for greater time spans. Short-range hearing is incapable of projecting large spans, because it does not perceive just those simpler elements upon which the far-reaching structure is to be based. Yet the genius's ability to encompass even the largest spans is not unduly astonishing. Anyone who, like the genius, can create the smallest linear progressions of thirds, fourths, and fifths abundantly and with ease, need only exert a greater spiritual and physical energy in order to extend them still further through larger and larger spans, until the single largest progression is attained: the fundamental line.

The transformation levels have the foreground as final goal, but, as they make their way to it, they also constitute a delaying, a *retardation*. As long as tension and content-expansion are maintained in the transformation levels, we are still far from the goal. Retardation therefore is one of the most valuable of compositional means [§§ 70, 90, 109].

Section 2: The Possible Forms of the Fundamental Structure in the Cases of $\hat{3}$, $\hat{5}$, and $\hat{8}$

§ **31.** The form of the fundamental structure in the case of $\hat{3}$

The fundamental structure in the case of $\hat{3}$ reads as follows:

Fig. 9

The linear progression of a third $e^2—d^2—c^2$, if based merely on the root of the I, would express only the single tone e^2, not the fundamental-line progression $\hat{3}—\hat{2}—\hat{1}$. The bass lacks arpeggiation and so any movement whatsoever.

The indivisibility of the fundamental line prevails over the inherent two-part quality of the bass arpeggiation (§§ 6, 18).

§ **32.** $\dfrac{\hat{3}—\hat{2}}{\text{I—V}}$ opens the prospect of prolongations by means of linear progressions of a third and of a fifth

The first two vertical intervals of this form of the fundamental structure—the tenth (third) and the fifth—contain within themselves the possibility of composing-out by means of a linear progression of a third and of a fifth ⟨Figs. 34c; 35,1; 39,2; 84⟩.

§ **33.** The first glimpse of form in the foreground

This type of fundamental structure can maintain itself undivided in the foreground and therefore result in an undivided form (§ 307).

However, the linear progression of a fifth, suggested by $\dfrac{\hat{2}}{\text{V}}$, presents, after an exploratory probe into the foreground, the possibility of a modulation (in the foreground sense) to the key of the dominant, which then would provide special support for the interruption form $\hat{3}—\hat{2} \| \hat{3}—\hat{2}—\hat{1}$ (§§ 87, 309 ff.).

§ **34.** The form of the fundamental structure in the case of $\hat{5}$

The form of the fundamental structure in the case of $\hat{5}$ is as follows:

Fig. 10

§ **35.** The $\hat{4}$ as a dissonant passing tone in the fundamental line $\hat{5}—\hat{1}$

Fig. 10,1 shows that the $\hat{4}$ is dissonant as it passes over the root. As a dissonant interval the $\hat{4}$ permits no composing-out, for an interval which is itself passing cannot at the same time serve as a primary tone of a linear progression. Such a primary tone must necessarily be consonant. Therefore in a dissonant state the $\hat{4}$ remains without the emphasis which a consonant interval receives: no linear progressions can be derived from it (§§ 169, 170) [§ 69].

§ **36.** The apparent subdivision $\hat{5}$—$\hat{3}$—$\hat{1}$; the unsupported stretch

Fig. 10,2: If after the dissonant $\hat{4}$ the $\hat{3}$ asserts itself as a consonance—as a tenth or third above the root—the semblance of a subdivision $\hat{5}$—$\hat{3}$—$\hat{1}$ immediately arises [§§ 77, 95].

In this context the first part of the fundamental line $\hat{5}$—$\hat{4}$—$\hat{3}$ has more the effect of a transiently filled space of a third; it is not quite like a linear progression of a third that is worked out with the help of a counterpointing bass progression. This creates a certain void, or unsupported stretch, at the very outset of the fundamental line of a fifth, and occasionally gives rise to the question whether the form of the fundamental structure is not actually $\hat{3}$—$\hat{2}$—$\hat{1}$ as it is shown in Fig. 9 [§ 116].

§ **37.** The apparent subdivision $\hat{5}$—$\hat{2}$—$\hat{1}$

Fig. 10,3: Lastly, through $\dfrac{\hat{2}}{V}$ an emphasis upon $\hat{2}$ results, which makes an especially strong contrast with the previous unsupported stretch. Thereby another subdivision seems to appear in the linear progression of a fifth: as though with $\hat{2}$ the linear progression of a fourth, $\hat{5}$—$\hat{2}$, had come into being [§ 76].

§ **38.** Affirmation of the indivisibility and unity of the fundamental line of a fifth despite any appearance of subdivision

However, the forward compulsion toward $\hat{1}$ still exists at the end of the fundamental-line segments $\hat{5}$—$\hat{3}$ or $\hat{5}$—$\hat{2}$. This necessity reaffirms the indivisibility of the progression of the fifth in the fundamental structure, no matter how much the appearance of a subdivision might seem to deny it (§ 6).

§ **39.** Tasks posed by the form of the fundamental structure in the case of $\hat{5}$

It follows from the foregoing paragraphs that the tasks of the middleground and foreground are to eliminate the unsupported stretch at the passing $\hat{4}$ by making that $\hat{4}$ consonant and composing it out, and ultimately to establish and fulfill the structural subdivision $\hat{5}$—$\hat{3}$—$\hat{1}$ or $\hat{5}$—$\hat{2}$—$\hat{1}$ [§ 170].

§ **40.** A glimpse of form in the foreground

In the possibility of the structural subdivision $\hat{5}$—$\hat{2}$ lies the root of the interruption-form $\hat{5}$—$\hat{2}\,\|\,\hat{5}$—$\hat{1}$ in the middleground (§§ 95 ff.) and also in the foreground [§ 192].

§ **41.** The form of the fundamental structure in the case of $\hat{8}$

This form is shown in:

Fig. 11

§ **42.** The appearance of several subdivisions

Fig. 11,1: Since $\hat{5}$ and $\hat{3}$ are consonant with the root of the triad, an effect of several subdivisions arises.

Fig. 11,2 and 3 show that the unsupported stretch is apparent to a much greater degree than in the case of $\hat{5}$—$\hat{1}$. For this reason doubt often might arise as to whether we are instead confronted with a linear progression of a third or a fifth.

Fig. 11,4 and 5: Even when the root of V is placed under $\hat{7}$ or $\hat{5}$, the phenomenon of the unsupported stretch has not been eliminated.

§ **43.** The task posed by the fundamental structure in the case of $\hat{8}$

Above all, the unsupported stretch must be eliminated in order to establish that the fundamental line $\hat{8}$—$\hat{1}$ actually exists. This can be achieved through the subdivision $\hat{8}$—$\hat{5}$—$\hat{1}$ with two arpeggiations in the bass (Figs. 19b; 27, a and b).

§ **44.** The $\hat{7}$ is diatonic

The $\hat{7}$ in a linear progression $\hat{8}$—$\hat{1}$ must be strictly diatonic if a genuine fundamental line is involved [§ 102] and not merely an octave line in a coda, where a lowered seventh may appear (Fig. 73, 4).

Part II

The Middleground

Chapter 1

The Middleground in General

§ 45.   Assignment of names

A name or term always implies a simultaneous verbal and logical connection, an essential unity. Therefore the assignment of names to concepts is of utmost importance in intellectual discourse.

For the sake of continuity with my earlier theoretical and analytical works, I am retaining in this volume the words of Latin derivation *prolongation* and *diminution* as designations for the voice-leading levels in the middleground. However, as in the past, I shall also utilize German terms for these concepts, as, for example, *Stimmführungsschichten* (voice-leading levels), *Stimmführungsverwandlungen* (voice-leading transformations), or shorter, *Verwandlung* (transformation), *Mehrung* (increase of content), *Auswicklung* (unwinding), *Auflösung* (dissolution), *Umwandlung* (reshaping), *Umbildung* (recasting), and similar ones.

§ 46.   Voice-leading transformations also spring from a vital natural power

The fundamental structure shows us how the chord of nature comes to life through a vital natural power. But the primal power of this established motion must grow and live its own full life: that which is born to life strives to fulfill itself with the power of nature. For this reason, it is not artistically accurate to consider the voice-leading transformations merely superficial variations (§ 30).

§ 47.   Freedom of the prolongations

A particular form of the fundamental structure by no means requires particular prolongations; if it did, all forms of the fundamental structure would have to lead to the same prolongational forms. Indeed, the choice of prolongations remains essentially free, provided that the indivisibility and connection of all relationships are assured [§ 183].

The rapport between the particular form of the fundamental structure and the later levels—ultimately also the foreground—determines the choice of prolongations more specifically. It is this rapport which forms the actual picture of the background, middleground, and foreground (§ 29).

Fig. 12

Thus, the neighboring-note harmony at the beginning may have arisen in the composer's imagination together with the first tone of the fundamental line.

Fig. 13

Similarly, the setting of the first arpeggiation might have originated together with the first tone of this fundamental line [1] [§§ 125–27]. In any event, it is the fundamental structure which guides the composer.

§ 48.   The number of structural levels

It is impossible to generalize regarding the number of structural levels, although in each individual instance the number can be specified exactly, as I have shown in many examples in my work. In any event, the first two levels already contain the branching-out into the particulars of a work of art. Moreover, there are some prolongations which would occur only at the first level, others which take place only at the second. The prolongations at the later levels evolve from those at the first two levels [§§ 183–85].

§ 49.   The danger of confusing structural levels

Merely to discuss prolongations orally or to suggest them is a rather fruitless undertaking. One must write them out, take hold of them with the fingers, in order to bring them most accurately to one's consciousness. Only when a very exact picture is laid out on paper do questions arise which demand clarification, especially those concerned with the smallest details of the voice-leading. The composer who lacks the gift of true ingenuity knows from experience how he stumbles in the foreground—stumbles, indeed, over the foreground itself, over the difficulties of creating diminutions. Let him go forth and learn their laws!

The illustrations which I have called *Urlinie-Tafeln* (literal translation: graphs of the fundamental line) diagram the penultimate prolongational level, after which follows the foreground.[2] Those who feel no desire to expend effort in exploring the background and middleground should confine themselves to the *Urlinie-Tafeln*. Readers who have acclaimed my presentation of the foreground (e.g., in my monograph on Beethoven's Ninth Symphony) because it has revealed to them new relationships, will surely approve of the *Urlinie-Tafeln* for the same reason. And yet, I recommend that everyone take the trouble to feel his way from the foreground to the middleground and background; he need only employ the familiar method of reducing more extensive diminutions, as taught in textbooks and schools. So he will arrive at shorter and shorter versions, and finally the shortest, the fundamental structure!

§ 50.   Rejection of the conventional terms "melody," "motive," "idea," and the like

Great composers trust their long-range vision. For this reason they do not base their compositions upon some "melody," "motive," or "idea." Rather, the content is rooted in the voice-leading transformations and linear progressions whose unity allows

---

[1]. Chopin's op. 31, usually referred to as the Scherzo in *Bb* Minor because of its initial harmony, must be regarded as being in the key of *Db* major ⟨§ 303⟩. (Schenker)

[2]. Schenker refers here to illustrations in previous publications, *Der Tonwille*, the three volumes *Jahrbücher (Das Meisterwerk in der Musik)*, and finally the *Five Graphic Analyses (Fünf Urlinie-Tafeln)*. Compare the presentation of three voice-leading levels in Fig. 22b. Due to limitation of space, however, the fundamental structure and the first level are not specifically shown in this example.   (Oster)

no segmentation or names of segments ⟨§§ 308, 311, 313⟩. Every linear progression, provided it does not quickly pass by in sixteenths or thirty-seconds, presupposes a certain extended vision, and has nothing to do with "melody" or "idea." While fashioning linear progressions, the great composer feels secure and does not fear momentary obviousness or incompleteness, nor does he act precipitously from helplessness in the midst of a linear progression. Without shame, he often places the simplest kind of composing-out at the very beginning of a work, one which the least gifted composition student would reject as too uninteresting. Of course, the great composer already hears the continuation, and with it a series of composings-out. These form a *totality* and present a melody of far higher order and greater inevitability than a "melody" or "idea" could provide. What is to be designated as "melody" or "idea" in those pieces whose entire course is identical with the fundamental structure (§ 26)?

One cannot speak of "melody" and "idea" in the work of the masters; it makes even less sense to speak of "passage," "sequence," "padding," or "cement" as if they were terms that one could possibly apply to art. Drawing a comparison to language, what is there in a logically constructed sentence that one could call "cement"? How does one distinguish an "idea" from "cement"?

It is certainly not out of place here to distinguish "fundamental structure" composers from "idea" composers. The latter must always be concerned with the effect of the moment; they ramble constantly instead of deriving higher entities from the background and middleground. They frequently defend their inability by saying that that is precisely how they wanted to write and thus give one to understand that they could compose just as well as the masters if they so desired. If only they would once attempt to create a truly organic work! Under extreme duress, however, they take refuge in emotion, where they believe themselves to be unassailable; I should consider them unworthy of an attack.

It is impossible to present in specific and perceptible forms all the events which occur through the miraculous rapport of fundamental structure with foreground—especially in forms which would satisfy the superficial interest of the curious. A wonder remains a wonder and can be experienced only by those blessed with special perception. Its secrets are inaccessible to every sort of metaphysics; they are neither teachable nor learnable. Up to the present we have not even learned to comprehend those events which lie on the surface. The simplest linear progressions in the foreground are still inaccessible even to very sensitive ears.

§ **51.** The status of music history

Music history, as I have repeatedly indicated, should pursue the questions of where, when, and how musical material found the path from incoherence to coherence: when did the first creative ear develop a sense for linear progressions as the essential unities, complete with their constraint to move forward in the horizontal dimension? When did composers begin to demonstrate the sustaining power of these linear progressions by constructing more and more extended prolongations? When one considers the art of such prolongations, it becomes immaterial whether (as the historians suppose) J.S. Bach composed monothematically or Beethoven composed polythematically. Despite the eternal sameness of the linear progressions, there is still room in the art of music for countless gifted composers!

But the historian should avoid placing the master and the man of moderate ability on the same level: such a grouping has led to a false concept of culture. The master composer enters the scene in isolated instances—the man of moderate ability is always there. Never can there be a connection between them! When genius has been absent, mere talent has always plodded onward. But even the simultaneous presence of genius and talent has never meant true culture for the average man.*³

*3. Passage (L), omitted here, is supplied in Appendix 4. (Rothgeb)

§ **52.**   The present situation

On the one hand, the battle against diminution is raging. Since musicians can no longer cope with diminution, they simply abolish it. Composers attempt to return to the technique of those first contrapuntal creations which exhibit the first traces of diminution. They imagine a rebirth of the primitive, a bond with the old masters. Such composers never realize that only the diminutions in the masterworks of the epoch of genius represent the truly creative in music, music's actual nature and significance [§§ 251–66]. Moreover, in today's desperate struggle to expand content, diminution certainly does not have the worth of even those first efforts; then the power of diminution was still youthful and yearned to create linear progressions. Diminution today is the product of withering imitation alone, pursued without talent. For the same reason, we find constant misunderstandings in today's editions of the masterworks and in the performance of their diminutions.

On the other hand one hears the cry for melody—most frequently meaning a tasty aural bonbon. It is amusing to watch those persons who woo melody also striving to attain a wide span. They somehow sense that music needs a certain length in which to expand and soar. But melody and length always will remain at odds, and so they devise theories to justify themselves in producing length artificially and force themselves to expand material whose nature is extreme brevity. There is hardly a compositional technique more fraught with danger than that of the "wide span of melody."

Chapter 2

Specific Characteristics of the Middleground: The First Level

Section 1: The Combination of Fundamental Line with Bass Arpeggiation

(a) An Unprolonged Fundamental Line Combined with an Ascending Bass Arpeggiation I—V That Is Prolonged by Contrapuntal-melodic Means

§ **53.** The contrapuntal-melodic prolongation in the ascending arpeggiation

By the word *melodic* I do not mean "melody" in its customary sense (§ 50), but a filling-in of the space from I to V in the bass. This space-filling motion serves to counterpoint the fundamental line, which is as yet unprolonged (§ 20).

Because the fundamental line remains unprolonged, one scarcely notices the space-filling motion with which the bass goes beyond the I—V—I of the fundamental structure. Yet, since it is a prolongation of the bass, we must regard the new contrapuntal structure as part of the first level.

§ **54.** Ways in which the bass reaches the V

The following illustration shows the possible space-fillings:

Fig. 14

In order to make this illustration understandable it is necessary to apply the concept of harmonic scale-degree here, though its systematic presentation can only come later (§§ 276 ff.) [§ 79].

§ **55.** Arpeggiation through the third

Fig. 14, Ex. 1: The paths in a) and b) represent an arpeggiation of the fifth through the third. This gives rise to the concept of a *third-divider*. The meaning of this third-divider changes according to whether it remains within the first harmonic degree, as at a), or whether it achieves the value of an independent root, especially when the third is raised (III♯), as at b). However,

29

in both instances the essential unity of the fifth-arpeggiation prevails over the third-divider.*1

§ 56.   The complete filling-in of the arpeggiation by means of seconds

Exx. 2a and 2b show the birth of seconds, which are the true bearers of the contrapuntal-melodic element. The arpeggiation is completely filled in as though it were an upper voice which is filled in by passing tones. In this way a certain state of indecision is generated between the fundamental harmonic arpeggiation and the melodic filling-in. However, this state of indecision eventually finds its resolution in the descending fifth V—I, which underscores the harmonic division of the triad more than does the melodic filling-in of the ascending arpeggiation.

Exx. 2a and 2b present the filling-in of the paths shown in Ex. 1. The filling-in can also take on other meanings, depending on the position of the tones of the fundamental line, as shown in Exx. 2c and 2d.

When, as in Ex. 2c, the fourth bass tone *F* is emphasized by a tone of the fundamental line, we then have, within the I—V motion, a linear progression of a fourth, *C—F*, with the effect of I—IV. I indicate this relationship by means of interlocking slurs, thus: I—IV—V. The V is the goal, the IV represents the subsidiary contrapuntal-melodic *step of a second* (*Jahrb. II*, pp. 21 ff.) [§§ 164, 186].

If, as at Ex. 2d, the second bass tone is made prominent by a tone of the fundamental line, there arises the relationship I—II—V, in which case I—II represents the contrapuntal-melodic *step of a second.*

§ 57.   The omission of the initial second

In Ex. 3, the illustrations of the omission of the initial second show at a) and b) an arpeggiation in thirds, corresponding to

*1. The special type of third-divider shown in Fig. 131 appears in conjunction with an interruption.   (Oster)

that shown in Exx. 1 and 2, a) and b). The illustrations at c) and d) show the effect of I—IV—V or I—II⁶—V, as in 2c) and d). In the latter two instances the third implies only a *passing-motion*, even though the second tone of the filling-in is missing, and even when, as at d), there is a ♯3; it is the stress upon the following second, given by a tone of the fundamental line, which reveals the true intention, the contrapuntal setting I—IV—V or I—II⁶—V (Fig. 15, 3c).

Those who still hear in terms of Rameau's concept of harmony obviously cannot bring themselves to disregard the third in favor of the fourth. This assuredly makes the foreground inaccessible to them. ⟨See Figs. 40, 1 and 56, 2e; also the comments on the Scherzo of Beethoven's Seventh Symphony in the translator's note following § 316.⟩

§ 58.   The omission of the final second

In Ex. 4 the result is the same as shown at a) and b) in Exx. 1, 2, and 3.

§ 59.   The omission of the first and second or the second and third passing tones

In Ex. 5 the effect is either I—IV—V or I—II⁶—V; in Ex. 6 it is I—II—V. Thus, these illustrations correspond essentially to c) and d) in Exx. 2 and 3 [§ 186].

§ 60.   The first two descending fifths

In Fig. 14, Ex. 6 there appear for the first time two descending fifths in direct succession—that is, if one considers that the ascending fourth comes about from the inversion of the first fifth. This first fifth is integrated into the arpeggiation in such a way that the melodic principle of filling-in is confirmed by the step of a second I—II. We can also regard 2d) in this same way, despite the actual filling-in of the space of a fourth.

The far-reaching significance of two such descending fifths will be demonstrated later (§ 74, §§ 276 ff.).

§ 61.   The arrhythmic nature of the contrapuntal settings in Fig. 14

All the contrapuntal settings in Fig. 14 are just as arrhythmic, ametric, and formless as the fundamental structure (§ 21) ⟨§ 67⟩.

§ 62.   The contrapuntal settings of Fig. 14 in relation to form at the foreground level

I have already mentioned that the unprolonged version of the bass of the fundamental structure suffices to achieve a form at the foreground level (Figs. 9–11). This is also the case with the contrapuntally prolonged versions shown in Fig. 14.

The transference of the bass patterns shown in Fig. 14 to individual scale-degrees at various structural levels, even in the foreground, heightens their significance and creates additional content (§§ 242 ff.).

§ 63.   Further interpolations and their abbreviation

Since the unity of the bass arpeggiation is so strong, further interpolations can occur in the filling-in motion. These take the form of descending fifths which move down to each principal tone of the melodic filling-in. The bass, in its own fashion, abbreviates these descending fifths, by drawing them together for easy contrapuntal handling, in such a way that melodically desirable seconds arise. Thus the resulting bass line appears only as a melodic enlivening of the ascending fifth ⟨descending fourth⟩ (§ 283 and Fig. 135, 1 and 2).

§ 64.   The difference between a contrapuntally prolonged bass and the bass of a *cantus firmus* exercise

Even the constant tendency of the bass to imitate the melodic characteristic of the fundamental line with seconds does not alter the fact that it must constantly and exclusively be concerned with the arpeggiation through the fifth. This is in sharp contrast to the bass of a *cantus firmus* exercise.

The approach to the dominant is also different in the contrapuntally prolonged bass from the analogous movement in the bass of a *cantus firmus* exercise. In the former it takes place through the step of a second, IV—V, whereas in the latter such a second is not required, nor is it always possible to execute it [§ 56].

Therefore, the step of a second from IV to V in foreground cadences stems from the contrapuntal aspect of music! At this point we can finally answer the question of the origin of this remarkable second. Although the spirit of the fifth (the harmonic aspect) can realize the scale-degrees, including the IV, only by means of the fifth (or the fourth as its inversion), this in no way denies the contrapuntal origin of the step of a second from IV to V. [§ 164; Figs. 37a and 44, 2.]

§ 65.   A prolongation of the descending arpeggiation V—I cannot occur at the first level

At the first structural level, $\dfrac{\hat{2}-\hat{1}}{\text{V—I}}$ provides no opportunity for a prolongation in contrapuntal-melodic terms (Figs. 15–18; §§ 74, 86, 189).

(b) Working-out and Consequences of the Contrapuntal Structure in the Case of $\hat{3}$, $\hat{5}$, or $\hat{8}$

§ 66.   The laws of strict counterpoint remain valid in the newly achieved structure

If an unprolonged fundamental line, beginning either with $\hat{3}$, $\hat{5}$, or $\hat{8}$, is to be coordinated with the contrapuntal basses shown in Fig. 14 to form a structure, it must be done according to the rules of strict counterpoint. Thus, the consonance remains the fundamental principle of voice-leading; the dissonance appears only as a passing tone or as a syncopation.

The intervals which are gained in the new structure indicate the tasks of the next structural level ⟨§ 170⟩.

§ **67.**   Two lines in contrary motion in the outer voices; the necessity of balancing them rhythmically

The descending fundamental line and the melodically rising bass constitute the first example of two linear progressions in contrary motion; this motion, regulated according to strict counterpoint, indicates the path for what follows ⟨at later levels⟩ [§§ 221 ff.].

The necessity to create a balance between the tones of the linear progressions, which may differ in number, leads for the first time to an intrinsically musical *rhythm.*

The roots of musical rhythm therefore lie in counterpoint! Since this is so, musical rhythm can be acquired neither by dancing nor by gymnastics. Only corrupted present-day musical thought could contrive such absurd methods [§ 21].

At the later levels rhythm undergoes corresponding changes until, still anchored in counterpoint, it receives its final form in the foreground, by the addition of meter (§§ 284–300).

§ **68.**   The relation of the bass to the inner voices

Here, as in strict counterpoint, the bass also establishes a relationship with the inner voices. The contrary motion in the outer voices prevents consecutive fifths and octaves as a matter of course, but these faulty progressions tend to arise between outer and inner voices. Because, from the beginning, the fundamental line is bound to its descending course, the danger of such errors is even greater here than in strict counterpoint. This is one reason why the composer, particularly in the case of $\hat{5}$ and $\hat{8}$, finds himself forced onto the path of the prolongations [§§ 161–64].

§ **69.**   Even in the newly achieved structure, tones of the fundamental line may sometimes appear as dissonant passing tones

Because of the rhythmic distribution of the intervals, tones of the fundamental line in the newly achieved structure can pass through in a dissonant state, exactly as in the form of the fundamental structure in the case of $\hat{5}$ (§ 35).

§ **70.**   Retardation by means of the prolonged bass

Since the prolonged bass-structure gives rise to new chords it has the effect, essentially, of a delaying, a retardation [§§ 30, 90].

§ **71.**   The new structure as polyphony

It is clear that we must acknowledge the existence of polyphony in the prolonged structure also, as in every example of strict counterpoint. Polyphony, after all, means nothing other than a series of intervals in their particular temporal ordering.

Incidentally, since dances (e.g., waltzes) also necessarily have their origin in a form of the fundamental structure and its prolongations, polyphony must also be ascribed to them, however difficult this may be to understand (*Kpt. I,* p. 7).

§ **72.**   Structural consequences in the case of $\hat{3}$—$\hat{1}$

The structural consequences in the case of $\hat{3}$—$\hat{1}$ are shown in

Fig. 15

These all signify life and growth, as many examples in the course of the presentation will verify.

§ **73.**   Commentary on Fig. 15

Ex. 1: The structure at b) shows the inner-voice progression which gives rise to a new chord (=III$^{\sharp\sharp}$) and assists the motion to the leading tone within V.

Ex. 2: The same remarks pertain to 2b) as to 1b).

With the first example under c) there appears the possibility of a IV, which brings with it a suspended seventh. This suspension establishes the concept of the *seventh-constraint,*[2] frequently found in the service of voice-leading within prolongations [§§ 82–84, 178, 180]. At the second example under c) the linear progression of a fourth (in the bass) at first gives the impression that its goal is IV$^7_5$. Therefore, at the entrance of $\hat{2}$ we sense a 5—6 exchange: IV$^{(5)-6}$, and thus an uncertainty as to whether we are dealing with IV, which is implied by the linear progression of a fourth, or II, which is emphasized by $\hat{2}$. An uncertainty of this kind is of course avoided when, as at d), the $\hat{2}$ appears above D in the bass.

Generally it is the progression of the inner voices which, as in the second example ⟨under⟩ c), decides between the IV$^{(5)-6}$ and the II [§ 280].

In the foreground the 5—6 exchange mentioned above can prove to be a rhythmic shift (§ 294).

Ex. 3: The structures shown in a) through c) have already been explained at 2a)–c) above. With regard to the skip preceding the passing tone at c) see § 57.

Ex. 4: This is similar to 1, 2, and 3.

Exx. 5 and 6: The explanation given for 2c) and d) also applies here.

§ 74.   Two descending fifths combined with the descending second $\hat{2}$—$\hat{1}$

In Fig. 15,6 it is highly significant that the step of a second, $\hat{2}$—$\hat{1}$, progresses together with the two descending fifths:

$$\frac{\hat{2}\text{———}\hat{1}}{\text{II—V—I}} \text{ (§ 60).}$$

*2. The necessity for the seventh to descend. (Oster)

In terms of voice-leading, the situation presents only the avoidance of parallel octaves by means of an interpolated fifth, 8—5—8 (§ 163). However, since the $\hat{2}$ is already present in the first octave, the two descending fifths accompany only one descending second of the fundamental line. Thus it is possible to strengthen the descent of the fundamental line by two descending fifths in the bass; at later levels this procedure can be transferred to an upper voice that prolongs a harmony on any scale-degree [§ 242 and Fig. 109a].

The fact that the first descending fifth *(D—G)* is expressed as an ascending fourth is allied with the striving of the bass to conform to the principles of counterpoint.

§ 75.   Structural consequences in the case of $\hat{5}$—$\hat{1}$

The structural consequences in the case of $\hat{5}$—$\hat{1}$ are shown in

Fig. 16

What was said in §§ 72–74 applies here also.

§ 76.   Structural consequences in the case of $\hat{8}$

In the case of $\hat{8}$, one must recognize significant differences between the fundamental-line segments $\hat{3}$—$\hat{2}$, $\hat{5}$—$\hat{2}$, $\hat{8}$—$\hat{2}$, all counterpointed by I—V:

Fig. 17

a) Here, because of the step of the second, a harmonic division of the fundamental-line segment $\dfrac{\hat{3}\text{—}\hat{2}}{\text{I—V}}$ does not yet occur. This second moves downward.

b) In $\dfrac{\hat{5}\text{—}\hat{2}}{\text{I—V}}$ a fourth is expressed. Harmonically it is equivalent to a fifth and also moves downward [§ 7].

c) Here, by contrast, instead of the descending motion $\frac{\hat{8}-\hat{2}}{\text{I}-\text{V}'}$ one would hear a rising second ($=c^2-d^2$); but an ascending step would be contrary to the progression of a fundamental line. This resultant effect of a rising second creates an ambiguity in all the settings of $\hat{8}$; none of them permits a thoroughgoing harmonic division of $\frac{\hat{8}-\hat{2}}{\text{I}-\text{V}}$ to occur (§§ 41–44, 100).

There are too many possible versions to present them all in one illustration. I have given only a few here:

Fig. 18

(c) The Combination of an Unprolonged Fundamental Line with Two Bass Arpeggiations

§ 77.   General considerations

In Fig. 10,2 and Fig. 11,2 and 3 lies the key to further prolongation of the bass: here the bass is provided with two arpeggiations instead of one. Though it was stationary during $\hat{5}-\hat{3}$, $\hat{8}-\hat{5}$, and $\hat{8}-\hat{3}$, the bass now forms its own cadence:

Fig. 19

Although the two cadences tend to emphasize an apparent structural division $\hat{5}-\hat{3}-\hat{1}$, $\hat{8}-\hat{5}-\hat{1}$, or $\hat{8}-\hat{3}-\hat{1}$, the fundamental line remains in an unprolonged state. This is in strong contrast to the prolongation of the fundamental line by means of an interruption (§§ 87–101).

If one can use a special bass arpeggiation with the first segment of the fundamental structure (in the case of $\hat{5}$ and $\hat{8}$), then one can also apply the same principle when the bass arpeggiation serves linear progressions that prolong individual harmonies (§§ 242 ff.).

§ 78.   Examples of the above

The graphic presentation of the examples in

Fig. 20

shows the fundamental line's progressions and the two bass arpeggiations in accordance with Fig. 19a and b. The beams serve this special purpose.

Ex. 1: In the composition the bass is only implied, but I have indicated it here.

Ex. 2: Here we have a case similar to Ex. 1. The beginning of the Fugue is preceded by a Fantasy, which in toto expresses the I, so that the fugue subject can enter on III in the middle of the first bass arpeggiation.

Ex. 4: This example is related to Fig. 19b, first example. Compare this also with J.S. Bach's Little Prelude no. 6 in *D* Minor (BWV 940) in *Jahrbuch I*, pp. 101 ff. The second example in Fig. 19b may be compared with the Little Prelude no. 12 in *A* Minor (BWV 942) in *Jahrbuch I*, pp. 117 ff.

(d) Conclusions

§ 79.   The contrapuntal aspect of the harmonic degrees

Of course, the descending fifths in the bass present the fifth as verified by nature. But upon considering the results of §§ 56, 57, 59, 60, 63, 73, and 74, we find that such fifths are also a necessary outgrowth of voice-leading. Thus they combine in themselves a harmonic and a contrapuntal principle. This becomes even more apparent in the case of fifths interpolated in the service of expanding diminutions. These foreground fifths, secured through both fifth-relationship and counterpoint, have the effect of harmonic degrees in the foreground. Therefore, *the harmonic degrees are inextricably bound up with counterpoint* (§§ 276 ff.).

§ 80.   The structures of Figs. 15, 16, and 18 in relation to form in the foreground

Though the voice-leading in Figs. 15, 16, and 18 may appear insignificant, it nevertheless has the capacity to develop foreground forms, not only of small but also of larger pieces (§§ 301 ff.).

§ 81.   Open and close positions at the first level

At the first level $\hat{3}$ represents open position, as in strict counterpoint, whereas the $\hat{5}$ and $\hat{8}$ represent the close position ⟨*Kpt. II*, III/1, § 21; *Harm.* § 13⟩.

§ 82.   Voice-leading constraint in prolonged structure

For the moment, let us disregard what the fundamental line means for diatony, for form and synthesis as a whole; what the bass means for the unity of the fundamental chord; and last, what their combination means for tonality and for the synthesis of the whole. These considerations aside, the prolonged structure at the first level displays the same inner necessity of the voice-leading which ensures onward motion as in any *cantus firmus* structure ⟨§ 73, *seventh-constraint*⟩.*3

§ 83.   Significance of the voice-leading constraint with regard to "tone-readiness"

*3. The title *Der Tonwille* expresses a similar thought: the tones have a "will" of their own, to which even the composer must submit.   (Oster)

The voice-leading constraint creates a certain "readiness" which imparts to music the same flow as language displays in its constant readiness for thought and word. In language, flow derives from the fact that the speaker knows in advance what he wants to say and therefore formulates it: if he were to delay thought until he spoke, only stammering would result. In music, however, there are even talented men, creators and interpreters, who are still far from a similar "tone-readiness." True musical fluency comparable to that in speech is to be found only in works of genius. All such readiness springs only from the voice-leading of the fundamental structure and its subsequent prolongations.

Tone-readiness is something quite different from what is commonly called "inventiveness"—the ability, for example, to invent isolated "motives." Tone-readiness presupposes the whole, whereas so-called inventiveness concerns itself only with separate elements, and with these only haphazardly. One sometimes speaks of "halting" inventiveness, or one which somehow falters. For a composer who possesses tone-readiness this cannot exist [§ 301].

Just as a pianist or a string or wind player prepares all motions of the arm, hand, finger, bow, and breath, and does not wait to form them until he has begun playing, so the composer ought to establish his linear progressions in advance.

§ 84.   Voice-leading constraint controls all individual harmonies

As a consequence of voice-leading constraint, all those individual harmonies that arise from the progression of the various voices are forced to move forward. All transient harmonies which appear in the course of a work have their source in the necessities of voice-leading [§§ 178, 180].

§ 85.   To create art by means of intellect alone is impossible

One might feel tempted to entrust musical creativity entirely to the intellect and expect favorable results. But every attempt in this direction must founder, for even prolongations bring with them occurrences intangible, inaccessible to the intellect. The true profundities of creativity are not attainable by intellect alone [§ 29].

(e) V—I at the First Level

§ 86. At the first level there is no contrapuntal prolongation within the bass progression V—I

With $\frac{\hat{2}}{\text{V}}$ the rhythmic adjustment between the fundamental line and the contrapuntal-melodic settings of the bass comes to an end (Fig. 14). Because of the step of a second in the fundamental line, the situation $\frac{\hat{2}-\hat{1}}{\text{V}-\text{I}}$ provides no occasion for any further rhythmic conflict. Only at later levels can possible prolongations of the $\hat{2}$ also provide opportunity for a special contrapuntal-melodic development of the bass. Yet, these new structures must lack the significance of the forms of the fundamental structure shown in Figs. 15, 16, and 18, because they have their origin in the descending fifth $\frac{\hat{2}-\hat{1}}{\text{V}-\text{I}}$, which has no contrapuntal power in its unprolonged state [§ 65] ⟨§ 189⟩.

Section 2: Division of the Fundamental Line

(a) Division by Interruption in the Case of $\hat{3}$

§ 87. Concept of interruption

As a linear progression of a third, the fundamental line $\hat{3}-\hat{1}$ represents the smallest range of composing-out, the ultimate unity which cannot be further split. Therefore, the fundamental line $\hat{3}-\hat{1}$ admits of only one form of division, the *interruption* $\hat{3}-\hat{2} \,\|\, \hat{3}-\hat{2}-1$. The initial succession $\hat{3}-\hat{2}$ gives the impression that it is the first attempt at the complete fundamental line.

Fig. 21

§ 88. The return to $\hat{3}$ is not a cadence

From the concept of interruption it follows that the return to $\frac{\hat{3}}{\text{I}}$ does not represent a cadence. If this return were really a full close, $\frac{\hat{2}}{\text{V}}$ would have to move down to $\frac{\hat{1}}{\text{I}}$ with the effect of a descending leading tone.[*4] Hence $\frac{\hat{2}}{\text{V}}$ appears as the limit of an initial forward motion of the fundamental line. The return to $\hat{3}$ affects us so strongly precisely because $\frac{\hat{2}}{\text{V}}$ signifies, in the case of $\hat{3}-\hat{1}$, the last possible point of interruption ⟨see also §§ 91, 106⟩.

The interruption has such a strong effect that no connective linear progressions or similar features can obscure it:

Fig. 22

a) Here we find an interruption ⟨in the fundamental line⟩, even though the bass shows a linear progression of a fourth, $e\flat$—$a\flat$, against it (cf. *Five Graphic Analyses*).[*5]

b) The bass reveals an arpeggiation of a fifth, descending through the third; however, the arpeggiation does not eliminate the interruption (§ 189).

*4. See § 17, fn. 7, concerning the "descending leading tone." (Rothgeb)

*5. Concerning the interrupted beams in the bass, compare Fig. 49,3. (Oster)

§ 89. The first V as divider

The conventional technical term *semicadence*, used to describe the first $\frac{\hat{2}}{V}$ in Fig. 21a, too easily suggests the concept of "cadence" in the sense of closure, which contradicts the true meaning of an interruption. In order to avoid this danger, and to indicate more clearly the prolongational significance of this dominant at the first level, I recommend the use of the term *dividing dominant,* or simply *divider.* This serves as a reminder that the bass, like the fundamental line, aims at only one arpeggiation, the quintal division of the triad [§ 279].

Because of the diatonic system, the dividing dominant in the minor mode is a minor chord. Its minor third is changed to a major third only for cadential purposes (*Harm.* §§ 20 ff., 45) [§ 314; Figs. 26b; 39,2; and 40,4].

§ 90. The voice-leading is interrupted at the first occurrence of $\frac{\hat{2}}{V}$

At the first occurrence of $\frac{\hat{2}}{V}$ the voice-leading undergoes an interruption. The interruption not only creates more content; it also has the effect of a delay, or retardation, on the way to the ultimate goal, $\frac{\hat{1}}{I}$ (§§ 30, 70) [§ 109]. The interruption is able to produce this effect only because it carries within it the fundamental structure, which must achieve its fulfillment despite all detours. Fig. 21b provides a precise view of the constant control that the fundamental structure exerts; only at the goal, $\frac{\hat{1}}{I}$, do we see through the game which the interruption has been playing with us. Now we understand that, with respect to the unity of the fundamental structure, the first occurrence of $\frac{\hat{2}}{V}$ is more

significant than the second.*6 This insight is decisive for the fashioning of larger forms and for the impression which they create (§§ 301 ff.).

⟨At the point of interruption⟩ the first $\hat{3}$—$\hat{2}$ represents a course already run; only the $\hat{1}$ is still lacking.*7

§ 91. The first $\hat{2}$ is not a neighboring note

Since it is associated with the fundamental structure, the first $\hat{2}$ remains true to the principle of the passing tone within the space of a third; it never takes on the character of a lower neighboring note. "Passing note" and "neighboring note" are entirely different functions ⟨§ 106⟩.

---

*6. This formulation only seems to contradict Schenker's description of the initial $\hat{3}$—$\hat{2}$ as a "first attempt" (§ 87). At the point of interruption, our first impression is indeed that the motion leading to it is "tentative"; the motion comes to a halt and remains incomplete, at least for the time being. But when we arrive at the final $\frac{\hat{1}}{I}$, we are compelled to revise this preliminary impression (§ 90). (Oster)

*7. Schenker's graphic presentation of the interruption scheme is inconsistent and may cause the reader some confusion. The form Schenker uses in Fig. 21b corresponds to the description given in § 90. But in the later examples Schenker uses this form only occasionally, for example, in Figs. 24 to 26; 154,4; and in measures 1–8 of Fig. 157. Figs. 22 and 23 show a different mode of presentation, one in which the restatement of $\hat{3}$—$\hat{2}$ is not subordinated to the overall fundamental line (see the parentheses in Fig. 21b). Rather, the two "branches," $\hat{3}$—$\hat{2}$ and $\hat{3}$—$\hat{2}$—$\hat{1}$, stand side by side, as though they were of equal weight and significance.

But the meaning is the same in both cases. When using the form of Figs. 22 and 23, Schenker did not intend to give the interruption principle an interpretation different from that shown in Fig. 21b. The reason for his frequent use of the second form is, perhaps, that it creates a simpler picture and is therefore more practical: the type of presentation of Fig. 21b is obviously not well suited to extended analyses (cf. Fig. 39,2 to Fig. 154,4). In addition, the second form is the one which Schenker used exclusively in publications preceding *Der freie Satz;* its frequent use here may very well be a carry-over from earlier times. (Oster)

§ **92.**   Upward register transfer of the seventh at $\dfrac{\hat{2}}{V^{8-7}}$

In the situation $\dfrac{\hat{2}}{V^{8-7}}$, if a passing seventh in the inner voice is transferred to the higher octave, it has, by virtue of its new register, an effect like that of an upper neighboring note to the $\hat{3}$:

Fig. 23

This neighboring-note effect is stronger when, as at a), the octave remains in the inner voice and only the seventh is transferred upward [§ 111, last paragraph].

When, however, both the octave and the seventh are transferred upward, as at b), then the original situation of the inner voice appears more clearly, and the neighboring note creates more the impression of a passing tone.

Nevertheless, in both cases the effect of a neighboring note is strengthened by the fact that the $\hat{3}$, the border tone in a neighboring-note configuration, is supported by a consonance, as in the case of a genuine neighboring-note figure in strict counterpoint (§ 108 and *Kpt. I*, II/2, § 5). Yet, a significant difference exists between the seventh transferred upward and the genuine upper neighboring note: the genuine neighboring note appears with a plagal bass motion (Fig. 32,3 and 4), or else with the arpeggiation I—V—I. In the I—V—I situation, the neighboring note usually shows itself first as an octave and eventually becomes a seventh above the V, thus: IV^8—V^7 (Fig. 32,5). Therefore, in Fig. 23, the interruption does predominate; it suppresses the deceptive effect of the seventh as a neighboring note.

When it is transferred upward, the diatonic seventh usually serves to cancel the chromatic alteration in the succession $II^\sharp$—$V^{\sharp 7}$ and, through its inherent voice-leading constraint, to regain the $\hat{3}$ in its original register.

Despite the deceptive appearance, the 8—7 succession at b) must not be grouped together with the subsequent fundamental-line tones $\hat{3}$—$\hat{2}$—$\hat{1}$ and thus construed as a linear progression of a fifth (§§ 205 ff.) [§ 116].

It is clear that an interruption occurs in the case of $\hat{3}$—$\hat{2} \parallel \hat{3}$—$\hat{2}$—$\hat{1}$. The reason that it cannot also occur in the form of $\hat{3}$—$\hat{2} \parallel \hat{2}$—$\hat{1}$ is this: in the true interruption, the succession $\hat{3}$—$\hat{2}$ is a second, but the $\hat{2}$ is understood as a passing tone in the space of a third. The succession $\hat{2}$—$\hat{1}$ lacks such a justification, since $\hat{2}$, originally a passing tone, cannot become the point of departure for a new linear progression.[*8]

In no way is the resumption of the linear progression $\hat{3}$—$\hat{2}$—$\hat{1}$ (in the case of $\hat{3}$—$\hat{2} \parallel \hat{3}$—$\hat{2}$—$\hat{1}$) to be regarded as a parallelism to the subsidiary linear progression which may descend from the first $\hat{3}$ (§ 254). Indeed, in such an instance as Beethoven's Sonata op. 27 no. 2 (Fig. 7a), the first tone of the fundamental line is reached through an arpeggiation, which makes it unnecessary for the composer to form a subsidiary linear progression from the first $\hat{3}$; nevertheless, the linear progression $\hat{3}$—$\hat{2}$—$\hat{1}$ appears in the second part.

§ **93.**   The principle of the primary tone

The first $\hat{3}$, which is the *primary tone* of the total fundamental line $\hat{3}$—$\hat{1}$, although not expressly retained, is taken up again by the second $\hat{3}$, as primary tone of the resumed linear progression which now leads to $\hat{1}$. The actual retention of a primary tone (in order to make the inner connection quite apparent) would conflict with the nature of diminution, which requires motion. Thus, the primary tone combines within itself a mental retention, that is, a motionless state, and an actual motion of the linear progression—an invaluable source of compositional technique! ⟨See *Kpt. II, III/2*, § 2.⟩

---

*8. More exactly, the $\hat{2}$ can become the point of departure only for a linear progression belonging to a later level; see § 118 and Figs. 34b and 35,1. (Rothgeb)

To appreciate this principle of the primary tone, that is, to recognize its dual function based in voice-leading ⟨first, as a passively retained tone and second, as the generator of a linear progression⟩, demands that one turn away from the visual impression of the notation, something not easily achieved by beginners [§§ 301, 315].

§ 94. Interruption as a source of form in the foreground

Interruption has the quality of heightening the tension toward $\hat{1}$; particularly, it opens the way to two- or three-part forms, a_1—a_2 or a_1—b—a_2. It is even the basis of the extended form of the sonata, with exposition, development, and recapitulation (§§ 301 ff.).

(b) Division by Interruption in the Case of $\hat{5}$

§ 95. Interruption takes the form $\hat{5}$—$\hat{2}\,\|\,\hat{5}$—$\hat{1}$ only

As in the case of $\hat{3}$—$\hat{1}$, the interruption of $\hat{5}$—$\hat{1}$ must push forward to $\frac{\hat{2}}{V}$:

Fig. 24

For an explanation of the difference between this interruption form and the seeming division $\hat{5}$—$\hat{3}$—$\hat{1}$ see § 36. All other divisions belong to later levels.

§ 96. The initial $\hat{5}$ as primary tone

Besides resting on $\frac{\hat{2}}{V}$, the interruption of $\hat{5}$—$\hat{1}$ rests also on the first $\hat{5}$ as the primary tone of the linear progression $\hat{5}$—$\hat{2}$,

just as though the line of a fourth were not present between these two points.*9

§ 97. The return from $\hat{2}$ to $\hat{5}$ involves no cadence

The return from $\hat{2}$ to $\hat{5}$ no more involves a cadence than did the return from $\hat{2}$ to $\hat{3}$ in the case of $\hat{3}$—$\hat{2}\,\|\,\hat{3}$—$\hat{2}$—$\hat{1}$. In both instances the return has its psychological root in the fact that at $\frac{\hat{2}}{V}$ the descending leading tone does not follow its inherent tendency (§ 88).

§ 98. The octave transferred upward at $\frac{\hat{2}}{V}$ does not have a neighboring-note effect

The upward register transfer of the octave at $\frac{\hat{2}}{V}$ is shown in:

Fig. 25

There can be no neighboring-note effect here ⟨cf. Fig. 23b⟩.

The direct transfer of the octave is often replaced by an ascending linear progression:

Fig. 26

This linear progression can begin either with the next-to-last tone, as in a), or with the last tone, as in b), of the descending fourth.*10

*9. This means that the $\hat{5}$, the primary tone, could actually appear above the $\hat{2}$—and not only conceptually as in the case of $\hat{3}$. (Jonas)

*10. Both cases occur predominantly in the minor mode, particularly Fig. 26a. In Fig. 26b there is usually a transformation of the $V^{\natural 3}$ into a $V^{\sharp 3}$ (§§ 89, 249, and 314). Compare 26a with Fig. 154,3 and 7. Compare 26b with Fig. 152,6. (Jonas)

§ 99. $\hat{5}$—$\hat{2}$ ‖ $\hat{5}$—$\hat{1}$ as a source of form in the foreground

Interruption first of all points to the two-part form, a_1—a_2.

The initial linear progression already encompasses four tones of the total line. This distance provides the opportunity to prolong, step by step, each tone of the line (especially the $\hat{3}$ and even more so the $\frac{\hat{2}}{V}$). One can even create the effect of modulation and a new key in the foreground or reinforce the entire fourth-progression by repeating it. All these emphases and delays only intensify the desire to reach the final $\hat{1}$. Generally such prolongations lead to three-part form, as shown in Fig. 26a and b. Thus we see that three-part form develops out of two-part form, which in turn is brought about by interruption—all again tracing back to the undivided fundamental structure (§§ 34 ff.). Again, one must marvel at the inexorable control of the fundamental structure and the logic of the resulting development.

The apparent halt after $\hat{5}$—$\hat{4}$—$\hat{3}$ in Fig. 26a does not denote an interruption of the linear progression of a fourth in the strict sense of the concept; the unity of the line extends to $\hat{2}$. For example, in the first movement of Mozart's *G*-Minor Symphony (*Jahrb. II*) we have:

$$\hat{5} \quad \hat{4} \quad \hat{3} \quad \Big] \quad \hat{2} \quad \Big(\quad \Big) \quad \hat{1}$$
$$d^2 \quad c^2 \quad bb^1 \qquad a^1 \qquad\qquad g^1$$

Exp.————————Dev.———Recap.

The linear progression of a fourth forces itself through the exposition and development, even in the larger forms, no matter how much this motion may be concealed by a return to $\hat{5}$ [§ 313, explanation of Fig. 154,3; also Fig. 154,4].

(c) Divison by $\hat{8}$—$\hat{5}$—$\hat{1}$ in the Case of $\hat{8}$

§ 100. Linear division in the case of $\hat{8}$

The linear progression of an octave $\hat{8}$—$\hat{1}$ makes an interruption at $\frac{\hat{2}}{V}$ impossible. The reason for this has been given in § 76.

As a substitute for the interruption at $\frac{\hat{2}}{V}$, the division $\begin{array}{c}\hat{8}-\hat{5}\ \ \hat{5}-\!\!-\!\!-\hat{1}\\ \text{I—V—I—V—I}\end{array}$, in the form shown in the first example of Fig. 19b, is used.

§ 101. The linear division $\hat{8}$—$\hat{5}$ ‖ $\hat{5}$—$\hat{1}$ as a source of form in the foreground

This division gives rise to a two- or three-part form:

Fig. 27

In both of these divisions, prolongations in the $\hat{7}$—$\hat{6}$—$\hat{5}$ succession bring about even stronger effects of modulation and key in the foreground.

Section 3: Mixture

§ 102. Mixture at the third of the fundamental line is mixture of the first order

In the fundamental structure (Figs. 9–11), the fundamental line remains strictly diatonic. At the first level, however, it can contain a *mixture* of the major and the minor third. In this regard, it makes no difference whether the fundamental line begins with $\hat{3}$, $\hat{5}$, or $\hat{8}$:

Fig. 28

Mixture at the sixth of course cannot occur in the case of $\hat{3}$ and $\hat{5}$. It is not feasible even in the case of $\hat{8}$—$\hat{1}$: the fourth $\hat{8}$—$\hat{5}$ is artificial (§ 7), and, specifically, the interval succession 6—5 [*11] makes the decisive cadential figure I—V—I impossible:

Fig. 29

However, in the foreground, particularly in a coda, one is free to use mixture at the sixth of an octave-progression.

A possible chromatic alteration of the fifth in the inner voice, as in Fig. 15,1, 2, 3b, has no bearing upon mixture of the third in the fundamental line.

Fig. 30

The examples in Fig. 30 refer to Fig. 28a. Compare also Brahms's "Auf dem Kirchhofe," Chopin's Prelude in *Db* Major, and his Waltz in *C♯* Minor.

In connection with Fig. 28b, note Beethoven's Seventh Symphony, Allegretto; Haydn's Symphony no. 103 in *Eb (Drum Roll)*, Andante; and his Andante and Variations in *F* Minor for piano.

---

11. In the first edition, the interval succession is displayed as follows:

$$\hat{6}\text{—}\hat{5}$$
$$6\text{—}5.$$

The second German edition reads (paradoxically) the interval succession "$\hat{6}$—$\hat{5}$." The meaning of the sentence as a whole is somewhat obscure: the cadential progression I—V—I is no more readily available for a diatonic $\hat{6}$—$\hat{5}$ succession than it is for one involving mixture at the sixth ($b\hat{6}$—$\hat{5}$). And there are several reasons against assuming that Schenker has in mind a I—V—I progression relating to V in the sense of a tonicization.   (Rothgeb)

§ 103.   Relation of mixture of the first order to form

The mixed third does not represent a linear progression or a neighboring note. It provides no occasion for a cadence, but can only give form the opportunity to set off two or three sections against one another. Certainly, this also means a delay, a tension, but, in a strict organic sense, mixture is less form-indicating, less form-generating than division or interruption [§ 312].

Section 4:   The Phrygian $\hat{2}$ in the Fundamental Line

§ 104.   The $b\hat{2}$ at the first level

In the fundamental structure a Phrygian $\hat{2}$ can no more exist than can a mixture. At the first level, however, because of the constant rapport with the middleground and foreground, the voice-leading frequently creates the necessity of admitting the $b\hat{2}$, just as mixture may be admitted [§ 194].

§ 105.   The setting of the $b\hat{2}$ and the so-called Neapolitan sixth

In accord with Fig. 9, the harmonic-contrapuntal setting of the $b\hat{2}$ would read as in a) of

Fig. 31

In this way, either an augmented fourth or a diminished fifth would result in the bass line. Also, because of the cross-relation, the root of the bII would make it difficult to adjust the $b\hat{2}$ by restoring diatonic $\hat{2}$. In order to avoid all these difficulties, a sixth (the bass tone which is also the root of IV) is placed below the $b\hat{2}$—as in Fig. 31b). This sixth has been misunderstood and introduced into theory as the "Neapolitan sixth." It is, however, an event that originates only in voice-leading and has nothing to do with a Neapolitan school (*Harm.* § 50) [§ 280, below commentary on Fig. 132,4].

Section 5: The Neighboring Note

§ 106.   Only the upper neighboring note is possible at the first level

If it occurred in the fundamental line, the lower neighboring note would give the impression of an interruption [§ 91]. The upper neighboring note, however, is free from the danger of such misunderstanding. Hence it alone can appear at the first level, as a neighboring note of the first order. At the same time, it provides a glimpse into the next higher tone-space without working it out completely [§ 112]. Thus the essential space in the case of $\hat{3}\overset{\text{Nbn}}{-}4-\hat{3}-\hat{2}-\hat{1}$ remains $\hat{3}-\hat{1}$.

In the case of $\hat{5}$, since the interruption-form $\hat{5}-\hat{4}\,\|\,\hat{5}-\hat{1}$ is impossible, only the upper neighboring-note 6 can occur. This does not alter the essential space $\hat{5}-\hat{1}$.

In the case of $\hat{8}$ the upper neighboring note can never occur, because it would overstep the bounds of the octave space. As substitution for $\hat{8}\overset{\text{Nbn}}{-}9-\hat{8}$, a neighboring note may appear at a later level as an embellishment to the $\hat{5}$.

A final observation: the neighboring note of $\hat{3}$ is dissonant to the I, whereas the neighboring note of $\hat{5}$ is consonant. This affects not only the harmonic-contrapuntal setting of the neighboring note, but also, indirectly, the form [§§ 111, 175, 247].

§ 107.   The position of the neighboring note of the first order

The neighboring note of the fundamental line thus belongs to the primary tones $\hat{3}$ or $\hat{5}$. Hence, the following forms are impossible: $\hat{3}-\hat{2}\overset{\text{Nbn}}{-}3-\hat{2}-\hat{1}$ or $\hat{5}-\hat{4}\overset{\text{Nbn}}{-}5-\hat{4}-\hat{3}-\hat{2}-\hat{1}$. Thus, in doubtful cases only the neighboring note of the first order can decide whether $\hat{3}$ or $\hat{5}$ is the primary tone. The neighboring-note figure $\hat{3}\overset{\text{Nbn}}{-}4-\hat{3}$ is not, however, to be confused with a neighboring-note harmony which precedes the $\hat{3}$, such as that shown in Fig. 12 or Fig. 63,3.

Since, in the case of $\hat{8}-\hat{1}$, a neighboring note can appear only with the $\hat{5}$, one occasionally might misconstrue the $\hat{5}$ as the primary tone (§ 106).

§ 108.   The setting of the neighboring note

The neighboring-note concept, as understood in the second or third species of strict counterpoint, requires the return of the main tone with a consonant interval. Thus, the neighboring-note figure is based upon a consonance at the beginning as well as at the end. This is shown in Exx. 1 and 2 of

Fig. 32

The same requirement of strict counterpoint is also met in the Exx. 3 to 7, where we have:

$$\overset{\text{Nbn}}{\text{I}}\text{—IV—I},\ \overset{\text{Nbn}}{\text{I}}\text{—VI—I (3 and 4)};\ \text{I—IV}^8\overset{\text{Nbn}}{\overset{\frown}{-}}\text{V}^7\text{—I (5);}$$
$$\text{IV}$$

and finally a neighboring note arising from I—V$^{5-7}$—I (7).

§ 109.   The neighboring note as retardation

The melodic expansion of the fundamental line by means of the neighboring note (and the consequent illusion of a new tone in the fundamental line) has the effect of a delaying [§§ 30, 70, 90].

§ 110.   How the neighboring-note formation differs from an interruption

In contrast to the interruption, the neighboring-note formation remains at the same pitch level and thus reinforces the primary tone.

The neighboring note cannot be supported by the V in the same manner as can the $\hat{2}$ in the interruption shown in Figs. 21 and 24. Therefore, it lacks the weight of the $\frac{\hat{2}}{V}$ and stresses rather the effect of delay, particularly in cases where it is supported only by the IV or VI (Fig. 32,3 and 4). Where it has its own cadential bass (Fig. 32,5 and 6), the neighboring note is more organically established.

In interruption, the main part of the line has already run its course with $\hat{3}$—$\hat{2}$ or $\hat{5}$—$\hat{2}$. But in the case of the neighboring note, no matter how it is structurally supported, greater importance is attached to the descending line which follows the return of the main tone.

Since structural division and the neighboring note represent two different concepts, independent of one another, they can be combined. Thus, in the case of $\hat{8}$—$\hat{1}$ the employment of the neighboring note to $\hat{5}$ represents such a combination of division and neighboring note (§ 155).

§ 111.   The neighboring note as a source of form

The neighboring note, however humble it may appear to be in content and nature, carries within itself a fundamental musical idea, a great voice-leading occurrence.

The neighboring note of the fundamental line is in most cases form generative; its inherent delaying quality brings organic unity to that which in the foreground is a two- or three-part form.

The plagal setting in Fig. 32,3 and 4 is self-contained. Therefore, it is not permissible to read the neighboring-note harmony (IV or VI) together with the final V as a cadence. Nevertheless, the neighboring note in such a setting can be expanded at the foreground level to become the middle part of a three-part form.

The two cadences in the bass in Fig. 32,5 and 6, the first of which organically establishes the neighboring note, suggest a two-part form, which can eventually lead to a three-part form at the foreground level.

An interruption such as that in Fig. 32,7 indicates a two-part form, as does the apparent neighboring note brought about by the register transfer of the seventh. This does not exclude the possibility that a more significant working-out of the seventh could bring about a three-part form (§ 92 and Fig. 23a).

§ 112.   Preliminary discussion of the neighboring note at subsequent levels

At later levels a neighboring note can occur with any tone. The further it departs from the basic version found in strict counterpoint, the less form generative it is. It then serves only purposes of embellishment or expansion.

Section 6:   Linear Progressions

(a) General

§ 113.   A linear progression at the first level always relates to a tone of the fundamental line

A linear progression at the first level I call a *linear progression of the first order*.

An ascending or descending linear progression of the first order must, by definition, be related to a tone of the fundamental line. This can be any fundamental-line tone. In the case of a descending line, the fundamental-line tone will be the primary tone, the point of departure; in an ascending line, it will be the goal tone.

(b) Descending Linear Progressions of the First Order

§ 114. In the systematic presentation of linear progressions the descending line takes precedence over the ascending line

Because of the relationship of the descending linear progression to the all-encompassing descending fundamental line, it is appropriate to give the descending line preference in a systematic presentation ⟨§ 10⟩.

§ 115. The descending line of the first order signifies a progression from the upper to an inner voice

As a result of the continuing presence of the primary tone ⟨i.e., its mental retention⟩, a descending linear progression of the first order which departs from a tone of the fundamental line involves a progression from the upper voice to an inner voice: in the case of a third-progression, to the closest inner voice; in the case of a fifth-progression, to the second inner voice. The linear progressions present a horizontalization of the originally vertical intervals of the fundamental structure: 3 (10), 5. They form a new upper voice, which can only be understood as an offshoot of the fundamental structure.

Thus, the fifth and third of nature manifest themselves not only in the fundamental linear progressions $\hat{3}$—$\hat{1}$ or $\hat{5}$—$\hat{1}$ and in the counterpointing arpeggiation of the bass through the fifth, but also in fifth- and third-progressions which descend from a tone of the fundamental line. This agreement with nature and with the fundamental structure reveals itself even in the linear progressions of the transformation levels. Thus, on the way from fundamental structure to foreground, the unity of nature and art becomes stronger and stronger.

§ 116. Linear progressions of the first order display the characteristics of a fundamental line

All the characteristics of a fundamental line as found in the case of $\hat{3}$—$\hat{1}$ and $\hat{5}$—$\hat{1}$ also apply to descending linear progressions of the first order.

The relationships between the new upper voice of the linear progression and the new bass must be clearly defined, exactly as in the case of a fundamental structure. The possibilities of the linear progression must be fully utilized and thus fully realized [§ 36].

That which is both will and necessity in the fundamental line is also will and necessity in the derived linear progressions; in other words, the derived linear progression wants itself to be a true linear progression. A negative example, that of a tonal succession which has no will to be a linear progression, is to be seen in Fig. 23b of § 92 (also §§ 205–7).

Every linear progression shows the eternal shape of life—birth to death. The linear progression begins, lives its own existence in the passing tones, ceases when it has reached its goal—all as organic as life itself.

§ 117. The setting of linear progressions descending from $\hat{3}$ or $\hat{5}$

The support provided by I—V—I or by the prolonged bass forms shown in Fig. 14 imparts to the linear progressions which descend from $\hat{3}$ or $\hat{5}$ the effect of a fundamental structure or of a form of the fundamental structure as shown in Figs. 15 and 16 (§§ 242 ff.):

Fig. 33

Therefore, at the first level such linear progressions are chiefly encountered in connection with an interruption (Figs. 22b; 23) or with a neighboring note (Fig. 32, 3–7) ⟨Fig. 154, 3⟩. Quite apart from its expansion of content, the linear progression which departs from the first tone of the fundamental line exerts a special charm: the deceptive effect of a fundamental line, which it maintains until the interruption or the neighboring note enters upon the scene. This effect, so often sought, gives us an additional reason for giving first place to the descending progression in the systematic presentation of the linear progressions.

§ **118.**   Linear progressions descending from $\hat{2}$

The third-progression which departs from $\hat{2}$ leads to the ascending leading tone:

Fig. 34

a) If the $\hat{2}$ proceeds to $\hat{1}$ without an interruption, it fulfills melodically, by means of a third-progression, the requirement of three-part strict counterpoint that the tonic be entered by means of both leading tones (*Kpt. II*, III/1, § 27). The employment of the ascending leading tone, unattainable for the fundamental line in the fundamental structure, is made possible at the first level by the third-progression which departs from $\hat{2}$. It is clear that the ascending leading tone belongs to an inner voice.

b) The advantage of including the ascending leading tone in the composing-out is also provided in the case of an interruption (Fig. 7a).

c) Here, in addition to the line departing from $\hat{2}$, there is one which departs from $\hat{3}$. Examples of this follow:

Fig. 35

Occasionally, a third-progression from $\hat{2}$ is utilized in order to avoid an augmented second. The third-progression introduces the leading tone from above [cf. Fig. 74, 1]:

Fig. 36

§ **119.**   Relation to form

It is fairly evident that the linear progressions shown in Fig. 34 and in the examples of Fig. 35 lead the way to two- or three-part forms. This will be discussed further in the chapter on form.

(c) The Ascending Linear Progression

§ **120.**   The first tone of the fundamental line is the only possible goal for an ascending line

At the first level an ascending linear progression can move only to the first tone of the fundamental line: $\overset{\frown}{1\ 2\ \hat{3}}$, $\overset{\frown}{1\ 2\ 3\ 4\ \hat{5}}$, or, abbreviated, $\overset{\frown}{\hat{3}\ 4\ \hat{5}}$, $\overset{\frown}{\hat{5}\ 6\ 7\ \hat{8}}$. This I call an *initial ascent*.

Because of its ascending motion, this linear progression represents a basic conceptual contrast to the fundamental line; to confuse the two is impossible. Therefore, the tones of the initial ascent are never to be considered as tones of the fundamental line (with the exception of the final tone); they comprise, in relation to the fundamental structure, a *new upper voice* ⟨§ 115⟩:

Fig. 37

§ **121.**   The principle of the primary tone remains effective for the ascending line

The principle of the primary tone also applies to the ascending linear progression ⟨§ 93⟩. Thus, the ascending line contains both the primary tone and the goal tone, the latter having priority here because it is simultaneously the first tone of the fundamental line.

§ **122.**   The ascending line is a motion from the inner to the upper voice

Because of the principle of the primary tone, the ascending line is basically only a motion from the inner voice to the upper voice ⟨§ 115⟩. Therefore the first tone of the fundamental line comes into being through a melodic development, not in abbreviated chordal fashion (§ 12).

§ 123.   Structure of the initial ascent

The goal tones $\hat{3}$ and $\hat{5}$ prevent the effect of a complete close, such as is created by the descending line shown in Fig. 33. To be sure, the diatonic fourth-progression $\hat{5}$—$\hat{8}$ displays the leading tone, and so an effective close could be made even though the line ascends. But a complete initial ascent to $\hat{8}$ (1—$\hat{8}$) would result in too heavy a burden for the fundamental line $\hat{8}$—$\hat{1}$. There is no example of this in the literature of music. For $\hat{5}$—$\hat{8}$, see Fig. 20,4.

However, at a later level, a leading-tone effect may be achieved by means of a prolongational employment of chromatics, if such tones are aided by their respective dominants (§§ 244 ff.):

Fig. 38

Especially in an initial ascent to $\hat{5}$, the ♯4 is frequently employed. The $\hat{5}$ receives thereby an extra emphasis, particularly when in the foreground the chromatic event takes the form of a modulation to the key of the dominant (Fig. 38,b–d) [§ 167].

§ 124.   The initial ascent as retardation

The initial ascent represents a delaying at the very outset of the piece. This can serve various purposes:

Fig. 39

Ex. 1: The initial ascent virtually depicts the breathing ("atme kühl im Licht des Mondes, träume süss im stillen Mute"—

"breathing coolness in the moonlight, dreaming sweetly here in silence").

Ex. 2: Often it makes an onward movement of the bass possible, so that the first tone of the fundamental line appears over a degree other than I, effectively heightening the inner tension [§ 127].*12

[Ex. 3: Cf. § 277, last paragraph, and also Fig. 119,3 and Fig. 120,6a.]

Section 7:   Arpeggiation

§ 125.   An arpeggiation of the first order ascends to the first tone of the fundamental line

The only *arpeggiation* at the first level is that which ascends to the first tone of the fundamental line:

Fig. 40

§ 126.   The space of the arpeggiation

The ⟨vertical⟩ distance encompassed by the arpeggiation depends on whether $\hat{3}$ or $\hat{5}$ is the goal. Of course, an arpeggiation of a third may lead up to $\hat{3}$. However, such a broken third is often employed in the service of an unfolding (§ 140); this easily leads to misunderstanding ⟨compare Fig. 45⟩.

Fig. 40, Exx. 1 and 2: The arpeggiation of a tenth represents that of a third.

Exx. 3–6: The arpeggiation of a sixth up to $\hat{3}$ is properly understood as the upper part of an arpeggiation of a tenth. Root

---

*12. The small vertical brackets which appear above the section of the lower example pertaining to bars 30–38 are intended merely to draw attention to the vertical intervals with which they are aligned: they point out the succession of three fifths, which is eliminated by the interpolated sixths (cf. § 164). In general, vertical brackets are used in the examples to point out vertical intervals, while horizontal brackets point out motivic parallelisms.   (Rothgeb)

and third appear to be skipped over; the arpeggiation begins with the fifth (Fig. 7a).

Ex. 7: Octave arpeggiations beginning with the third are less frequently found (Fig. 13).

Exx. 8 and 9: The arpeggiation to $\hat{5}$ can move through a fifth or an octave.

§ 127.   The setting of arpeggiations of the first order

During an arpeggiation the bass can do one of three things:

1. It can remain on I (Fig. 40,4 and 5).
2. It can move according to one of the prolonged forms shown in Fig. 14, as follows:
    in Fig. 40,2 as in Fig. 14,3c;
    in Fig. 40,1 as in Fig. 14,3d;
    in Fig. 40,3 as in Fig. 14,5.
    (In the last example an arpeggiation leads downward by thirds from I to II.)
3. It can display an irregular prolongation; compare the neighboring-note harmony in Fig. 13 [§ 303].

§ 128.   The relationship of the first arpeggiation to possible later ones

The arpeggiation of the first order can evoke parallelisms:

In Fig. 40,10 the second arpeggiation f^2—bb^2 forms a parallelism to the initial e^{b2}—c^3.

In Fig. 40,9 the first ascending arpeggiation a^1—e^2 subsequently receives a droll reply in several descending arpeggiations, until, near the end, the ascending direction reasserts itself in the arpeggiations of the sixth and octave.

In Fig. 40,4 and 5, by contrast, the line descending from $\hat{2}$ does not represent a parallelism to the first arpeggiation rising to $\hat{3}$.

Section 8:   Reaching-over [13]

§ 129.   The nature of reaching-over

When a group of at least two descending tones is used to place an inner voice into a higher register, I call the phenomenon a *reaching-over (Uebergreifen)*. This can occur either in direct superposition or consecutively:

Fig. 41

The purpose of reaching-over is either to confirm the original pitch-level or to gain another.

The very statement of these purposes implies the necessity of rapport with both background and foreground.

§ 130.   The succession of reaching-over

The two-tone succession in the reaching-over must descend. An ascending succession would be contrary to the purpose of the reaching-over.

A reaching-over has obligation only to its goal. Thus, the individual entries are permitted complete freedom with respect to interval; from the final tone of one entry to the first tone of the next this interval can be a third, fourth, fifth, or whatever.

In order to clarify the visual representation of such irregular intervals, I have marked the individual entries with small slurs below the notes.

§ 131.   The setting of the reaching-over

Fig. 41a and Ex. 1: Here the direct superposition restricts the passage harmonically, since both the tones ⟨which show the contraction⟩ belong to the same chord ⟨cf. Fig. 65,6⟩.

*13. See the editorial comments after § 134.   (Oster)

Fig. 41, b–d, and Ex. 2: This reaching-over, which occurs consecutively, is less dense because the two tones involved may form different intervals with the bass. In this way the entries are more clearly defined.

Fig. 41e: Often, and particularly when fourths appear between the entries, an additional tone (with its structurally suitable bass tone) must be placed before the two-tone succession. This procedure then introduces the actual two-tone succession, which, however, creates the misleading impression of a three-tone succession ⟨§§ 205–7⟩.

§ 132.   Reaching-over at the first level serves the primary tone

In the service of the primary tone, a reaching-over can occur with the effect of—

1. a neighboring note (Fig. 41, a1, b1);
2. a linear progression which has the sense of an initial ascent (Fig. 41a, 2–4; b, 2 and 3; c and Exx. 1 and 2);
3. an arpeggiation (Fig. 41, d and e, and Ex. 3; also Fig. 47, 2).

The more the entries of the reaching-over restrict themselves to chord tones, the more the entries themselves resemble an arpeggiation. If greater freedom is employed, the arpeggiation becomes less obvious and the reaching-over predominates until the goal is attained, bringing complete clarification.

The amount of ⟨vertical⟩ space which the reaching-over occupies does not affect the concept. The intervals are determined by the particularities of the work involved: the rapport with background and middleground is decisive. Thus, the space of a reaching-over can even read: 1—3—5—8—5 (Bach, Two-part Invention in *E♭* Major).

§ 133.   The reaching-over differs from related prolongations: linear progressions, arpeggiations, register transfer

The freedom in the choice of intervals between the individual entries distinguishes reaching-over from other related prolongations: from a linear progression, where all the passing tones must be present, and from an arpeggiation, which rests on chord tones alone. Register transfer, in contrast to reaching-over, cannot make use of a motive ⟨the two- or three-tone succession characteristic of reaching-over⟩.

§ 134.   Reaching-over at later levels

In the presentation of later structural levels I shall show how the reaching-over technique can relate to tones other than the primary tone (§§ 231–32).

⟨Since Schenker's definition and presentation of *reaching-over* is somewhat lacking in clarity, a few additional editorial comments may be in order.

Uebergreifen means literally reaching over, or across, the top voice, in order to get hold of the following higher tone.

A reaching-over may appear in two basic forms (A and B):

A₁. The general scheme of this form is shown in Fig. 41, b2 and b3. The first tone of the top voice descends one or more steps, whereupon an inner voice crosses above, in order to establish the new pitch of the top voice. Here the main tone (c^2) generates the lower tone (b^1). Examples:

Fig. 41, Ex. 2: The reaching-over results in an initial ascent.

Fig. 41, Ex. 3: The reaching-over results in an arpeggiation.

Fig. 100, 3d: The reaching-over results in an ascending third-progression.

Fig. 101, 3: The descending group appears in the form of a third-arpeggiation (see Schenker's comments in § 232).

Fig. 101, 4: The descending group appears in the form of a third-progression.

Fig. 101, 5: See Schenker's comments in § 232.

A₂, a contraction of A₁. The last tone of the first group and the superimposed tone of the inner voice appear simultaneously. Thus, Fig. 41,a2 and a3 show the contracted forms of Fig. 41,b2 and b3. See also Figs. 65,6; 89,2; 101,1.

B. The general scheme of this form is shown in Fig. 41d. The superimposed inner-voice tone introduces a tone of the upper voice from above and so resembles an upper neighboring note. In this form, the lower tone is the main tone and is introduced by the upper tone. Examples:

Fig. 47,2: measures 14–18.

Fig. 53,5: a^1, e^2—d^2.

Fig. 102,3: eb^1, g^2—f^2 (see *Jahrb. III*, p. 39 and illustrations).

Fig. 123,5: $c\sharp^2$, e^2—$d\sharp^2$.

Fig. 153,3: measures 22 ff.

In Fig. 23b, the tones d^2, g^2—f^2 represent the basic idea of the reaching-over as it frequently appears in a sonata movement. See Fig. 47,2, measures 61 ff.; also Beethoven, *Eroica*, first movement, bb^2—ab^2 in measures 144–52 *(Jahrb. III)*.

C. Both forms described above at A₁ and B may appear in succession, as in Fig. 41,b1 (contracted: Fig. 41,a1) or at the beginnings of Fig. 41c and 41e. See Fig. 101,2; further Fig. 101,5 and the similar situation in Fig. 109,e6.   (Oster)⟩

Section 9: Motion from the Inner Voice

§ 135.   The nature of motion from the inner voice

Motion from the inner voice (Untergreifen) means a reaching-down to an inner voice at a lower register, in order to work back from there to the original register.

This procedure is used to introduce a certain slowing down into the motion of the upper voice, and to postpone arrival at the goal if for some reason it would be reached too soon.

As a result of this technique there appears on the surface a new voice which seems to spring forth from an unknown source. However, rapport with the fundamental structure makes it clear that this upper voice is only seemingly new. It is as though the original register were suspended until it is regained by the motion from the inner voice.

§ 136.   Motion from the inner voice at the first level

At the first structural level this motion from the inner voice cannot relate to the first tone of the fundamental line. It can only lead to a subsequent tone in the fundamental line or to a neighboring note. The specific means employed is in accord with the particular goal.

Fig. 42

§ 137.   How a motion from an inner voice differs from an initial ascent

An initial ascent applies only to the first tone of the fundamental line. As stated above, this relationship is denied to a motion from the inner voice at the first structural level.[14]

§ 138.   The motion from the inner voice combined with other prolongations

Most frequently, a motion from an inner voice at the first structural level appears in conjunction with other prolongations, for example with a neighboring note, as in Fig. 42 [§ 155].

---

[14]. This may appear to be only a terminological convention, but in fact it is something more. Following the definition given in § 135, the concept of *motion from the inner voice* includes the notion of *reaching-down* from an already established higher register in order to rise back to the original one. Clearly, no such reaching-down could occur at the first level without the prior establishment of the first tone of the fundamental line.   (Rothgeb)

§ **139.** A glimpse into later levels

At later structural levels the motion from an inner voice strives toward goals of various sorts.

Section 10: Unfolding

§ **140.** The nature of unfolding

An *unfolding* occurs in the following situations:

Fig. 43

1. when the vertical condition of a single chord is transformed into a horizontal condition in such a manner that a tone of the upper voice is connected to a tone of the inner voice and then moves back to the upper voice, or the reverse (a);
2. when in a succession of several chords a similar connection from the upper to the inner voice takes place (b to f).

By means of unfolding the upper voice is expanded; the basic meaning is revealed by the background [§ 234].

§ **141.** Commentary on Fig. 43

In Fig. 43 b–f the beams indicate the upper and lower voices of the original vertical successions.

Fig. 43b, 4 and 5: The two voices which are spread out in the upper or inner parts are not to be taken for a fourth-progression, since their origin lies only in the step of a second in the upper voice (§ 205). Observe also how the unfolding figure is counterpointed by itself and thus creates a two-part setting.

Fig. 43f, 2: Similarly here, the unfolding presents a third-progression in the upper voice, despite the apparent fifth-progression.

Fig. 43b, 3 and 43e: Compare Fig. 40, 3 and Fig. 7b.

See also the examples accompanying Fig. 43 as well as Fig. 103 [§ 234].

§ **142.** Unfolding at the first level

Unfolding at the first level applies only to the primary tone (Fig. 43, first example); to a series of fundamental-line tones, such as $\hat{3}$—$\hat{2}$ (Fig. 40, 3 and Fig. 43, second example); or to a neighboring note (Fig. 7b).

The use of unfolding has become almost a formula in particular endings:

Fig. 44

§ **143.** How unfolding differs from other types of prolongation

Arpeggiation (§§ 125 ff.) must move in only one direction, either ascending or descending.

Coupling (§ 152) is restricted to the octave, whereas in an unfolding other intervals can be expressed.

A procedure identical with unfolding may have another significance; only the rapport with the fundamental structure can determine the true meaning, as here:

Fig. 45

where the diminution above the actual upper voice is an instance of "boundary-play" (§ 260).

Compare Fig. 45 and Fig. 82, 2; also with Fig. 37a, measures 7–8.

§ **144.** Unfolding at later levels

Unfolding serves various purposes at the later levels. In the bass it plays a significant role, particularly in connection with

5—6 successions and the avoidance of parallel fifths (§ 234) [Fig. 103, 5a and b].

Section 11:   Substitution

§ 145.   The nature of substitution

Even at the first level, a tone which is not part of the fundamental line can substitute for a fundamental-line tone.

Such a *substitution* is generally combined with an interruption, an unfolding, or an ascending register transfer. However, it is easily recognizable as a substitution because the counterpointing bass arpeggiation clearly indicates the actual tone of the fundamental line, even though it is hidden.

§ 146.   Examples of substitution at the first level

For the most part substitution at the first level is to be found in short pieces. Most frequently the substitution applies to the $\hat{2}$ [§ 235]: *15

Fig. 46

Substitution for $\hat{1}$ is occasionally found in a work comprised of short pieces, for example in a set of waltzes, where it makes the connection of the parts smoother. See Schubert: *Valses Nobles* no. 4, where, at the end, the third, b^3, substitutes for $\hat{1}$, g^3.

Section 12:   Ascending Register Transfer

§ 147.   The nature of ascending register transfer

Ascending register transfer means a raising to a higher octave. The octave interval is the basis of this concept.

*15. This allows the upper voice to bring in the ascending leading tone. (Jonas)

§ 148.   Ascending register transfer at the first level

At the first level ascending register transfer is applicable to fundamental-line tones or their neighboring notes, and to a single tone or succession of tones of an inner voice.

§ 149.   Means of effecting an ascending register transfer

An ascending register transfer may proceed—

1. in direct fashion, by means of a simple raising to a higher octave, or;
2. in indirect fashion, by means of a connection to the higher octave through another prolongation at the first level, such as arpeggiation or reaching-over.

§ 150.   Examples

Examples of ascending register transfer are shown in

Fig. 47

A direct register transfer is shown in 1, an indirect register transfer in 2 and 3.

In Exx. 1 and 2 the fifth-progressions which descend from $\hat{2}$ arrive at the octave-doubling of V, which originally belonged to the inner voice but is now brought into the higher register also. Through 8—♮7 it then returns to the second $\hat{3}$ in the original register (Fig. 23). [Compare Fig. 47, 1 with § 313 and with Fig. 88, c.]

Examples of direct register transfer of fundamental-line tones, combined with a substitution for $\hat{2}$, are shown in Fig. 46, 1 and 2. The substitution itself is brought about by the ascending register transfer of a tone of the inner voice. Compare also Fig. 83, 3, where, at the end, an impossible vocal register is avoided by means of the register transfer $f\sharp^1$—$f\sharp^2$.

Finally, the frequent adjustment of $b\hat{2}$ by means of $\natural\hat{2}$ (as it appears in Chopin's Étude op. 10 no. 12, mm. 72–75) must be understood as a register transfer of the ♮5 of the V, originally in the inner voice ⟨compare Fig. 31⟩.

Section 13: Descending Register Transfer

§ 151. The nature of descending register transfer

In concept and its working-out, the *descending register transfer* is the reverse of the ascending register transfer:

Fig. 48

It can serve tones of the fundamental line, as in Ex. 1, but it also can be used in the bass, for example, for the purpose of coupling, as in Ex. 2.

Ex. 1: In this case there is a play between ascending and descending register transfers: first, the descending transfer from c^3 to c^2, then the ascending transfer to g^2 by means of c^3—bb^2—ab^2 ⟨mm. 15–16⟩, and finally the descending transfer to f^1 via c^2.[16] If we were to consider the register from c^2 to f^1 as the obligatory register, we would have to regard the g^2 (the $\hat{2}$) as transferred upward. The coda, however, confirms c^3 as the obligatory $\hat{5}$ [§§ 239, 268].

Ex. 2: In accord with Fig. 14,3 the third *(e)* should lie higher, that is, in the ascending direction toward the fifth. However, it is transferred downward in order to prepare the way for the coupling c^1—c. In the second part of Ex. 2, the situation is similar [§ 152].

Section 14: Coupling

§ 152. Concept of coupling

Coupling is the connection of two registers which lie an octave apart.

§ 153. Coupling at the first level

Coupling at the first level may serve tones of the fundamental line; it also plays an important role in the bass [Fig. 48,2].

§ 154. Interplay of registers

In view of the existence of an obligatory register (the primary octave in the fundamental structure), which usually is dependent on the position of the primary tone, it is possible to employ a coupling even at the first level (§ 268):

Fig. 49

In relation to the primary octave the coupled octave has only a reinforcing effect (Fig. 37,b; Fig. 41, Ex. 3).

Section 15: The Combination of Different Types of Prolongations at the First Structural Level

§ 155. The combination of different prolongations at the first structural level

Two or more prolongations can be combined even at the first level, yet each, independent of the others, brings its own nature and purpose to fulfillment: mixture and interruption; mixture and neighboring note; interruption and ascending register transfer; descending register transfer and substitution; reaching-over and ascending register transfer; interruption and linear progression.

*16. The dotted lines connecting the *c*'s in Fig. 48,1 indicate octave couplings. (Oster)

Part III

The Foreground

Chapter 1

The Concepts of Strict Counterpoint

Section 1: Perfect Consonances

§ 156. General observations

According to the presentation in parts I and II, the foreground has an organic relationship to the background and middleground; therefore strict counterpoint is implicitly present in the foreground.

Everything which has been said regarding the intrinsic properties of the intervals and the motion of the voices in my *Kontrapunkt*, volumes I and II, retains its validity in free composition. Consequently, the tonal events of free composition and their possible modifications will be presented, wherever feasible, in the same order as in strict counterpoint.

§ 157. The octave

In free composition, the octave remains only a change of register (*Kpt. I*, II/1, §§ 4, 8, 9).

In the course of foreground prolongations it acts as the significant bearer of transpositions and thus tends to confirm its essential nature as a change of register. Such transpositions do not exist in strict counterpoint.

In free composition the octave also makes the voice analogies soprano-tenor, alto-bass clearer than in strict counterpoint.

§ 158. The fifth

The fifth remains the boundary interval in free composition (*Kpt. I*, I/2, § 12; II/1, §§ 4, 8 ff.).

The prerequisite for this is that the fifth actually must relate to the lower tone as unequivocally as it does in strict counterpoint. However, free composition, in contrast to strict counterpoint, contains deceptive, inauthentic intervals which displace and obscure the actual intervals which originate in the middleground ⟨§ 261⟩.

§ 159. The fourth

The fourth has been shown to be a dissonance in strict counterpoint. For it has an ambiguous nature and so is subordinate to the perfect boundary interval, the fifth (*Kpt. I*, II/1, § 3). How free composition can provide this ambiguity with an unambiguous meaning is explained in the same section of my *Kontrapunkt.*

Here are further instances: Beethoven, Third Symphony, Scherzo, measures 15–17, where despite the thoroughbass figures $\frac{6}{4}$ the fourth is illusory, and similarly, in the Finale, measures 227 ff. (both passages are explained in *Jahrb. III*, pp. 65 and 81–82).

Fig. 50

Ex. 1: In a case like this Bach nevertheless avoids the fourth. Exx. 2 and 3: Here the fourths appear in passing.

§ 160.   Forbidden parallel octaves and fifths in strict counterpoint

Strict counterpoint maintains the unequivocal prohibition of parallel octaves and fifths. The reasons for this are given in *Kontrapunkt I* (I/2, § 12; II/1, §§ 7–14; II/2, § 11). Here I want to mention only that strict counterpoint forbids parallel fifths principally because the fifth controls the harmony. Counterpoint has no means of counteracting this controlling quality, since its intervals are still unequivocal [§ 16].

By contrast, thoroughbass permits open fifths even in the outer voices: see C.P.E. Bach, ⟨*Versuch über die wahre Art, das Clavier zu spielen*⟩, "Generalbass," chapter 2, section 1, §§ 21–23 ⟨in the English version *Essay on the True Art of Playing Keyboard Instruments* [New York: 1949] by W.J. Mitchell, p. 200⟩.*[1] For thoroughbass, in the service of a free composition, shares the greater freedom of that composition.

*[1]. But C.P.E. Bach speaks here only of the succession of a perfect and a diminished fifth, and the reverse.   (Jonas)

§ 161.   Successions of open fifths and octaves at the foreground level

Since the foreground is ultimately based upon the strict counterpoint of the background (§ 156), it too fundamentally prohibits parallel octaves and fifths.

However, the foreground prohibits these parallels only when the danger arises that the octaves and fifths will appear with the same unequivocal quality as in strict counterpoint—that is, when the tones which form the octaves or fifths relate as unequivocally to one another as in strict counterpoint. But where such a danger does not exist, voices at the foreground level, even the outer ones, can form octave or fifth successions with impunity. It is as if two people who have no contact with one another simply pass in the street without an exchange of greetings. Therefore, successions of this kind are not true parallel fifths or octaves. Beneath the outward appearance, in background and middleground there lies a faultless voice-leading based on other intervals. Composer and listener meet in the understanding of the true situation, which is concealed in the middleground.

Thus the long-disputed problem of parallel octaves and fifths is finally solved. The solution remains simple, despite the detour through middleground and background.

Conversely, the middleground frequently displays forbidden successions; it is then the task of the foreground to eliminate them.

Perhaps the phenomenon came about in this way—at first the linear progressions, in the act of expanding the content of the middleground (diminution), often tended to produce fifths: for instance, when two linear progressions, for some imperative reason of coherence, had to proceed in parallel motion:

Fig. 51

In such a passage each individual fifth would have the same unequivocal quality as it has in strict counterpoint. Since the two voices simultaneously present two different keys, should the ear listen to the upper or the lower line? (Compare Fig. 54, 15.)

The gross impossibility of such a situation can be illustrated with the aid of a familiar example:

Fig. 52

Should a setting such as this be heard in *G* major or in *C* major? *² Every composer avoids such parallel fifths as automatically as a writer avoids faulty grammar.

Brahms, in a study which he entitled *Oktaven, Quinten u. A.* (a posthumous publication, edited and provided with explanatory text by me), set himself in opposition to a theory which adhered unreservedly to the foreground, in the following words: "One sees and, more importantly, one hears that no succession of parallel fifths occurs here" (p. 5, in the printed edition p. 7).

Brahms expressed the following opinion about the origins of truly bad successions in the foreground (p. 2): "Apart from pure carelessness or error, whenever one finds truly bad parallel fifths, everything else is usually also so bad that the one mistake hardly makes any difference. See Ambros, *Lehre vom Quinten-Verbot*, p. 45, Trio by A." (There follows the example by Ambros in notation.)

Though he does not clarify what he means by "everything else," and though he bases his remark upon the contrasting examples which display only seemingly parallel fifths, Brahms, with these words, points to generally ungrounded voice-leading in the composition as a whole as the source of error.

In this regard, I really must add that, although I am several

*2. This error is also to be seen in the pernicious practice of counterpointing two independent and equally important motives against one another, as Wagner does in the Prelude to *Die Meistersinger*. It would be wrong to invoke fugal technique in justification of such a counterpoint, for the countersubject which accompanies the subject or the answer in a fugue is subordinate to them in importance.   (Schenker)

decades younger than Brahms, I am the first person who has solved this problem. The master's pages present merely a loose sketch. More significantly, I was the first to make clear the relationship between strict counterpoint and free composition, within which the problem of parallel octaves and fifths is also solved.

§ **162.**   The avoidance of parallel fifths and octaves in general

There are various circumstances which give rise to 8—8 or 5—5 successions. There are also various means for eliminating them. These means permit of a systematic presentation, which we attempt for the first time here.

1. Even in strict counterpoint we have had the experience that 8—8 and 5—5 successions, which somehow seem to be unavoidable because of voice-leading requirements, can be eliminated. We can eliminate them simply through contrary motion, or else through crossing of parts, interpolation, syncopation, or rhythmic displacement, and sometimes even by means of a rest (*Kpt. I*, II/2, § 11; II/4, § 15). One must take care ⟨even in free composition⟩ lest these devices exercise such a strong influence that they interfere with the flow of voice-leading. Strict counterpoint recognizes no other means for the avoidance of parallels.

2. It is evident that free composition can also employ the above-mentioned devices for preventing or removing 8—8 or 5—5 successions. In addition it has available an abundance of other means:

a) The foreground may contain 8—8 or 5—5 successions that would have to be considered faulty were their removal not achieved locally by foreground devices. Thus the foreground itself shows both the faulty succession and its means of removal, different from, yet belonging to each other.

b) The foreground does sometimes show 8—8 or 5—5 successions. But these are only seemingly parallels. The successions are justified by the voice-leading in the middleground and background from which they originate, where 8—8 and 5—5 successions are nonexistent. In this sense, the apparent parallels in the foreground must be sanctioned because their middleground and background successions are correct [Fig. 123, 1a].

Within this category we can find some seemingly parallel octaves and fifths whose correction and justification does not lie far from the foreground, and others whose justification lies at deeper structural levels, that is, concealed in deeper relationships.

§ 163.   The avoidance of parallel octaves in general

Examples of the avoidance of parallel octaves follow. These are arranged in the order of § 162, 1, 2a and b *3:

Fig. 53

Ex. 1: This clearly shows contrary motion ⟨between the octaves *D, E, F♯, G♯*⟩. It is refined and improved through an apparent ⌢7 suspension ⟨d^2 in m. 2⟩, which is resolved in the bass, in conjunction with an afterbeat effect. ⟨Resolutions in the bass are marked with slurs.⟩

Ex. 2: This shows octaves on the offbeats following the ⌢7— 6 suspensions. They are nearly obliterated by the suspension series.

Interpolations, such as 8—10—8—10—8 (Mozart, Sonata in *A Minor*, 1st mvt., mm. 88 ff.), 8—6—8—6—8 (Mozart, Rondo in *A Minor*, mm. 118–20), or 8—5—8—5—8 (Bach, Brandenburg Concerto No. 5, 2nd mvt., mm. 24 ff.), are encountered very frequently. They are easily recognized in the foreground (cf. Fig. 40, 9 and 10; Fig. 41, Ex. 2) [§ 74].

Ex. 3: The tones forming the octaves (mm. 124–39) also have the effect of offbeats. In contrast to Exx. 1 and 2, the octaves

*3. Paragraphs 1 and 2a of § 162 apply to Examples 1, 2, and 5 of Fig. 53; Examples 3 and 4 can best be understood in terms of paragraphs 1 and 2b; and Example 6 is unique in that the octaves are justified by the formal division which separates them.   (Rothgeb)

show themselves in the background only; it is the events of the middleground which justify these octaves. There is a wealth of hidden relationships—parallelisms—in this mazurka (see the brackets). [§ 310, b 4]

Ex. 4: Here, likewise, the interpolation cannot be perceived as an interpolation without insight into the middleground and background. This insight makes the extended 8⌢10—8 in measures 14–26 understandable. The 8—10—8 progression also shows that the last quarter note in the bass of measure 25 is unquestionably an *Ab*, despite the absence of the flat in Chopin's autograph (see the footnote in the *Urtext-Ausgabe*, Breitkopf und Härtel).*4

Ex. 5: Bach avoids the parallel octaves ⟨between measures 3 and 6⟩ with a reaching-over ⟨a^1—(e^2)—d^2⟩; afterbeats soften the octaves in measures 4 and 5.

Ex. 6: $\dfrac{E^8}{V}$ and $\dfrac{F^8}{VI}$ are without direct relationship; V closes like a dividing dominant, and a new attempt at a cadence begins with VI. Hence, there are neither parallel octaves nor a deceptive cadence. Because of other relationships, the octave successions in the coda of Beethoven's Third Symphony (1st mvt., mm. 551 ff.) are also not parallels in a true sense (see *Jahrb. III*, p. 53).

§ 164.   The avoidance of parallel fifths in particular

Examples of the elimination of parallel fifths follow, also arranged in the order of § 162, 1, 2a and b:

Fig. 54

Ex. 1: The means here is a simple arpeggiation of a third.

Ex. 2: The means here is a fifth-arpeggiation $\left(\begin{smallmatrix}6\\4\end{smallmatrix}\right)$ in the manner of an auxiliary cadence (§ 244). The means of breaking up

*4. However, in the first autograph (which Schenker apparently did not know) a natural sign stands before the *A* in the last quarter of the right-hand part, even though it would not be necessary there.   (Jonas)

the fifths in Exx. 3–7 are easily recognized in the foreground as syncopations.

Ex. 5: Compare *Five Graphic Analyses.*

Ex. 6: Compare Fig. 53,3, where measures 124–32 show the tone-space of a sixth which encloses the parallel fifths. The consecutive sevenths which accompany the fifths make it necessary to assume an underlying progression $5, 4\frown5, 4—5$. These implied syncopations justify the fifths. Compare further *Kontrapunkt I*, Ex. 184; Brahms's *Oktaven, Quinten u. A.*, p. 8 (p. 10 in the printed edition) under "Klaviersatz"; Schumann in his review of Chopin's op. 30.*5

Ex. 7: Compare Fig. 117,1.

Interpolation must also be included among the means of elimination which are easily recognized in the foreground. The most frequent interpolation is the so-called 5—6 exchange. However, this means of avoiding 5—5 successions must not be confused with the simple change of harmony 5—6 (§ 175).

Ex. 8: A 5—6 exchange can be employed, as here, in the outer parts (cf. Fig. 39,2) or in situations such as $\begin{smallmatrix}8\\5—6,\end{smallmatrix}\begin{smallmatrix}8\\5—6;\end{smallmatrix}$ $\begin{smallmatrix}10\\5—6,\end{smallmatrix}\begin{smallmatrix}10\\5—6\end{smallmatrix}$ ⟨cf. Fig. 135,3⟩.

Ex. 9: A similar situation exists here: $\begin{smallmatrix}10\\5—6,\end{smallmatrix}\begin{smallmatrix}10\\5—6.\end{smallmatrix}$

Ex. 10: Occasionally a third is added below the root of the $\frac{6}{3}$ chord, which somewhat conceals the 5—6 exchange.

Ex. 11a: The 5—6 exchange plays a special and important role when the harmonic degrees proceed by seconds:

$\begin{smallmatrix}5—6—5\\I\text{———}II—V\end{smallmatrix}$; this is particularly so in the cadence $\begin{smallmatrix}5 — 6 — 5\\IV—(II)—V\end{smallmatrix}$, no matter whether the $\frac{6}{3}$ remains a $\frac{6}{3}$ (Figs. 37a; 44,2) or the root of the II actually appears [§ 280].

Other interpolations are possible: 5—8, 5—8 (Fig. 30b); *6 5—7—5 (Fig. 62,2); or the interpolation of a passing tone that has been made consonant (§ 170).

Ex. 11b: This shows the reverse, a removal of parallels by means of omission.

Of course, all of these devices can also be more or less hidden in the middleground. Particularly the 5—6 exchange is often so obscured in the foreground that it can only be understood from the middleground.

Entirely of middleground nature are the solutions to parallel fifths which arise out of incidental encounters in the foreground: a principal note with an accented or unaccented passing tone or with a neighboring note; a passing tone with an anticipation, with an accented passing tone, or with a neighboring note; a neighboring note with another neighboring note, with the concluding turn of a trill, or with a suspension; the resolution of a suspension with a passing tone, with another suspension, and so forth. The Brahms study mentioned above shows numerous examples.

Ex. 12: The first acceleration in the form of two quarter notes in measure 2 brings about two further quarters which restore the rhythmic balance.

Ex. 13: The diminution which extends from the first measure

---

*5. ". . . the sudden close with the fifths, over which the German schoolmasters will wring their hands. . . . Naturally, a chromatic succession of fifths of this kind, if it be extended for some twenty measures, should be regarded not as admirable, but as deplorable. At the same time, one must not take such things out of context, but rather hear them in relation to what has gone before, as a part of the whole." Only with the last words does Schumann come close to the solution. (Schenker)

*6. The voice-leading shown in Fig. 30b seems to present a 5—10—5—10 succession rather than the 5—8—5—8 indicated beneath the example. The latter indication apparently derives from the fact that eb^1 in measure 1 basically moves to db^1 in measure 2; this is clarified in the composition by the vertical thirds f^1/db^1 in measure 2. The impression of an ascending step $eb^1—f^1$ indicated by the slur in the example results from the descending line in the top voice from c^2 to f^1. Thus the progression $eb^1—f^1$ is, in a sense, produced by reaching-over (§§ 129–34). (Rothgeb)

(second and third quarters) to the second (first quarter) represents b^2. Therefore, the middleground shows only

$\dfrac{b^2 - b^2}{D - E}$ and not the parallel fifths of the foreground

$\overline{(6-5)}$

$\dfrac{c\sharp^3 - b^2}{F\sharp - E}$ (cf. Fig. 40,1; Fig. 56,2e).

$\overline{(5-5)}$

Ex. 14: The reinforcement $eb^1 - f^1$ counteracts the parallel fifths $\dfrac{eb^2 - f^2}{a^1 - bb^1}$. The resulting sixth chords tend to absorb the parallel succession. Such a reinforcement belongs to keyboard style.

Ex. 15: Often it is the task of the foreground to circumvent a succession of fifths which threatens in the middleground (cf. Ex. 15b with Fig. 51).

Section 2: Imperfect Consonances

§ 165. General considerations

In the outer voices of the foreground, the advantage provided by imperfect consonances is obvious, just as in strict counterpoint. The refined employment of these intervals is one of the characteristics of a good outer-voice structure (*Kpt. I*, II/1, § 19; *Kpt. II*, III/1, § 20; IV/1, § 2).

Sixths, in particular, may have their origins in other intervals (e.g., in parallel fifths at an earlier level); this phenomenon in no way prevents the use of sixths in an extended succession. Indeed, these successions are necessary to the composing-out process, which encourages more sixths-in-succession than the series of three which strict counterpoint permits ⟨Fig. 96,4⟩.

§ 166. Open position in connection with the sixth

The necessity for composing-out leads to the use of the open position of the sixth chord, that is, with the tenth between bass and upper voice. This applies not to an extended succession of sixth chords but rather to a single sixth chord which is to be prolonged:

Fig. 55

The fifth between the upper and inner voices (a) represents a $\frac{5}{3}$ area of its own and provides a welcome tone-space for a composing-out ⟨Fig. 88c⟩.

§ 167. Succession of two major thirds

In free composition, too, the adverse effect of a succession of two major thirds is to be avoided (*Kpt. I*, II/1, § 18). However, even in strict counterpoint, two major thirds are permissible if the continuation of the voice-leading shows that the augmented fourth is not the sum of these intervals (*Kpt. I*, Ex. 196). This applies even more to free composition. Compare Beethoven, Fifth Symphony, Finale, measures 122–130–132: $\dfrac{e^2 - f\sharp^3 - g^3}{C - D - G}$ [especially in the case of I—II$^\sharp$—V; § 123 and Fig. 38].*7

*7. With a certain justification, our forefathers established the prohibition of *mi contra fa* and maintained that two hexachords were incompatible (solmization); thus, when there occurred a *mi-fa* within the *G* hexachord *(B—C)* they would not admit a *mi-fa* from the *C* hexachord *(E-F)* at the same time. They possessed as yet no real sense of key and no genuine tonal system, since, above all, they lacked the octave which contains the space of a fourth 5—8. This fourth-space would have necessitated a new hexachord. We, however, have the octave, containing two semitones which formerly would have belonged to hostile hexachords. From the standpoint of the octave, there are no grounds for opposing the two groups of semitones against one another. Therefore, I pointed out in *Kontrapunkt II* that *mi contra fa* was an empty fabrication, like the fallacies of the ecclesiastical modes and numberless intervals. Every prohibition based upon such reasons should be cast aside. Only the disagreeable total interval of an augmented fourth such as in *Kontrapunkt I*, Ex. 195, need cause the rejection of two successive major thirds.   (Schenker)

Section 3: The Passing Tone at the Foreground Level

§ 168.   General remarks

Strict counterpoint requires a stationary tone for the verification of a consonant or dissonant passing tone, whether in the upper or the lower voice. This requirement can be dropped in free composition, where there is the possibility of transforming an originally stationary tone into a succession of moving tones ⟨Fig. 56,2⟩. Thus, we must add the nature of background and middleground to the reasons already given for greater freedom in free composition.*8 Considerations of background and middleground are the final determinants; they also provide the greatest liberty.

§ 169.   Impossibility of composing out a dissonant passing tone

The dissonant passing tone, including the passing seventh, is itself a means of composing-out. Therefore, as long as it retains its dissonant quality, it cannot at the same time give rise to a further composing-out; only the transformation of the dissonance into a consonance can make composing-out possible. Such an opportunity was lacking in strict counterpoint [§ 35; Fig. 62,9].

§ 170.   The transformation of a dissonant passing tone into a consonance; the consonant passing tone

The fundamental structure exhibits the first transformation of a dissonant fundamental-line tone into a consonance: above all, $\hat{2}$ is changed into a consonance $\dfrac{\hat{2}}{V}$ by the counterpointing

bass arpeggiation of the tonic triad. When the fundamental line begins with $\hat{5}$ and $\hat{8}$, the originally dissonant passing tones $\hat{4}$ and $\hat{7}$ also await the transformation into consonances which will make composing-out possible (Figs. 5, 10, 11).

This principle continues through all levels of the middleground, creating more and more new levels which present new possibilities of prolongations for dissonant passing tones either in the outer or in the inner voices. Finally the foreground, with its greatest freedom, shows voice-leading events which are not understandable as passing motions unless one refers to relationships in the middleground and background ⟨§ 66⟩.

The voice-leading transformations are based upon the principle of the primary tone (§ 93). Its power completely controls the linear progressions; it alone permits understanding of the original, dissonant condition.

Examples:

Fig. 20,2, measure 2: The inner voices $\dfrac{g}{e}$, originally dissonant passing tones in relation to the F of the preceding measure $\left(\dfrac{9}{7}\right)$, are made consonant in the foreground through the $C\left(\dfrac{5}{3}\right)$. This change into a triad is more favorable to the composing-out.

Fig. 20,4, measures 16–36: In $\begin{smallmatrix} 8 & 47 & 46 & 5 \\ \hline A \end{smallmatrix}$, the passing seventh g appears in measure 21 first as a consonance (10). Compare, in addition, Fig. 35,1 and 2.

Passing sevenths in the case of IV$\underline{^{8—7}}$V (Fig. 22b, m. 2) and II$\underline{^{8—7}}$V (Fig. 49,2; Fig. 53,3, m. 21) are usually transformed into consonances.

The passing tones in I$\underline{^{8\hat{7}6\hat{5}}}$ (Fig. 11,1) often undergo a transformation. A beautiful example of this is to be found in Bach's Little Prelude No. 12 in A Minor (BWV 942) (*Jahrb. I,* p. 117).

*8. *Kpt. I,* II/2, § 6; *Kpt. II,* III/2, §§ 2, 3; III/3, § 1; VI/1, § 2 under (2), § 3; VI/2, § 3; also "Erläuterungen" in *Tw.* 8/9, 10 and in *Jahrb. I, II.* (Schenker)

Fig. 42,2: The neighboring note eb^2 (marked n.n.) is shown in the middleground as the seventh over V. In the foreground, however, it appears as part of a IV in a cadence.

Further examples:

Fig. 56

Ex. 1, a–c: These show descending passing tones made consonant. In Ex. 1a, the c^2—bb^1—g^1 differs from the five-note melisma known as the *nota cambiata* (*Kpt. I*, II/3, § 7, especially Exx. 357–60).

Ex. 2, a–f: These show ascending passing tones which are made consonant. In relation to d) and e) see §§ 244 ff., Fig. 40,1 and Fig. 54,13.

Ex. 2, g and h: In g) the passing $\frac{8}{4}$ is avoided; in h) the passing motion is combined with a chromatic alteration (*Tw.* 3, p. 5).[9]

§ 171. Major seconds

The corroborative power of linear progressions which stems from the middleground and background extends to the foreground, where it imparts conviction even to a series of major seconds in the upper or lower voice (cf. *Kpt. I*, II/1, § 18, Exx. 200, 201):

Fig. 57

§ 172. Leaps that form part of a passing motion

The concept of a *leaping passing tone* ⟨a leap combining with a dissonant passing tone⟩ emerged first in the combined species (*Kpt. II*, VI/1, § 3).[10] The clarifying power of the mid-

dleground explains more irregular leaping passing tones in the foreground:

Fig. 58

Ex. 1: ⟨Both e^2 and d^2 are passing tones in a descending sixth $f\sharp^2$—$a\sharp^1$; the lower voice follows (§ 221) in sixths.⟩ In the lower voice, a different progression (such as g^1—a^1, $f\sharp^1$—g^1) would of course be possible. However, leaping into $c\sharp^2$ ⟨and thus joining the passing tone e^2⟩ instead of proceeding to a^1 provides not only a ⟨melodically⟩ suitable skip of a fifth but also the fifth of the subsequent chord $\frac{7}{5}$.
      3

Ex. 2: The last four sixteenths of the lower voice should actually read g—a—$f\sharp$—g (see the countersubject in m. 4 of the Fugue), but it is clear that the skip of a fifth, a—d, into the next measure is more desirable than the skip of a fourth, g—d, which would have resulted.[11]

Ex. 3: In the bass, Ab, Gb, and F ⟨in particular, the leaping passing tone Gb⟩ are completely subordinate to the main third-progression db—cb—Bb.[3]

§ 173. Tendency of passing motions to give rise to parallel formations

Even the combined species reveal the tendency of passing tones to strengthen and intensify their effect by moving together, thus forming an almost independent contrapuntal setting of $\frac{6}{3}$ or $\frac{6}{4}$ chords (*Kpt. II*, VI/1, §§ 1–2,7; VI/2, § 10). In the foreground, this tendency is furthered and reinforced by

---

*10. See also *Kontrapunkt II*, Ex. 283,1, measures 4, 6, 8 (quoted in Felix Salzer and Carl Schachter, *Counterpoint in Composition*, Ex. 9–60, b. (Oster)

*11. Since a in the bass would have been due at the beginning of measure 13, one might hear the last sixteenth of measure 12 as an anticipation rather than a leaping passing tone.   (Oster)

*9. With respect to Fig. 56, compare what is said in § 282 about Fig. 134,1 and 2. (Jonas)

the parallelistic bent of diminutions, whether in relation to the succession of intervals or to the composing-out process. Here belong the frequent 6 6, 10 10 sequences which arise as a result of exchange of voices [Fig. 105], as well as others which will be discussed in § 236. Compare Fig. 43b,4, 5; Fig. 43c,4, 5.

§ 174.　The accented passing tone

Since the *cantus firmus* exercise of strict counterpoint knows neither genuine meter nor genuine rhythm, it provides no opportunity for an accented passing tone, that is, a passing tone on the strong beat in a genuinely metrical situation. However, one might perhaps conceive of a passing dissonance on the third quarter in third species as the origin of the accented passing tone (*Kpt. I*, II/3, § 1, Ex. 332). The accented passing tone is thus a foreground concept.

The necessity of bridging skips, whenever or in whatever voice they occur, easily produces accented passing tones. The strong beat need not be the downbeat but may, by implication, be a first or third eighth also, or even a sixteenth note:

Fig. 59

Ex. 4: A fifth-progression and a fourth-progression appear in contrary motion (§§ 227 ff.); at a) the db^2 is shown as an unaccented passing tone, at b) as an accented passing tone. At the foreground level db^2 is placed in measure 5, which is metrically strong. This imparts to it a tension—basically only the tension of a passing tone!—which carries through to c^2 in measure 11.

Section 4:　The Change of Harmony 5—6

§ 175.　The change of harmony 5—6

Like 6—5, the 5—6 succession in the second and third species is not adequate to eliminate parallel fifths. Rather, both successions signify the only natural change of harmony ⟨in counter-

point⟩; such a change often has the simultaneous effect of a passing tone or a neighboring note (*Kpt. I*, II/2, § 13; II/3, § 8; *Kpt. II*, III/2, § 3) [§§ 108, 110].

However, in thoroughbass, which of course presupposes a free composition (*Harm.* § 92), the succession 5—6 often becomes the means for the elimination of 5—5 successions—and this also applies to the foreground (§ 164). Yet even the foreground occasionally shows a simple change of harmony like that in strict counterpoint. An example:

Fig. 60

Section 5:　The Seventh

§ 176.　The seventh in strict counterpoint and in free composition

In strict counterpoint the seventh appears either as a passing tone on a weak beat or as a ⌒7—6 syncopation on the strong beat. It also appears in these two forms in the foreground. Hence, it is the fifth that forms the boundary of any given chord in the foreground, and never the seventh. Even where the seventh is placed above the fifth in the foreground—that is, in cases where conventional harmony speaks of a seventh chord—the seventh must be considered only a passing tone whose primary tone, the octave, is understood.*[12]

Fig. 61

To reduce this to the shortest formula: where the seventh is not a suspension (syncopation) (*Kpt. II*, III/4, § 2), it is a passing tone. As such it has not the slightest relationship to the seventh overtone, which many textbooks hold to be identical with the seventh (*Harm.* § 10). ⟨As to Fig. 61b, see also end of § 287.⟩

---

*12. See C.P.E. Bach, ⟨*Versuch*,⟩ "Generalbass," chapter 13, section 1, § 20 (in the English version by W.J. Mitchell, pp. 273 ff.); compare also Fig. 23. (Rothgeb)

§ **177.**   Transformations of the seventh in free composition

Since it is a dissonant passing tone, the seventh cannot be composed out (§ 169). The change of the seventh into a consonance has been discussed in § 170. Here are examples showing other means of transforming the seventh [§ 215]:

Fig. 62

Exx. 1–4 show the composing-out of a seventh chord, upwards from the root to the seventh (Exx. 1 and 2), as well as downwards from the seventh to the root (Exx. 3 and 4).

Ex. 1: The composing-out is carried through by means of chromatic passing tones. The return of the root $B\flat$ in measure 115 divides it into root-third-seventh, that is, $b\flat^1$—$(d\flat^2)d\natural^2$ and d^2—$a\flat^2$ (see *Five Graphic Analyses*).

The transformation of all passing tones into individually prolonged consonances results in a very rich unfolding of detail in the foreground. The question of what specific diminutions the prolongation employs in its details is less important than the direction of the path of the whole prolongation.

Ex. 2: Only the first space of a third, g^1—b^1, is filled in by chromatic passing tones. The further course of the prolongation shows the arpeggiations b^1—d^2 and d^2—f^2. In measures 9–14 there is an event of marvelous beauty: the first passing tone, $a\flat^1$, undergoes a transformation into the interval of an octave, that is, into the $A\flat \; {}^{8}_{5}{}_{3}$ chord, and upon this harmony, the first four bars of the "Florestan Aria" are sounded; the chord shapes itself into a virtual stage, and on it Florestan, arisen from a dream, takes up his song. Evidently, Beethoven did not consider it sufficient to relate the overture to the opera by quoting those measures only in the course of the Allegro: hence he strove to make the quotation distinctly more logical by anticipating it with another in the introductory Adagio. Thus the circle of relationships within the overture is closed; it is as though the overture had no need of the opera. Beethoven achieved the effect of the vision in the Adagio by placing it in a passing tone of chromatic origin, which is more remote than the diatonic $a\natural^1$. It is this which makes the vision more distant, more visionary. To a genius, a simple prolongation can create who knows what unseen opportunity!

Ex. 3: See pp. 43 ff. and Figs. 2 and 3 in *Jahrbuch III*.

Ex. 4: The descending composing-out actually begins in measure 66 with $a\flat^1$ but then rises to $a\flat^2$ in the higher octave. With the exception of f^1—$(e\flat^1)$ in measures 73–74, this octave then contains all the remaining passing tones. Into the prolongation there comes a "programmatic" note: the "Lebewohl" motive, which stands at the beginning of the introductory Adagio and comprises the three tones g^1—f^1—$e\flat^1$, corresponding to the three syllables, is shortened by one tone in the development section. The third syllable is lost, as though in a sob—thus, only $a\flat^1$—g^1, $a\flat^2$—g^2, f^1—$e\flat^1$, $e\flat^2$—$d\flat^2$, $d\flat^2$—c^2, c^2—$c\flat^2$, $c\flat^2$—$b\flat^1$. The bass moves in contrary motion from the root to the third, D, which is preceded by the neighboring note $E\flat$ (m. 83). A remarkable series of intervals and harmonies results from the contrary motion of the two prolongations, that in the upper and that in the bass voice.*[13]

---

*[13]. In a short note among his unpublished papers, dating from the late 1920s, Schenker calls this descending seventh a "true seventh-progression"; but he also calls it a "harmonic sin" and contrasts it with the seventh-progression shown in Fig. 62,1. What Schenker seems to indicate is this: in order to be composed out (either through a descending linear progression or in some other way), the tone which represents the seventh would first have to appear as a consonance (see § 169; Fig. 62,9, and Fig. 42,2 as discussed in § 170). But Beethoven immediately presents $a\flat^2$ in measure 66 as a seventh and then proceeds to prolong this dissonant position. In the Haydn, the situation is different: the seventh, $a\flat^2$, appears only at the end of the ascending linear progression and, continuing the $b\flat^2$ of measure 64, goes straight on to g^1 of the recapitulation. Thus, this seventh is not composed out in the same strict sense as is the one in op. 81a. Fig. 62,3, of course, shows the same procedure as Fig. 62,4. But in *Jahrbuch III*, from which the *Eroica* example is taken (published 1930), Schenker does not remark on this specific problem of the seventh.   (Oster)

Exx. 5–11 show arpeggiations as means of prolonging a seventh chord: in Exx. 5–7 ascending arpeggiations in the upper voice (5—7, 3—7, 1—3—5—7), and in Exx. 8–11 descending arpeggiations in the bass (3—1, 5—1, 7—5—3—1).

Exx. 5 and 6: See *Five Graphic Analyses*.

Ex. 7: This shows the chromatic alteration eb^2—$e\natural^2$ (*Jahrb. III*, pp. 77 ff.).

Ex. 8: See *Jahrbuch III*, p. 76; also Fig. 111a.

Ex. 9: Here we see the technique most frequently employed in the middle sections of song forms: the arpeggiation from fifth to root in the bass (mm. 13–19) makes it possible to introduce as a consonance (10) the tone which is to become the seventh. Thus, as in strict counterpoint, a preparation of the seventh is attained: $3(10)—7$ [§ 169].

Ex. 10: See *Jahrbuch III*, p. 38.

Ex. 12: The seventh chord arises through the combination of the bass arpeggiation I—IV with a rhythmic displacement. This type of prolongation takes the place of the more basic IV^{8-7}, in which the 8 appears on the downbeat. Similar events which are possible in combined species were discussed in *Kontrapunkt II*, VI/1, § 5.

Ex. 13: The $\frac{4}{3}$ inversion in "scattered" position (f—b—d^2—a^2 instead of f—a—b—d) makes the tenths between upper voice and bass $\begin{smallmatrix} a^2—g^2 \\ f \quad \end{smallmatrix}$ much clearer (cf. *Erläuterungsausgabe* op. 111). Regarding the "scattered" position of inversions see C.P.E. Bach, ⟨*Versuch,*⟩ "Generalbass," chapter 7, section 1, § 8 and also chapter 8, section 2, § 6 (in the English version by W.J. Mitchell, p. 235 and p. 251) ⟨also see Fig. 64, Ex. 3⟩.

§ 178. Closure of the passing seventh

Since it originates in the octave, the seventh must move onward in the descending direction [§ 73].

§ 179. Strict counterpoint remains in control despite deviations

From §§ 176–78 it follows that in free composition the necessity of composing-out seldom permits a seventh to remain stationary above the root.

Section 6: The Syncopation

§ 180. General observations

In *Kontrapunkt I* (II/4, § 12) I referred to the significance of the syncopation in free composition in the following words: "In their instinctive search for technical means which would expand the length of a tonal structure (*Harm.* § 88, note), musically creative minds were occupied with voice-leading practices which, apart from their own laws, did not yet manifest any higher necessity. Still, they found in the constraint of preparing and resolving a dissonance a most welcome means of simulating a type of musical causality and inner necessity, a means which operated at least from consonance to consonance [§ 73]. Of course, the germ of such a need to move onward lay also in the simplest passing tone—when studying the nature and history of music as an art, one must always keep in mind the problem of the creation of length—but it is clear that the constraint of the dissonant syncopation is incomparably stronger and more cogent." *14

Fig. 63

Ex. 1: Because of the chord progression in the foreground, a suspension over IV must be assumed, even though the bass tone is not stated until two measures later.

Ex. 2: The principle of the "root property" ⟨the inclination to

---

*14. One recalls the corrections which J.S. Bach made in his arrangements of works by other composers. He expended the greatest care upon suspensions.

Such necessary suspensions are lacking especially in contemporary organ improvisation. Even Bruckner was wanting in this respect. (Schenker)

become a root⟩ of the lowest tone, which is also operative in free composition—as well as the meaning derived from middleground and background—reveals this to be a double suspension. The fact that the bass moves on under e^2 does not alter the situation (compare Fig. 65,2 and *Kpt. II, III/1, § 11*).

Ex. 3: A 6—5 is combined in a most artistic way with the free double suspension $\dfrac{11-10}{9-8}$. This can be understood only from middleground and background [§ 107].*15

§ 181.   The composing-out of suspensions

Examples of the composing-out of suspensions are given in

Fig. 64

Ex. 1: Here a^2, the $\hat{5}$, is followed by the neighboring note bb^2, whose setting is $IV^{10}\frown V^{9-8}$ (the 9 being tied over as in strict counterpoint). However, the foreground divides the 9 into a C^7 (=♮VII) and an A^7 (=V♯³) ⟨§ 246, Fig. 111c⟩. See *Jahrbuch I*, pp. 37–38, Fig. 19; also *Jahrbuch I*, p. 79 (Bach, Violin Partita III).

Ex. 2: Here we see that the tying-over of a ninth may have great consequence also in free composition. Chopin originally wrote a ninth eb^1 (at c, m. 7), and this ninth still appears in many editions. Yet, it can only have been Chopin himself who finally replaced the eb^1 by the octave d^1— and with good reason: since it is not tied over (compare to sketch d), the intended ninth eb^1 has rather the effect of a sixth below c^2 (see the diagonal lines at d).*16 In addi-

*15. In connection with this section see text and examples in *Kpt. I*, II/4, §§ 5, 7, 8, 10, 15 and in *Kpt. II*, III/4, §§ 2, 4–6; VI/3, §§ 2–8.   (Schenker)

*16. The first German edition (Breitkopf) and the first French edition (Schlesinger) were published almost simultaneously. Schlesinger has eb^1, Breitkopf, d^1; and this d^1 could very well be due to an engraver's error. Musicological reasoning alone is probably unable to decide with certainty in favor of either eb^1 or d^1, and one has to make one's decision on purely musical grounds. (Oster)

tion, the example shows a tying-over of the passing tone g^1 (at b) against which the bass executes an unfolding.

Ex. 3: The "scattered" position ⟨§ 177, Ex. 13⟩, with its vertically interlocking sevenths Eb—db, bb—ab^1, and db^2—c^3, makes it possible to exploit the rich sound-potentialities of the piano. Failure to recognize such a "scattered" position leads to the false theory of eleventh and thirteenth chords.

An example of the composing-out of $\frown\dfrac{6}{5}$ is found in Fig. 54,3. Here the coda-like descent $c♯^2$—$c♯^1$ (=8—1) brings with it the diatonic ♮7. Yet the $\frown\dfrac{6}{5}$ at $g♯^1$ provides the opportunity to make use of the leading tone $b♯$. This establishes the bass progression as a line which, in the service of 8—5, departs from $C♯$ and returns by way of $F♯$—E—$D♯$ to $C♯$ (cf. Fig. 11,5). The circumstance that the lowest tones of $\frown\dfrac{6}{5}$ configurations are thirds of the actual root permits the employment of chromatics in the sense of leading tones [cf. § 247]. This advantage does not exist in the case of $\frown\dfrac{4\ 5}{2}$.

§ 182.   Preparation and resolution

Examples of preparation and resolution of suspensions are given in

Fig. 65

Ex. 1: In measure 86 the seventh is, in essence, tied over and prepared, not merely passing. The actual appearance of the II in measure 90 between VI and V reveals that a similar preparation of the seventh is implied in measure 86.

Exx. 2–4: Formerly it was taught that no other tone should lead to the tone of resolution in similar motion. The erroneousness of this idea ⟨for free composition⟩ is indicated by Ex. 2. After the f^2 was led to e^2 via the embellishing octave g^2, the composer deemed it necessary to employ this embellishment further for the diminution of the upper voice (see the brackets). Whoever hears the g^2 in measure 7 as an embellishment will also accept what follows, regardless of the ⌒7—6 sequence in the lower voice. Thus the upper voice presents merely a doubling, and the tied-over seventh is the essential part in this passage; the tying-over of a suspension is more cogent than the skips of thirds in the upper voice. In Ex. 4 the playfulness of the doublings, realized in a different way, is easily recognized.

Ex. 5: The resolution of the suspension ⌒$^{6—5}_{4—3}$ is rhythmically delayed. The root of V moves through a descending arpeggio and reaches the root of I before the suspension resolves—a particularly imaginative solution!

Ex. 6: The tied-over ⌒7 is only seemingly forced upward. In actuality, e^2 is introduced through superposition *(reaching-over)* and becomes the ascending passing tone ⟨cf. Fig. 41, a4⟩.

Ex. 7: The resolution is omitted (see a) and thereby a rhythmic imbalance (as at b) of the two-tone groups db^2—c^2 and gb^2—f^2 is avoided.

Ex. 8: The fifth is missing at the close, and the piece ends without a complete resolution of the ⟨triple⟩ suspension.

Specific rhythmic events in the foreground which take place within the meter admit of a very free play with tyings-over of a merely rhythmic nature, be they in the service of leading tones, passing tones, or ascending and descending arpeggiations. These, however, are not genuine suspensions (*Kpt. I*, Exx. 397, 420–22, 426, 427).

Chapter 2

The Later Structural Levels

A. THE LATER STRUCTURAL LEVELS IN GENERAL

§ **183.**   Content of the later levels

The content of the second and the subsequent levels is deter-mined by the content of the first level, but at the same time it is influenced by goals in the foreground, mysteriously sensed and pursued. The second level, even more clearly than the first, reveals how a work branches out into its own special characteris-tics. Yet I reiterate that the way in which the composer arrives at his initial inspiration—whether he derives it from an earlier or from a later level, perhaps even from the foreground—is one of the unfathomable secrets of creativity. This in no way affects the logical sequence of the levels, but rather gives evi-dence of a veritable clairvoyance which envisions a more distant level before the nearer one is clear in the consciousness. Only genius can command such far-reaching forward and backward perception (§ 47) [§ 29].

§ **184.**   Reappearance of first-level prolongations

Such prolongations as are met at the first level can appear also at the later levels and undergo a further development. But new types of prolongation may appear as well—for exam-ple, exchange of voices, and combinations of all kinds of prolon-gations.

§ **185.**   Prolongation of the bass

All manner of prolongations found in the upper voice may occur also in the lower voice—always, however, in keeping with its particular contrapuntal purposes (§ 20) [§§ 53, 64, 210, 257].

B. THE PROLONGATIONS OF THE LATER LEVELS IN PARTICULAR

Section 1:   Prolongations of the Bass Arpeggiation

§ **186.**   Inversions within the bass line I—V

Some of the steps of the prolonged versions of I—V shown in Fig. 14 admit of inversion at the later levels:

Fig. 66

Ex. 1: Only in the later levels, which gradually work out the obligatory register, can it be decided whether or not the descending sixth at a) and b) serves a register transfer ascending or descending.

Ex. 2: The descending fifth at a) is conceptually equivalent to the fourth in Fig. 14,5 (I—IV). The succession IV—V counterbalances the fifth with a melodic second—a purely contrapuntal means which arises when an ascending fifth-progression is filled in by passing tones (Fig. 14,2c). Therefore, when a descending fifth is filled in by passing tones—even including a chromatically altered tone, as at b)—one must recall that this descending fifth has its origin in the contrapuntally ascending fifth-progression. For this reason, in the so-called cadence I—IV—V—I in free composition, the V has preeminence because of its prior development as arpeggiation tone of the harmony, whereas *the placement of IV before V stresses the step of a second, and hence, primarily the contrapuntal element* ⟨§§ 56, 64⟩!

Ex. 3: This illustration is related to Fig. 14,6.

§ **187**   Inversion of the ascending fifth I—V to a descending fourth

The whole ascending fifth in the bass can also be transformed into a descending fourth. Several possibilities for the structural consequences of such a fourth-progression in the bass in the case of $\hat{3}$ or $\hat{5}$ are shown in

Fig. 67

§ **188.**   The combination of various inversions

The combination of various kinds of inversion is shown in

Fig. 68

Especially when the contrapuntal bass formula is transferred to individual harmonies in the foreground, one must be careful to note whether the arpeggiation I—V is expressed in ascending or descending form; only thus can a combination be recognized (§§ 242 ff.).

§ **189.**   The arpeggiation of the descending fifth V—I proceeds through the third only

Prolongations of V—I become possible only at the later levels. The arpeggiation of this descending fifth V—I *can proceed through the third only:*

Fig. 69

Exx. 1–4: These are the possible forms. They represent a reversal of the prolongational forms of the ascending arpeggiation I—V, as shown in Fig. 14,1–4. Such arpeggiations through the third are to be found in all prolonged descending fifths at the later levels, in the middle sections of three-part song forms (Fig. 22b) as well as in the development sections of sonata movements, such as that of Beethoven's Violoncello Sonata op. 69, first movement, measures 94   127   152

$$\frac{E — C\sharp^{\flat 3} — A}{V\rule{3cm}{0.4pt}I.}$$

Exx. 5–6: Arpeggiations such as these, which reverse Fig. 14,5–6, would be impossible.

Ex. 7: In contrast, an arpeggiation through the third can occur in the simplest descending fifth.

Of course, a descending arpeggiation is not the only means of prolonging V in the case of V—I. Sometimes this can also be effected by a neighboring note with interpolations, as, for example, Fig. 62,3, and 11; Fig. 76,9; Fig. 154,5; Fig. 158.

In relation to this section, see §§ 65 and 86; also § 230, Fig. 100,3.

§ 190.   Inversion of the descending fifth V—I to an ascending fourth

The descending fifth V—I can be inverted to an ascending fourth. This remains indivisible, because the fourth, in contrast to the fifth which is based in the overtone series, must be brought into being artificially by voice-leading [§ 212].

Fig. 70

§ 191.   The so-called deceptive cadence

The so-called deceptive cadence is shown in

Fig. 71

Ex. 1: With the succession V—VI, the bass in a) sets out in the direction of the ascending fourth-progression (Fig. 70b)—but it can be led back by means of interpolated fifths into the direction of the descending fifth V—I, as in Fig. 71b.

Ex. 2: Another means for the overcoming of V—VI is repetition in the form of an auxiliary cadence (§§ 244 ff.).

Section 2:   Structural Division

§ 192.   Structural division at the later levels

Linear progressions which depart from $\hat{3}$, $\hat{2}$, or $\hat{5}$, as shown in Figs. 33 and 34, also admit of interruption at the later levels, by virtue of the principle described in § 117, thus:

1st Level: $\begin{cases} \hat{3}\text{————}\hat{2} \| \hat{3}\,\hat{2}\,\hat{1} \\ 3\text{———}2\ 1 \end{cases}$

2nd Level: 3 2 ‖ 3 2 1

Compare Fig. 42,2; Fig. 73,3; also Chopin, Étude op. 10 no. 8, in *Five Graphic Analyses*.

In other words, any and every third-progression or fifth-progression can undergo an interruption in the strict sense, 3 2 ‖ 3 2 1 or 5—2 ‖ 5—1, as though it were the fundamental line. This is the key to the application of the outer-voice forms with their prolongations, including interruption, to each individual harmony in the foreground (§§ 242 ff.).

Such strict forms of interruption must not be confused with forms such as those in

Fig. 72

These must be considered diminutions in concept (§§ 251 ff.). ⟨Compare Fig. 72,1 and 2 to Fig. 87,5.⟩

Section 3:   Mixture

§ 193.   Mixture at the later levels

At the later levels mixture has even less potential for creating form than it did at the first level (§ 103). It usually enters the composing-out process only to embellish and extend.

Fig. 73

Ex. 1: The upper voice follows the chromatic passing tones in the bass with $e\natural^2$—eb^2, a final parallelism (Fig. 12).

Ex. 2: The tonicizing chromatic bass tone ♮IV provides opportunity for the use of the minor seventh db^2, which, within the framework of the fundamental line, is a mixture at the third ⟨m. 33 of the composition⟩. Since, however, the chromatic alteration of the bass tone belongs to the second level, the mixture in the fundamental line belongs there also. The readjustment of the $b\hat{3}$ is achieved through a composing-out of the $\hat{2}$, which presents an unfolding—in this case, a succession of sixths between the voices (Fig. 43 f; *Jahrb. I*, pp. 31 ff.).

Ex. 3: In the context of the upper voice, the bb^1 in measure 6 represents only a chromatic passing tone, but it is necessitated here by the tonicizing chromatic tone $c\sharp^1$ of the inner voice (= $\sharp VII^{b7}$ of D major). Despite Haydn's slur from bb^1 to d^1 and the omission of a^1 in measure 7, there can be no doubt that bb^1 nevertheless progresses to a^1, which is the $\hat{2}$; the a^1 can remain absent in measure 7 because its presence is even more urgently required in measure 9 above the seventh, c.

Ex. 4: The octave-progression constitutes the coda of the Étude. It includes a minor seventh ($b7$), which is inadmissible in the fundamental line $\hat{8}$—$\hat{1}$. This chromatic alteration tonicizes the IV, but is retracted at V^{b3} (§ 44). See also Chopin, op. 10 no. 8, in *Five Graphic Analyses*.

Section 4: The $b\hat{2}$

§ 194. Rectification of the $b\hat{2}$ by $\natural\hat{2}$ at the later levels

At the later levels, the $b\hat{2}$ can be rectified by the diatonic $\natural\hat{2}$:

Fig. 74

Ex. 1: The adjustment is achieved by means of a skip of a third or a third-progression, and results from the simple fact that the $b\hat{2}$ is followed by V, which contains only the perfect fifth (§ 105, Neapolitan sixth) [§ 118].

Ex. 2: The special effect of this whole Mazurka depends upon the following fact: that the tension of $\natural\hat{2}$ persists until the last measure, where the diatonic $\sharp\hat{2}$ finally appears. (See also Chopin, op. 10 no. 12, mm. 72–75, in *Five Graphic Analyses*.)

This way of converting the $b\hat{2}$ into a diatonic situation is employed not only in a fundamental line, but also at a prolongational level or in the foreground when the forms of the fundamental structure are transferred to individual harmonies (§§ 242 ff.). Compare also the inner voice d^2—$c\sharp^2$—$b\sharp^1$ in Fig. 44,2, measures 11–12, as well as a similar event in Fig. 53,3, measures 21–31.

Ex. 3: Instead of a third-progression bb^2—a^2—$g\sharp^2$, this example shows a descending register transfer bb^2—f^2—$g\sharp^1$. Furthermore, at the entrance of V in the next measure, the perfect fifth is missing altogether; it is, however, understood.

§ 195. The reverse succession $\natural\hat{2}$—$b\hat{2}$

Once the diatonic structure of a composition is firmly established, the composer can, for the sake of a special effect, place a $b\hat{2}$ even at the end, as though the entire piece were in the Phrygian mode:

Fig. 75

Section 5: The Neighboring Note

§ 196. The neighboring note at the later levels

Obviously the basic form of the neighboring note as it appears in strict counterpoint can also serve at the later levels for the expansion of the content (§ 108 and Fig. 32). However, when the main tone in a neighboring-note figure returns at a dissonant interval or in an accented-passing-tone progression 6—5, altering the original dissonant seventh (Fig. 76,1), then a five-tone diminution results in which the neighboring note appears to fall away. In such cases the neighboring note lacks form-generating power (§§ 111, 112).

§ 197.   Examples and comments

At the later levels the neighboring-note figure can relate to tones with various meanings:

Fig. 76

Ex. 1: The neighboring-note figure relates to a primary tone. A neighboring note of this kind can render a third-progression from the first $\hat{3}$ superfluous (Fig. 49,2), but need not do so (Fig. 32,3–7; Fig. 64,1).

Ex. 2: Here, in an interruption $\hat{3}—\hat{2} \parallel \hat{3}—\hat{1}$, the neighboring note relates to the second primary tone (as in Fig. 22a); it can, however, also relate to the first (as in Fig. 22b).

Ex. 3: In the case of an interruption $\hat{5}—\hat{2} \parallel \hat{5}—\hat{1}$, the neighboring note is occasionally associated with the $\frac{\hat{2}}{V}$ (in contrast, see Fig. 26a and b).

Ex. 4: In the case of $\hat{8}—\hat{5} \parallel \hat{5}—\hat{1}$, the neighboring note pertains to the second $\hat{5}$ (compare Fig. 19b).

Ex. 5: If there is a form-generating neighboring note at the first level (or, as in Fig. 30a, a form-generating mixture), neighboring notes at the later levels can relate to all primary tones.

Ex. 6: Here an illusory neighboring-note figure, brought about by an ascending register transfer (see Fig. 23a), comes to a close over the VI in measure 2. This VI, however, represents merely the middle of the arpeggiation $C—A—F$, and should really be regarded as an added bass tone under the C^{5-6}.

Ex. 7: The neighboring note often accompanies the transfer of forms of the fundamental structure to individual harmonies (§§ 242 ff.).

Ex. 8: The example shows how neighboring notes can lead to a play of expansion and rhythm of the most varied sort.

Ex. 9: A neighboring note in the bass is of special significance and can even be generative of the form, as in this case (§ 189, last paragraph) ⟨§ 324, Fig. 158⟩.

Ex. 10: A neighboring-note figure is particularly attractive when it appears in the same durational values as the main tones. In Bach's chorale settings, such figurations in the bass give rise to strange thoroughbass notation which can be understood only when the equality of the note values is disregarded (Fig. 125,1). The same holds true for similar figurations in instrumental music (Fig. 142,1 and 2).

In rondo form the neighboring note plays an important role in the connection of the individual sections (§§ 318 ff.).

§ 198.   The neighboring-note motion 3—4—3

The neighboring-note motion 3—4—3 can be combined with 5—6—5 and 8—9—8 simultaneously, provided the fifth is not in the soprano—such a position would of course produce consecutive fifths.

Fig. 77

§ 199.   The syncopated form of the neighboring-note motion 3—4⌢4—3

From earliest times, composers tended to introduce a neighboring-note motion on the third when they wanted to retard the flow at a given point:

Fig. 78

With correct instinct they avoided the form shown at a), preferring instead the syncopated form 3—4⌢4—3 as at b), which already, as at c), hints at a third voice (Palestrina, *Missa Papae Marcelli*, Gloria, mm. 9–10).

§ 200. Combining the neighboring-note figure 3—4⁀4—3 with other voices

The figure 3—4⁀4—3 can also be combined with 5—6—5, 8—9—8, 8—7—8, 8—$\frac{9}{7}$—8 or with ♭7—6—5, ♭7—6—♮7—8, 7—6⁀6—5, or with a neighboring-note motion of the bass:

Fig. 79

§ 201. Free use of the neighboring-note motion 3—4⁀4—3

Extensions and delays of this kind can appear in connection with I, IV, and V, as well as with other degrees and individual harmonies:

Fig. 80

§ 202. Linking of several 3—4⁀4—3 figures

In the practice of the great masters, particularly in preludes and fugues, such neighboring-note motions are often linked together, generally in such a manner that the accidentals for the third at the beginning and end of the neighboring-note motion change, thus affording opportunity to interlock groups such as ♯3⁀4—4—♮3⁀4—4—♭3. Examples: Handel, Suite in *E* Major (Prelude, mm. 16–18), Fugue no. 6 in *C* Minor (m. 7); Haydn, Sonata in *E*♭, Hob. XVI:52, first movement (*Tw.* 3).

Section 6: Linear Progressions

(a) General

§ 203. Linear progressions at the later levels

In the succession of voice-leading transformations we move farther and farther away from what was the new upper voice ⟨§§ 115, 116⟩ and so gain new levels. Consequently, the purpose of the linear progressions undergoes a change, as the new goals dictate.

Whatever the goal may be, the qualities inherent in the fundamental line and in the linear progressions at the first level remain the same at the later levels: a linear progression is, above all else, the principal means of creating content in passing motions, that is, of creating melodic content. The descending linear progression always signifies a motion from the upper to the inner voice; the ascending linear progression denotes a motion from the inner to the upper voice.

§ 204. Unity of the linear progressions

In all linear progressions, whether descending or ascending, the principle of the primary tone holds (§ 93): the mental retention of the primary tone achieves coherence. Each previous level vouches for the succeeding one, thus guaranteeing the indivisibility and unity of the linear progressions at the later levels: unity prevails in the foreground as well as in the background.

Whether a linear progression occurs in the upper, lower, or inner voice, its unity signifies a horizontal totality, before which the vertical retreats in importance.

Fig. 81

Ex. 1: Only by mentally retaining the primary tone db^1 can one understand a succession such as that of the tenor at c) as a third-progression in the inner voice.

Ex. 2: This example shows a very expanded third-progression. Four small third-progressions, measures 1–5, 5–9, 9–15, and 15–18 carry g^2 down to $f\sharp^1$ and e^1 (see a and b). The goal and effect of the overall third-progression could not have been achieved if the bass had not supplied its own organic prolongations. One of these is the arpeggiation $E—C—A$ (as I—IV) in measures 1–5–15: C appears in measure 5 exactly with e^2, which represents the conclusion of the first third-progression as well as the beginning of the second. Note also the octave-progression c—c^1 in measures 5–15, which holds together the second and third third-progressions.

The rhythm of the above groupings is an organic element which also deserves attention. In measures 5–8 we have two 2-measure units, then an acceleration to four whole notes in measures 9–12, and finally to four halves in measures 13–14. The accelerated third-progressions c^2—a^1 in measures 9 and 11 prepare the third-progression in halves in measures 13–15, where the second tone b^1 is prolonged by its own special third-progression b^1—a^1—$g\sharp^1$. The four halves in measures 13–14 also prepare the fourth-successions in measures 15–16, which are finally surpassed by the fifth-progression b^1—e^1 in measures 17–19.

(b) Illusory Linear Progressions

§ 205. The essential characteristic of a genuine linear progression

At the later levels, too, a genuine relationship must exist between the first and last tones of a linear progression, a relationship determined by the earlier levels. This interval relationship must be at least the size of a third, for not only the fundamental line, but every linear progression must contain a passing motion. The same applies to a fifth-progression, to a fourth-progression when it is equivalent to a fifth-progression, and to an octave-progression.

§ 206. The composing-out of a second simulates a linear progression

Where a relationship of this kind is lacking, the succession is not a genuine linear progression [§ 141]. Therefore, a succession of passing tones, even if it is subdivided, does not constitute a linear progression if its ultimate result is only the interval of a second above or below. A prolongational connection of this kind represents only an indirect ascending or descending register transfer (§§ 147 ff. and 151 ff.).

In connections of this kind there is indeed a goal, but there is no harmonic relationship between the point of departure and the final tone. A ninth therefore stands for a second, ascending as well as descending. The same is true of a seventh, except that a descending seventh stands for an ascending second, an ascending seventh for a descending second:

Fig. 82

Exx. 1 and 2: The ninths stand for descending seconds [in relation to Ex. 2, see Fig. 134,8].

Ex. 3: At b) the ninth d^1—eb^2 (mm. 35–42) is equivalent to an ascending chromatic passing tone [§ 238].

Ex. 4: The example shows a seventh which means a step of a second.

Ex. 5: In contrast, it would be incorrect to read the bass motion shown at b) in measures 9–10 as an ascending ninth d—e^1, since the unfolding shown at a) determines its meaning. At c) the end of the fifth-progression c^1—f in the bass coincides with the beginning of the fifth-progression a^2—d^2 in the soprano (m. 3). Therefore it would be incorrect to read the bass motion here as c^1—d ($=c$—$c\sharp$—d) in measures 1–4.

§ 207. The composing-out of a third, fourth, fifth, or octave occasionally simulates a linear progression

Whether or not the filling-out of a harmonic space constitutes a true linear progression thus depends upon the relationships revealed by the structural levels.

Fig. 83

Ex. 1: This is only seemingly a third-progression.

Ex. 2: Since g^2 represents a neighboring note at an earlier level, we cannot read the succession $bb^2—f^2$ in measures 9–12 as an interrupted fourth-progression (cf. Fig. 76,5 and §§ 212, 217). For this reason the successions which introduce g^2 and f^2 are not genuine third-progressions.

Ex. 3: In the same manner the successions preceding E and $F\sharp$ in the bass do not constitute genuine linear progressions, despite the outward appearance of fourth- and fifth-progressions. Nor, incidentally, is the strict concept of an unfolding applicable to the soprano. The necessary ascending register transfer, $f\sharp^2—(c\sharp^2)—b^1$ instead of $f\sharp^1—(c\sharp^1)—b$, must be assumed [see § 238]. The bass is determined by the motion $\begin{smallmatrix}(B)—d—e—f\sharp—B\\ \text{I}———\text{II}—\text{V}—\text{I}\end{smallmatrix}$ [with reference to N.B., see § 261, commentary to Fig. 125,3].

(c) The Ascent and Descent of Linear Progressions

§ 208. Descending linear progressions

From descending linear progressions of higher order, further descending linear progressions are logically derived:

Fig. 84

The division $\hat{3}—\hat{2}\,\|\,\hat{3}—\hat{2}—\hat{1}$, including the linear progressions indicated by stems pointing downward, belongs to the first level (§§ 117 and 118, Figs. 33, 34). In contrast, the linear progressions which descend from g^2 and the first stemmed f^2 belong to the second level, as does the division of the fifth-progression (§ 213).
See in addition: Fig. 42,2; Fig. 30a; Fig. 73,3; Fig. 76,3.

§ 209. Ascending linear progressions

After having established rapport with the foreground, the initial ascent to the first tone in the fundamental line can subsequently become a diminutional entity, which comes to full flower in the form of ascending linear progressions. These do not lead to tones of the fundamental line and hence belong to the later levels:

Fig. 85

[Compare § 279, commentary to Fig. 130,3.]

§ 210. Linear progressions in the bass

Linear progressions can also appear in the bass when the spaces of its arpeggiation are filled in with interpolations and passing tones (§ 257). Here, too, one must distinguish between ascending and descending linear progressions; both forms have, as always, their respective primary tones and goal tones. In the bass, however, a descending linear progression can never simulate a fundamental-line progression, since the bass and the fundamental line are separate entities:

Fig. 86

I cannot recommend strongly enough the study of the bass motions in the works of J.S. Bach. One should begin with the *Generalbass-Büchlein* and attempt to ascertain the linear progressions implied in these seemingly simple basses. One should then study the basses of other masters in a similar manner, at first leaving out the question of fundamental line while seeking to ascertain the logic of the bass. In the final analysis, of course, the true situation can be determined only by a study of the contrapuntal relationship of the bass with the soprano [§ 3, footnote].

(d) The Individual Linear Progressions

§ 211. Third-progressions

Third-progressions at the later levels are composed-out chiefly by means of the interruption $\hat{3}—\hat{2}\,\|\,\hat{3}—\hat{2}—\hat{1}$ and the neighboring note (see Figs. 42,2; 22b; 30; 73).

§ 212.   Fourth-progressions

Fourth-progressions at the later levels can have various meanings:

Fig. 87

Ex. 1: The examples demonstrate that the identity of the fourth-progression can only be ascertained with finality by considering both counterpoint and harmonic degree. In both examples the changes of harmony make it impossible to mistake fourth-progressions for fifth-progressions.*1

Ex. 2: The fourth-progressions 8—5 and 5—8 above a I or V require special attention. The same holds for other harmonic degrees which for various reasons assume the character of a I or a V.

Ex. 3: When the fourth-progression occurs in the bass, the counterweight of the harmonic degrees is less perceptible, less powerful. The unity of the fourth-progression is determined more by its melodic succession than by the clear statement of harmonic degrees. It is as if the progression took place in an upper or inner voice which moved above implied harmonic degrees far below ⟨*Kpt. II*, III/2, § 2⟩.

a) Thus, this fourth-formula, which was often used in older music to connect movements of a suite or concerto grosso, is ambiguous; only from the emphases of the particular composition can it be determined whether I—V or I—II♯—V is intended.

b) Despite the $\frac{6}{3}$ over B♭, which represents the I in *g* minor, the fourth-progression in the bass imparts to B♭ the significance of the root of III which moves to VI; for only B♭

as III can be the initial tone of the fourth-progression which is undeniably present here.*2

c) In the *Eroica* this fourth-progression unifies measures 28–93 of the Scherzo. The arpeggiation B♭—*f*—*d*—B♭ belongs exclusively to B♭. The tension of the long fourth-progression is resolved only with the terminal tone E♭.

d) The descending fourth-progression leads to the minor V more convincingly than the ascending fifth-progression would, because of the presence of the chromatic G♯.

Ex. 4: For the fourth to be heard as an indivisible entity, no emphasis must be placed on the third tone of the progression that would cause it to be understood as the goal of a true third-progression; it must, rather, be understood as a passing tone (Fig. 14,3c and d; Fig. 40,1, mm. 1–7; Fig. 114,2b).

Ex. 5: The fourth-progression does, however, admit of subdivision. In this example it would be incorrect to read the first tone of the second third-progression as a neighboring note, since the counterpoint emphasizes the parallelism of the subordinate linear progressions. This parallelism subdivides the fourth-progression, but does not represent an interruption in the strict sense (§ 192, Fig. 72,1; Fig. 157).

§ 213.   Fifth-progressions

In addition to interruption (§ 192), fifth-progressions may exhibit freer divisions:

Fig. 88

Ex. 1: This schematic interruption is illustrated by the musical example at a) (mm. 41–61), which also includes a particularly effective mixture.

*1. Schenker refers here to the augmented fourths in the top voices.   (Oster)

*2. In his personal copy of the Chaconne, Schenker wrote the III at the second beat of measure 6. This may serve as a clue to the understanding of Schenker's reading.   (Oster)

Ex. 2: Compare Figs. 41,3; 72,3.
Ex. 3: Compare Fig. 30b.
Ex. 4: This scheme fits musical example b).*3

At c) there is no subdivision, but rather an expansion which occurs through the interpolation of yet another fifth-progression descending from the primary tone (Figs. 104,3; 40,4) [§ 93].

The example at d) shows a masterly interlocking of two fifth-progressions.

In the bass too, the fifth-progressions may contain all manner of free division. As in the fourth-progression, the ascending fifth-progression in the bass may reveal a conflict between the melodically unified character of the progression and the harmonic degrees ⟨Fig. 87,3a⟩.

§ 214. Sixth-progressions

Examples of sixth-progressions at the later structural levels are given in

Fig. 89

Ex. 1: The division of the sixth-progression is counterpointed by a seventh-progression in the lower voice.
Ex. 2: The sixth-progression d^2—f^1 is subdivided by means of two fifth-progressions.
Ex. 3: The sixth-progression really consists of a fourth-progression which continues into a lower inner voice.
Ex. 4: In contrast to Ex. 3, the sixth-progression here is to be understood as the inversion of a third.

§ 215. Seventh-progressions

*3. Compare Schenker's reading of the bass in *Jahrbuch II*, p. 17, which is, in my opinion, better than the one given here, although it is slightly self-contradictory. In this earlier reading, Schenker closely relates A♭ to F (in the manner of B♭—G in Fig. 111a) and reads 5—7—5 above A♭—F—G. (Oster)

Fig. 62,1–4 shows examples of seventh-progressions. These differ from the composing-out of a seventh which stands in place of a second (as in Fig. 82,4) in that they emphasize their harmonic intervals, at least the third.

§ 216. Octave-progressions

Wherever an octave-progression is used, its unity is commonly affirmed by a complete cadence.

Fig. 90

Basically, the upper voice remains stationary on $g\sharp^1$. Compare Fig. 54,3; Fig. 73,4; Fig. 95,e4 [as well as § 260, next-to-last paragraph].

§ 217. The freest form of interruption

In addition to the interruption forms 3—2 ‖ 3—1, 5—2 ‖ 5—1, 8—5 ‖ 5—1 and the freer divisions, as in Fig. 72,1 and 2, and in Figs. 88–90, there is a type of interruption which is probably the freest. Its distinguishing feature is that the setting again takes up its initial position:

Fig. 91

(e) The Closure of Linear Progressions

§ 218. General

Linear progressions in an upper, inner, or lower voice are at an end as soon as they have reached, in ascent or descent, the goal determined by the context.

Specifically, descending fifth-progressions come to an end only when they reach the fundamental tone (and not in the middle of the progression, at the third, even if a change of harmony occurs there). This is a natural outgrowth of the fact that all fifth-progressions are modelled after the fundamental line, which, regardless of its division, closes only with $\hat{1}$ [§ 245]:

Fig. 92

Ex. 1: The recognition of the first fifth-progression, that is, that it concludes only with f^1 in measure 2, is particularly important for the understanding of the middle section of this fugue [mm. 22 and 30].

§ 219. Anticipation of the closing harmony

The unity of a linear progression in the lower voice makes it possible for the upper voice (by means of an arpeggiation or other diminution) to anticipate the chord which belongs only to the final tone of the linear progression.

Fig. 93

The root *F* remains in effect through the passing tones *E* and *D*. However, these passing tones provide the opportunity for the composing-out of the *C* triad, and the individual intervals conform to the principles of strict counterpoint—a very unusual and bold voice-leading.

§ 220. Further application of the principle of closure

The principle of closure also applies to the motion of a second, even though the step of a second is not a linear progression; only when the last tone is actually reached is the motion completed:

Fig. 94

(f) The Combination of Two or More Linear Progressions

§ 221. The concept of a leading linear progression

When two or more linear progressions are combined, it is essential to determine—from background, middleground, and foreground—which of them is *the leading progression*. In relation to this leading progression the others must be considered only as counterpoints, whether they proceed in parallel, oblique, or contrary motion, in outer or inner voices. Once one has decided whether the leading linear progression is in the lower or in the upper voice, one must understand the counterpointing progressions as upper or lower thirds, tenths, or sixths.

§ 222. Rejection of the concept of double counterpoint at the tenth and twelfth

From the concept of a leading linear progression counterpointed by upper or lower thirds or sixths, it follows that the concept of so-called double counterpoint at the tenth or twelfth can have no validity. Double counterpoint therefore takes its place in the ranks of such fallacious concepts as the ecclesiastical modes, sequences, and the usual explanation of consecutive fifths and octaves (§ 229, Fig. 99, 1).

§ 223. The inner voice

In weighing the relative significance of the linear progressions in the upper and lower voices it is important to determine whether the motion of the inner voice agrees with the primary harmony throughout or whether it is opposed to it at the beginning or the end.

§ **224.** Linear progressions in parallel thirds (tenths)

In a progression in parallel thirds (tenths) one must take into consideration whether it remains within the same harmony or moves to another, as well as the dimensions and extent of the progression.

Fig. 95

a) Third-progressions are shown in Exx. 1–8: ascending or descending, involving one or two harmonies.*4 Exx. 2 and 4 show the lower voice moving in lower tenths. Exx. 7 and 8 show a substitution for the first and last tenths, respectively. Exx. 5, 6, and 7 demonstrate the ever-present danger of parallel fifths in three-part settings.

b) Fourth-progressions are shown here. Exx. 1–3 show lower and upper tenths involving one or more harmonies. The examples under 4 contain liberties of various kinds: in the first a change from 10—10 to 6—6 supplies the third of the C_3^5 harmony instead of the nonharmonic sixth a^1 which would result were the tenth-motion to be continued as at Ex. b1. Conversely, the Mozart example shows the motion continuing to the fourth tenth, where in order to regain $c\sharp^2$ the octave d^2 would have been required ⟨as shown in Fig. 72,3⟩.

c) Fifth-progressions are shown here. At 1, we must hear the succession V—I despite the first tenth which arises in conjunction with the leading upper voice.*5 The third

*4. The asterisks in Fig. 95, a2, 4 and b1, 2 indicate tones resulting from the parallel motion, which are in opposition to the primary harmony. (Oster)

*5. The example is incomplete. In his unpublished analysis of the Suite, Schenker understood the bass $g\sharp$ at the end of measure 18 as the beginning of the V, which extends as far as $g\sharp$ in measure 20. The remainder of the bass tones represent tenths below the leading upper voice, as shown in the example. (Oster)

tenth provides an opportunity for a kind of cadence in place of the fourth tenth, without, however, disturbing the underlying V—I succession.—In the examples under 2 the lower voice leads. In version β, at the third tone of the fifth-progression the inner voice introduces the $\frac{6}{3}$ position of the harmony belonging to the final tone of the progression. In a setting of this kind the fifth-progression need not run its full course.—The example at 3 is controlled by a fifth-progression in the upper voice. At the second chord, a tenth replaces the less welcome octave, as though the passage were about to move in tenths.

d) Sixth-progressions are shown here. At 1, lower tenths associate themselves with the leading sixth-progression in the upper voice, while the inner voice enters at the third. Thus, with the first of the tenths there arises a $\frac{5}{3}$ chord, which, however, in terms of the harmony of the leading sixth-progression, must be understood only as an appoggiatura 6 (—5). Of course, it is necessary to eliminate by some means the parallel fifths arising out of the motion of inner and lower voices.—At 2, the inner voice begins on the fourth as an appoggiatura and, together with the first tenth, produces the double appoggiatura $\frac{6}{4}$. Here, too, the parallel fifths between the upper and inner voices must be eliminated.—Ex. 3 shows how a sixth-progression provides opportunity for the "ejection" of tones, that is, the placement of inner-voice tones above the upper voice, so that despite the descent of the sixth-progression, the original register can be retained (Fig. 90) [§ 260, next-to-last paragraph].

In the Bach example for Fig. 43b, the first third of the unfolding is expressed by an ascending sixth, the last three tones of which are transferred to the lower octave for the sake of the unfolding. The bass moves in lower tenths, except that a sixth is set under the b^1 in place of the tenth.

e) Octave-progressions are shown in these examples. In 1 and 2 the danger of parallel fifths arises, whether the inner voice enters at the fifth or at the sixth. These parallels must be eliminated in the foreground.—At Ex. 3, we must consider the bass as the leading voice since it is subdivided at g. The upper voice e^2—e^1 does prolong the primary tone of the fundamental line, but we cannot assume a subdivision at b^1 since this tone is foreign to the C harmony (cf. *Five Graphic Analyses*).—Ex. 4, beginning with N.B. (m. 5) shows the same situation as in Ex. 2, save that the handling of the foreground brings about a register transfer of the last tones of the bass line (*Jahrb. II*, pp. 85 ff.).—In Ex. 5 the leading octave-progression in the bass is counterpointed by an arpeggiated sixth and by a sixth-progression in the top voice which moves in upper tenths.

§ 225. Linear progressions in parallel sixths

Examples of linear progressions in parallel sixths are shown in

Fig. 96

Ex. 2: The example demonstrates that fourth-progressions in parallel sixths lend themselves to chromatic alteration.

Ex. 3: This is similar to Fig. 53,2, except that there an interval succession 6—5 occurs at the next to last tone of the leading fifth-progression in the upper voice; as a result, the counterpointing fifth-progression of the lower voice closes in the manner of a cadence (=II—V—I).

Ex. 4: The example shows the leading sixth-progression e^1—$c\sharp^2$ as a motion from the inner voice, even though the line would seem, at the foreground level, to represent the upper voice. At the beginning of the progression, the vertical situation $\begin{smallmatrix} e^1 \\ A\sharp \end{smallmatrix}$ suggests the danger of parallel fifths. The 5—6 exchange overcomes this danger and leads into a progression in parallel sixths.

§ 226. Linear progressions in parallel thirds or sixths where the outer voices move obliquely

Linear progressions in parallel thirds or sixths with the outer voices moving in oblique motion also constitute a self-contained area. In such a case the stationary tone often expressly confirms a situation which can only be generally implied when the linear progressions are in the outer voices. Occasionally, however, a modification is required, which brings about a certain freedom in the treatment of the parallel settings.

Fig. 97

Ex. 1: The ascending fourth in the upper voice (5 6 7 8) is the leading progression. The inner voice moves in lower thirds, but at the end it avoids the sixth, the a^2, which would contradict the harmony (Fig. 95b,1 and 4).

Ex. 2: On the other hand, in a descending fourth-progression in the upper voice (8 7 6 5), $\begin{smallmatrix} 8 \\ 3 \end{smallmatrix}$ often replaces $\begin{smallmatrix} 8 \\ 6 \end{smallmatrix}$ in order to avoid the nonharmonic sixth. At N.B. is shown an example from C.P.E. Bach's ⟨*Versuch*,⟩ "Generalbass" (chapter 3, section 1, § 17 a, b) ⟨in the English version by W.J. Mitchell, p. 215⟩ which Bach employs to explain the so-called Telemann bow in the ensuing § 19: the linear progression in the upper voice is accompanied by lower thirds, but the third which thoroughbass would ordinarily require at $\begin{smallmatrix} 8 \\ 6 \end{smallmatrix}$ is to be omitted.

Ex. 3: Despite the appearance of fourth-progressions, only third-progressions with appoggiaturas are to be read here.

Ex. 4: The example shows the nonharmonic e^2—a "Viennese note"—within the parallel sixths formed by the upper and inner voices.

§ 227. Linear progressions in contrary motion

The forms of the fundamental structure already exhibit linear progressions in contrary motion (Figs. 15,2; 16,2; 18,2).

The contrapuntal organization of the contrary motion in the foreground depends primarily upon the adjustment of balance in the number of tones ⟨§ 67⟩; but also, in individual instances, the particular requirements of a prolongation may determine the contrapuntal setting.

§ 228. Examples

The following examples show the contrapuntal organization of linear progressions which contain equal or unequal numbers of tones:

Fig. 98

Ex. 1: A comparison of a) and b), which both express a single harmony, points up the difference between the commonplace setting at a), so one-sided and summarily harmonic, and the truly contrapuntal way of writing at b) which seems to produce independent chords and even endows the middle one with its own figures.*6 Insignificant as the example may appear, it suffices to indicate the decline of our musical sense.

Ex. 2: A fourth-progression in the lower voice is at variance with a third-progression in the upper voice. The third-progression interpolates the chromatic passing tone ab^2, thereby achieving balance with the four-note pattern.

Ex. 3: At a) and b) a fourth-progression is balanced with a fifth-progression. In c) the lower voice traverses a fifth, the inner voice a fourth. The top voice moves parallel to the inner voice in upper thirds.*7

Ex. 4: At a) there occur within the two octave-progressions first a fifth- against a fourth-progression, then the reverse: a fourth- against a fifth-progression. At b) the diagonal lines indicate the actual intervals.

Ex. 5: The fifth-progression of the inner voice eb—bb, with its line of upper thirds, is counterpointed against the octave-progression of the lower voice.

Compare Fig. 56,1c, where the sixth-progression of the inner voice moves against the third-progression in the lower voice. See also Fig. 89,1, where the sixth-progression $b\sharp^1$—$g\sharp^2$ in the upper voice and the seventh-progression $f\sharp^1$—$g\sharp$ in the lower voice adjust to one another.

§ 229. Linear progressions in mixed motion

Combinations of linear progressions in various motions are given in

Fig. 99

Ex. 1: We see here the combination of a fifth-progression in the bass with a fourth-progression in the tenor which moves in contrary motion. The fourth-progression is accompanied by the alto in upper thirds, while the bass is accompanied in upper tenths by the soprano. It is only the fifth-progression in the bass which leads here, including the upper tenths

*6. The setting at b) comes from C.P.E. Bach; the one at a) was supplied by Schenker. (Oster)

*7. Ex. c) is not a direct quotation from C.P.E. Bach, but is rather Schenker's interpretation of the voice-leading shown in one of Bach's examples. (Rothgeb)

belonging to it. The fifth-progression also leads in b) and c). In the light of this evaluation, the specific teachings of double counterpoint become somewhat less significant (§ 222).

Ex. 2: The octave-progression f^2—f^1 in measures 1–4 is followed by a series of reachings-over, aiming at the neighboring note gb^2 in measure 8. This reaching-over is counterpointed by an octave-progression in the bass, producing partial linear progressions which move in parallel sixths and tenths.

Ex. 3: The outer voices show the combination of a fifth- with a sixth-progression in parallel motion; the sixth-progression in the bass, however, represents a rising third-arpeggiation. While this arpeggiation of the c-minor chord is continuing toward completion, a sixth-progression in contrary motion begins in the upper voice over the bass Eb. At the third tone of the sixth-progression, eb^2, the bass arpeggiation arrives at the octave c, the root of I. From this point the bass moves down to a V by means of a fourth-progression. The sixth-progression also reaches its end at the V, and over this V the octave g^1 moves to the passing seventh (8—7) which leads to the Allegro.*8

Section 7: Arpeggiation

§ **230.** Arpeggiation at the later levels

The following examples show different types of arpeggiations: ascending or descending in an upper, inner, or lower voice, resulting in a triad or four-note chord.

Fig. 100

---

*8. For a more detailed discussion of the "dissonances" in this Introduction, see Oswald Jonas's commentary in Schenker's *Harmony,* p. 346. (Oster)

Ex. 1: The first arpeggiation, which leads to the first tone of the fundamental line, belongs to the first level. In contrast, the second arpeggiation, leading to the $\hat{2}$, belongs to a later level, primarily because it has the effect of a parallelism (Fig. 40,10; Fig. 93).

Indeed, for the most part, arpeggiations appear in parallelistic fashion—connecting one or more inner voices with the upper voice. They may be integrated and concealed in a diminution, or they may be produced by a reaching-over (cf. Fig. 47,2; also Haydn, Sonata in Eb Major, Hob. 49, in *Five Graphic Analyses*). Especially in the works of the older masters, the polyphonic style frequently obscures the arpeggiations (cf. J.S. Bach, Sonata III for Solo Violin, Largo, in *Jahrb. I,* p. 61).

Ex. 2: The ascending arpeggiations ⟨in the upper voices⟩ here develop into four-note harmonies. They reveal their own power, a power which enables them to support such neighboring-note harmonies ⟨as those in a)⟩ and such intervals ⟨as those in b)⟩.

Ex. 3: We see here how each descending arpeggiation of a fifth ⟨at a) and b): g^2—eb^2—c^2 and bb—gb—eb⟩ is equivalent to the formula V—I, no matter what specific harmonic degrees or prolongation each individual situation may express. All of these arpeggiations add up to triads (Fig. 69).

Ex. 4: Here are descending arpeggiations which develop into four-note harmonies.

Ex. 5: This presents a descending register transfer by means of an arpeggiation through the fifth below, which basically can be regarded as a neighboring note of the third (Figs. 79, 80).

Ex. 6: Here we have a descending register transfer by means of three major thirds ⟨Fig. 114,8⟩.

In addition, compare Figs. 30b; 37a; 40,3; 40,6; 68a; 76,6; 81,2; 96,4; 103,1; 104,1.

Section 8: Reaching-over[*9]

§ 231. Reaching-over at the later levels

Despite the descending direction of the entries, reachings-over at the later levels serve (a) to maintain the original pitch, (b) to produce an ascending motion in order to gain an upper neighboring note, (c) to prevent a descending arpeggiation from moving beyond its goal.

We must remember that, at the later levels too, a reaching-over can occur either in direct superposition or in succession (§§ 129–33 and Fig. 41).

§ 232. Examples

Examples of reachings-over at the later levels, all in succession, are given in

Fig. 101

Ex. 1: The pitch level g^1 is maintained by means of a reaching-over.

Ex. 2: The reaching-over produces the effect of a neighboring note, since the interval between the final tone of the first and the initial tone of the second entry is a third, e^1—g^1.

Ex. 3: In this example, we see a fourth arising between the final tone of one entry and the initial tone of the next: the reaching-over results in a series of seconds leading upward to the neighboring note $\langle c\sharp^2 \rangle$. In measures 1–2, the suspended e^1 of the opening entry continues into $d\sharp^1$, a fifth below the initial tone of the next entry.

Ex. 4: The reaching-over occurs in the form of three-tone successions.[*10]

[*9.] See editorial comments after § 134. (Oster)

[*10.] The left arrows in Ex. 4 would seem to serve the same purpose as those in Ex. 5 and may, simply through an engraver's error, point to the suspension rather than its resolution. (Oster)

Ex. 5: The reaching-over aims at the arpeggiation of the triad a—$c\sharp^1$—e^1. Thus, there would normally be fourths between the individual entries $\langle a$—d^1, $c\sharp^1$—$f\sharp^1 \rangle$. Mozart combines a reaching-over-in-succession $\langle d^1$—$c\sharp^1 \rangle$ with a sort of contracted reaching-over $\langle g\sharp$—$d^1 \rangle$: he precedes the second and third entries with fifths, which make the superimposed reaching-over possible. Compare Figs. 23; 47,2; 53,5; 65,6.

Section 9: Motion from the Inner Voice

§ 233. Examples

Examples of motions from the inner voice at the later levels are given in

Fig. 102

Ex. 1: By means of the motion from the inner voice the pitch level b^1 is maintained.

Ex. 2: Here the next higher tone—a neighboring note—is reached (b^2—c^3—b^2).

Ex. 3: Similarly, eb^2 moves via g^2 to f^3.

Ex. 4: The motion from the inner voice leads to the next lower tone: f^2 to eb^2.

Exx. 5 and 6: Direct chromatic steps (Exx. 5 and 6) and a direct enharmonic change (Ex. 6) are avoided by a motion from the inner voice (§§ 248 ff.) $\langle$ § 303 $\rangle$.

Ex. 7: Compare Fig. 62,2.

Compare also Figs. 39,2; 54,15; 64,3; 96,4.

Section 10: Unfolding

§ 234. Examples

Examples of unfoldings at the later levels, with references to the schematically presented forms in Fig. 43, are given in

Fig. 103

Fig. 104

Ex. 1: Compare Fig. 43, b1 and also Fig. 76, 2.

Ex. 2: As stated in § 141, the usual setting of the form of unfolding in Fig. 43, b4 consists of an exchange of voices, giving rise to the sequence 10—10, 6—6 (§ 236). When the setting is freer, as here at a), this type of unfolding may be somewhat ambiguous; at b) ⟨which is similar to Fig. 43, d3 and 4⟩ it is less ambiguous ⟨since it involves intervals larger than thirds⟩. Compare the unfolding of two sixths in Fig. 53, 3.*[11]

Ex. 3: Compare Fig. 43, b5. We encounter this kind of unfolding of thirds at different points in a composition, at the beginning, as well as in the middle or at the close. The example at d) shows an unfolding of 8—6.

Ex. 4: Compare Fig. 43, c1. The example shows two ascending thirds.*[12]

Ex. 5: Compare Fig. 43, c2. This unfolding makes use of a 5—6 exchange in order to avoid parallel fifths (§ 164).

Ex. 6: Compare Fig. 43, c5. Usually an exchange of voices accompanies this form of unfolding. However, when the unfolding takes place between upper and inner voices, as in this example, the bass may counterpoint more freely.

Ex. 7: Compare Fig. 43, e2.

Section 11:   Substitution

§ 235.   Examples

Examples of substitution at the later levels are given in

Ex. 1: The tenth which arises at the first $\hat{3}$ suggests further tenths (§ 173); thus the neighboring note g^2 is covered by the bb^2 (m. 9). The leading tone $c\sharp^2$ substitutes for the missing $\hat{2}$ (Fig. 20, 1; also § 146).

Ex. 2: In order to avoid a seventh, as at a), or a fourth, as at b), during the descending register transfer of the third of the triad, the composer employs a consonant passing tone, which substitutes for the chord tone in the arpeggiation (§ 170, Fig. 56, 2; § 186, Fig. 66, 1b; Fig. 68b, mm. 9–14) [see also Fig. 109, e2, m. 5].

Ex. 3: The substitution of the lower third for the $\hat{3}$ of the descending fifth-progression is reminiscent of the cadential pattern in strict counterpoint in which the tonic enters before the descending leading tone (*Kpt. I*, Ex. 136, 2; Fig. 40, 4 in this book).

Section 12:   Exchange of Voices

§ 236.   The nature of exchange of voices

The necessity for exchanging voices arises only at the later levels. Here the diminutions have expanded considerably, and so it frequently becomes necessary to bring the demands of the diminutions and the requirements of the voice-leading into agreement with one another [§ 173].

§ 237.   Examples

Several examples are provided in

Fig. 105

Exx. 1–3: Exchange of voices makes it possible to remain within the harmony (cf. Fig. 95b, 1 and 4).

*[11]. Schenker seems to refer here to the foreground unfolding $d\sharp^2$—$c\sharp^2$, $f\sharp$—e in measures 136–37, 138–39 of the same **Mazurka**. This unfolding is not shown in Fig. 53, 3. It is a prolongation of the second sixth of the larger unfolding in measures 124–39, which belongs to the middleground.   (Oster)

*[12]. The ascending thirds are ab^1—c^2 and c^2—eb^2; however, the thirds with respect to which this example is related to Fig. 43, c1 are d^2—$b\natural^1$ and c^2—eb^2.   (Rothgeb)

Ex. 4: Occasionally exchange of voices is used in order to achieve, via a detour, an expansion of the upper voice.

Ex. 5: In the bass, the necessity to regain an earlier register can lead to an exchange of voices (in the event that the register became too low as a result of a descending line or coupling).*[13] Compare Handel, Prelude in $B\flat$ Major, measures 29–31, in *Jahrbuch I*, p. 32.

Section 13: Ascending Register Transfer

§ 238. Examples

A desire to exploit the brilliance of an instrument, the establishment of a relationship between registers, the general necessity of creating new content, the accentuation of formal divisions—all these lead to an ascending register transfer at the later levels.

Fig. 106

Ex. 1: The coda is stressed by the ascending register transfer.

Ex. 2: The basic form of an unfolding assumes quite another appearance through the transfer of the inner voice to the higher octave. The higher position can obscure the meaning of the unfolding and cover even the obligatory register.

Ex. 3: The register transfer at a) serves to produce an expansion and a singular and highly declamatory diminution. At b) the highest register of the étude is employed because of the close of the composition. See also Fig. 82,3b: d^1—eb^2—e^3, as well as Fig. 83,3, measure 3, where the nature of the human voice sets a limit to further descent—hence the ascending register transfer $f\sharp^1$—$f\sharp^2$.

*[13.] *E* and *D* are placed into the inner voice, which is not shown in the example. (Oster)

Section 14: Descending Register Transfer

§ 239. Examples

Examples of descending register transfer at the later levels are given in

Fig. 107

The neighboring note c^3 descends to b^1, the $\hat{2}$. This descent comprises two fifths, the first of which is realized in a very complicated fashion through an octave-arpeggiation downward followed by a seventh-arpeggiation upward (Fig. 100,2a and 6a). What a remarkable compulsion toward diminution, and how organic the effect of the constant rapport with the voice-leading shown in Fig. 76,3!

Observe in Fig. 76,2 the descending register transfer b^2—c^2—b^1. Also note the varied interplay of ascending and descending register transfers in the coda of Haydn's Variations in F Minor. These even surpass the play of registers in the theme (§ 151, Fig. 48,1).

Section 15: Coupling

§ 240. Coupling at the later levels

Although the purpose of a coupling is only the connection of two registers, it nevertheless requires a composing-out of the connective passage. The significance of a coupling lies in the role which it plays as a generator of content. A fleeting connection between octaves, an interplay of registers such as that in J.S. Bach's "Aria Variata," is foreign to the coupling.

§ 241. Examples

Examples of couplings are given in

Fig. 108

Ex. 2: A most magical coupling! Fundamentally, the $_1B\flat$ in measure 98 is intended to support the last six measures of the Adagio and to ring through them. However, since the close requires an echoing of the two-line and three-line octaves, the left hand must temporarily abandon the $_1B\flat$ register to follow the right hand. Yet the final eighth note in the left hand manages to give the impression that the $_1B\flat$ has been ringing throughout! In addition, the final measure appears to be filled to the brim—a relationship to the first measure always borne in mind by the masters. Thus, the coupling here serves the obligatory register (§ 268).

Chapter 3

Specific Foreground Events

Section 1: Transference of the Forms of the Fundamental Structure to Individual Harmonies

§ 242. General

The tendency to propagate the forms of the fundamental structure (as shown in Figs. 9–11 and 14–19) goes through all voice-leading levels. Hence, such transferred forms appear in greatest abundance in the foreground. Every transferred form has the effect of a self-contained structure within which the upper and lower voices delimit a single ⟨tonal⟩ space. Self-contained units of this kind are often difficult to decipher; dividing dominants and other interpolations can often be confusing before one has learned to understand them in relation to the middleground and background (§§ 28, 117, 188, 192, 194).

§ 243. Specific examples

The multiplicity of transference of forms of the fundamental structure is shown in

Fig. 109

a) Exx. 1 and 2 show transferences which have the effect of the linear progression $\hat{3}\ \hat{2}\ \hat{1}$ or the interruption $\hat{3}\ \hat{2}\,\|\,\hat{3}\ \hat{2}\ \hat{1}$ (Fig. 42,2). The situation is similar when the tones of the fundamental line $\hat{7}\ \hat{6}\ \hat{5}$ are set in the same way as $\dfrac{\hat{3}\ \hat{2}\ \hat{1}}{\mathrm{I\ V\ I}}$ (Figs. 20,4; 76,4).

b) The example shows the fifth-progression $\hat{5}\ \hat{4}\ \hat{3}\ \hat{2}\ \hat{1}$ (Figs. 35,2, mm. 5–8; 89,2). It is also possible to transfer the interruption form $\hat{5}—\hat{2}\,\|\,\hat{5}—\hat{1}$ and the freer division forms $\hat{5}—\hat{3}\,\|\,\hat{5}—\hat{1}$ and $\hat{5}—\hat{3}\,\|\,\hat{4}—\hat{1}$ (Figs. 42,1; 87,5; 88,4 and b; 103,1).

c) Octave-progressions in coda sections merit special attention, even when the fundamental line reads $\hat{3}—\hat{1}$ or $\hat{5}—\hat{1}$ (Figs. 54,3; 73,4) [§ 304].

d) However, transferring the prolonged bass of the fundamental structure alone will guarantee unity, even where the soprano shows no linear progression and instead takes the form of:

87

an *initial ascent* (Figs. 37a; 39,1; 46,2; 104,1).

In Fig. 39,2 the bass holds together both the initial ascent and the first third-progression which descends from the $\hat{3}$;

an *arpeggiation,* no matter how expressed (Figs. 40,6; 41,3);

an *unfolding* (Fig. 43a and b); or

a *diminution* which, as in Fig. 109,d1, represents a stationary tone (cf. Fig. 99,2, mm. 1–4). A similar diminution is to be seen in Fig. 109,d2, where the coloratura passage forms a self-contained unit (cf. Fig. 90). It lies between the initial ascent and the descent of the fundamental line, clearly indicating an expansion of a^2. This clarification should satisfy those who might object to the coloratura passage at this point in the aria. Its purpose here is not to relate to form, nor does it represent a main element of the aria—it is merely an interpolation, an expansion.

e) Since the one-voice configurations of the foreground represent several voices, it is not difficult to perceive the bass progressions hidden in the settings:

e2: The example would seem to express a stationary tone in the upper voice (cf. d1 and d2). With regard to the passing $F\sharp$ on the second quarter in measure 5, see Fig. 104,2.

e3γ: Compare Fig. 33a.

e4: See the commentary upon Fig. 109a.

e5: Particularly in fugue subjects it is most important to understand the implied bass formula. It ⟨determines the countersubject and⟩ pervades the entire fugue. Compare the presentation of the *C*-Minor Fugue from the *Well-Tempered Clavier,* book I, in *Jahrbuch II;* also Fig. 20,1 and 2; Fig. 92,1.

e6: Even the so-called elaborated cadenza (at a fermata) has a structure of its own (see C.P.E. Bach's ⟨*Versuch,*⟩ "Vom Vortrage," §§ 30–31) ⟨in the English version by W.J. Mitchell, pp. 164 ff.⟩. In order to gain an under-standing of such a passage and its bass, it is necessary temporarily to disregard the bass tone which underlies the cadenza, usually V^{6-5}_{4-3}.

Section 2:   Incomplete Transference of the Forms of the Fundamental Structure; Auxiliary Cadences

§ 244.   General

It would be too great a burden for the synthesis if each transference of a form of the fundamental structure had to begin with $\hat{3} \atop I$ or $\hat{5} \atop I$. The transition from harmony to harmony is made smoother by the omission of the I, the first tone of the bass arpeggiation. When this tone, which generates and underlies the development, is omitted, the following abbreviated forms arise:

Fig. 110

From our experience of the ascending arpeggiation we understand, in retrospect, that the fundamental tone is *C* in all such cases, especially since *C* ultimately appears. The voice-leading is "closed off" from what precedes it: that is, the IV, III, and II are related only to the forthcoming I; they point only to it. However, despite the degrees which belong to the forthcoming root, the space up to its actual entrance belongs conceptually to the preceding harmony. In a sense, the territory of the previous harmony provides a base for the preparation of the following one (cf. § 219, Fig. 93). The relationships of earlier levels make this clear [see also § 279].

§ 245.   Specific examples

Fig. 110a: Even though the bass form which begins with I is the only true image of the fundamental structure, the bass can, if the synthesis requires, occasionally start with the

V, provided a fifth-progression in the upper voice defines the specific harmony. The meaning remains the same even when the I appears as soon as the $\hat{3}$ sounds, thus subdividing the fifth-progression of the upper voice, as in Fig. 92,2; in any event the bass, with descending fifth-motion, finds true completion only when the $\hat{1}$ is reached in the soprano. It is apparent that the abbreviated form V—I can be applied to any descending fifth in a given tonality, whatever the harmonic degree. For example, it can occur in connection with II$^{(\sharp\flat)}$—V (= V—I), as in the Haydn symphony at 1.

a3: This example shows the complete composition. The piece is a true prelude: it represents a fifth-progression over V—I only.

a4: Since a descending fifth of this kind entails a motion of the upper voice, suspensions or incomplete neighboring notes often arise. These, of course, could have appeared simply above the root; now they rest upon their own bass tone, namely the fifth, which has been advanced from its normal position. Thus, we speak of suspension harmonies or neighboring-note harmonies. In any event the harmony which has been placed ahead is to be heard together with the basic chord. Whether the fifth precedes or follows ⟨§ 279, Fig. 130⟩, the fact that it really belongs to its root always creates an organic connection; its ultimate explanation lies in the original vertical situation. This is what makes the above-mentioned "closing-off" of the voice-leading possible, and it further makes clear the auxiliary nature of the embellishment. It is in this sense that I speak of *auxiliary cadence.*

Figs. 54,2 and 56,2e may be cited in this connection. Because in the latter example we have really
$$A \overset{c\sharp^3 - d\sharp^3 - e\sharp^3}{\underset{10\ -5\ -10}{- G\sharp - C\sharp,}}$$
the $d\sharp^3$ passes through the third-progression with the effect of an accented passing tone ⟨in relation to $C\sharp$, the I of the auxiliary cadence $G\sharp - C\sharp$⟩ (Figs. 40,1 and 54,13).

Fig. 110,b3: [See also § 309.]

Fig. 110c: In the first example the abbreviated bass formula, an auxiliary cadence, supports a fifth-progression; in the second it supports a third-progression. Despite the root $B\flat$ in measure 4 of the first example, it would be incorrect to assume III at this point; III appears only at the end as the product of the auxiliary cadence (Fig. 82,5c, mm. 3–4, 7–8).

Fig. 110d: In the first example the auxiliary cadence introduces a new chord in the service of more extended relationships. The second example shows an auxiliary cadence as the basis for the so-called second theme of a sonata movement, while the third shows such a cadence supporting even an entire piece (Fig. 39,2, mm. 13–21; Fig. 73,3, mm. 7–8).

Fig. 110e: In the first example auxiliary cadences, worked out in fourth-progressions, lay out the path to the fifths above I and V, namely, A and E; that D and A are only tones of the arpeggiation I—V is determined by the middleground (Fig. 103,5b).

In the second example the first theme of the movement enters over an auxiliary cadence.[1]

The third example is particularly instructive: the main tones of a large arpeggiation, the goal of which is c^3 as $\hat{3}$, are established by means of auxiliary cadences [§§ 303; 309].

In the fourth example, the Introduction shows first a descending third-progression as a unity above an essentially stationary bass tone. In the Allegro, however, the bass proceeds with II—V—I; thus the Introduction is, so to speak, connected, as if it were a prophecy, with the main section by the auxiliary cadence.

§ 246. The descending third, VII—V

[1]. Anton Bruckner was not capable of starting a musical thought, much less a whole first movement, with the aid of an auxiliary cadence. Thus the impression of a rigid succession of thought in his work: the ideas usually come in blocks, each one with a new tonic at the beginning. (Schenker)

The descending third VII—V differs in essence from the descending third that divides a descending fifth:

Fig. 111

a) In the major mode the diatonic chord which is presumably built upon the VII can be altered chromatically.

b) In the minor mode the chromatic change is inherent. The second example shows a skip of a fifth upward from the III, giving the appearance of a connection from III to ♮VII, whereas in actuality the ♮VII belongs to V♯3 in the sense of an auxiliary cadence.*2

c) A descending third of this kind can even produce the effect of a ninth, while it avoids the vertical form ⌒9—8 (Fig. 64,1).

d) It is occasionally possible for IV—I to replace V—I, if IV $\frac{5}{3}$ is omitted and the passing tones are placed over the root of the IV. An illusory VII is thus created. One can only understand the true situation when one considers the omission.

Section 3:   Addition of a Root

§ 247.   Examples

Voice-leading may also arrive at roots by actually adding ⟨inner-voice⟩ tones that are implicit in the context, that is, by placing them underneath the lowest voice.*3

Fig. 112

Ex. 1: When a chromatic tone has the effect of a leading tone, the third below, the root, is often added. The chromatic

*2. See also Figs. 53,3 (mm. 95–97); 62,8; 113,1b; 114,1a,5c and d.   (Jonas)

*3. In this process, then, an original $\frac{6}{3}, \frac{5}{5}$, or even a $\frac{6}{4}$ position that results from voice-leading is transformed into a root position.   (Oster)

passing tone is thus somewhat concealed, and in addition the stronger effect of a descending fifth is achieved ⟨cf. Fig. 152,4; also J.S. Bach, *WTC I*, Prelude in *C* Major, mm. 10 and 18, in *Five Graphic Analyses*⟩.

Exx. 2 and 3: In both these examples we find chromatic passing tones as part of a series of thirds. Once again, these chromatic passing tones have the effect of leading tones, and, as they move, they suggest roots below. Once the roots are added, they naturally form a series of auxiliary cadences [Fig. 106,2d]. The prolongational meaning of such a series of thirds derives from the contents of the previous levels. The series may mean an actual linear progression, or only a connection between the two tones of a register transfer, as in the present examples. In relation to Ex. 2, see Fig. 106,3c. In Ex. 3, measures 1–6 of the Trio represent an augmentation of measures 1–2 in the main section— see the brackets at N.B.

Chromatic tones are not the only ones which provide opportunity for the addition of a root. Fig. 102,5 shows added roots in a series of ascending diatonic thirds. In Fig. 107 (cf. Fig. 76,3; Fig. 100,2a and 6a) the $\frac{6}{3}$ chord supporting the neighboring note suggests the root *C*. Once this *C* is added, it becomes possible to return in an ascending motion to the root of V, which contains the major third *g*♯[1]. Thus the direct succession *G*♮—*G*♯ is avoided (§ 249). [For further reference to neighboring-note motions with added roots, see §§ 106, last paragraph, 108, 110, and 175.]

Ex. 4: A series of descending thirds also can suggest added roots, and richer possibilities of prolongation may so arise. Even though the addition of the roots results in descending skips of fourths, these represent in actuality skips of fifths upwards—like dividers or projected fifths (§ 279; Figs. 35,2; 82,1). The meaning of the total motion is established by the previous levels.

Section 4: Chromatic Tones

§ 248. Examples

The use of chromatic tones with leading-tone effect has already been illustrated in Figs. 38a–c; 39,3; 48,1; 62,1, 3, and 7. Chromatic tones which occur as ♭2—♮2 in connection with ♭II—V(♮5) or ♮II—V(♯5) have been illustrated in Figs. 31; 44,2; 48,1; 54,8; 64,2; 74.

Various other uses of chromatic tones are shown in

Fig. 113

Ex. 1: Here we see a chromatic tone arising as a mixture of the third (♭3—♮3 or ♮3—♯3) used in connection with any harmony, as though that harmony were I. A mixture of this kind provides opportunity for prolongation.

Ex. 2: Even so basic a degree-progression as I—III♯3—♮V in major, and the same progression in minor with III♮5 and V♯3, brings about a conflict of chromatic tones (Figs. 15,1b, 2b and c, 3b and c; 20,2; 37b; 41,2; 76,3; 100,3d).*4

Ex. 3a: Here, in the case of V8—7, the bass is arpeggiated a third upward, and this third is lowered so as to avoid the diminished fifth. This procedure creates a major triad. When the chromatic tone has fulfilled its function for the prolongation of this major triad, it is revoked. In this way the forthcoming seventh first appears as the fifth of such a major triad [§ 314].

Ex. 3,b and c: A ninth appears first as a minor seventh if the bass is arpeggiated a third upward.

Ex. 3d: The point of departure here is $\overset{\frown}{\underset{\natural 3}{\flat 9}}$. The third-arpeggiation upward in the bass then gives rise to a seventh chord. This is a very unusual kind of voice-leading.

*4. Compare also the comments on Beethoven's op. 53, following the discussion of Fig. 154,4 in § 313. (Oster)

Ex. 4: The root of V can also descend a third, once again providing opportunity for a chromatic change.

Ex. 5: This quotation from C.P.E. Bach's ⟨Versuch,⟩ "General-bass" ⟨chapter 3, section 1, § 20; in the English version by W.J. Mitchell, Fig. 257⟩ shows a chord which has the effect of ♯IV♭7 in G major, and must have the V as its continuation. In prolonging such a ♯IV one can avoid a possible augmented second, c♯—b♭, by using the major second c♯—b♮ in its place. If in addition the diatonic c♮ is used (as is the case here), it forms the interval of a diminished octave in relation to the raised root C♯.*5 Such a diminished octave can be used in a composing-out process or in the realization of a figured bass, but in no way does it constitute an harmonic concept (Fig. 80,1; Harm. §§ 53 ff.).

[In relation to Fig. 113,2 and 3, see also § 279, Fig. 131.]

Section 5: Avoidance of Chromatic Steps

§ 249. Examples

The prohibition of chromatic steps in strict counterpoint no longer holds in free composition. However, since in free composition direct chromatic successions are generally avoided (thus affording the possibility of more abundant prolongations), the prohibition is in a certain sense reestablished.

Various means for the avoidance of direct chromatic steps are shown in

*5. Compare also Exx. 1–4 in the same section of C.P. Bach's work, which show ♯IV♭7 chords.

I have completely paraphrased the first three sentences of this section. The original reads: "In the composing-out of a chord which has the effect of ♯IV♭7, the augmented second is avoided by the use of the diatonic major second (8)—♯$\overline{7}$—♯6—5 in its place. Thus a diminished octave arises if the diatonic seventh is placed above the raised root ♯IV." Schenker must surely have meant these figures and the diatonic seventh in relation to D, the V of G. (Oster)

Fig. 114

Ex. 1: The examples confirm the freedom to use chromatic steps in all voices.

Ex. 2: The direct chromatic succession is avoided by the interpolation of a neighboring note. This note can be supported—by a consonant passing tone or other means—or remain unsupported. Thus, in Ex. 2b the bass which supports the neighboring note must be considered only a passing tone. Ex. 2d gives evidence of a very special aural awareness (Figs. 7b; 71,2; 100,4a). All these examples illustrate that the issue is only the avoidance of direct chromatic steps; no further significance is attached to the chords.

Ex. 3: The chromatic step can also be avoided by means of two neighboring notes (cf. Fig. 89,1).

Chromatic steps are frequently separated by means of linear progressions (Ex. 4–6):

Ex. 4: The descending skip of a third makes it possible to achieve the required chromatic alteration diatonically in the following ascent (Fig. 102,5; compare also Beethoven, op. 57, 1st mvt., mm. 217–20, ab-$a\natural$; also Chopin's Étude op. 10 no. 12, mm. 23–27, in *Five Graphic Analyses*, where the upper voice leaps down a sixth and the chromatic tone $e\natural^3$ is reached only at the completion of the ascending sixth-progression).

Ex. 5: As Exx. a and b show, two descending third-progressions make it possible to avoid the chromatic step represented by their boundary tones (§ 260). Exx. c–f show two simultaneous third-progressions with the effect of VII—V (§ 246): while the lower of the two voices traverses the path to the root of the chord which contains the chromatic tone, the upper proceeds to the chromatic tone itself. This is one of the most frequently employed means for avoiding direct chromatic successions. Yet such a case must not be regarded as a cross-relation (§ 250). In Ex. e, a third voice is expressly introduced in order to achieve the diatonic ad-

justment of the bb^1. Ex. f shows an inversion of these progressions: the upper voice leads to the root, the bass descends to the chromatic tone—this removes the chromatic succession $V^{\natural—\sharp}$ (cf. Figs. 39,2; 40,4; 82,2) [§ 247 and Fig. 107].

Ex. 6: By means of an ascending and descending progression in the bass the chromatic step is avoided. The resulting harmony over Ab is not, however, to be considered a $\frac{5}{3}$.

Ex. 7: Occasionally an enharmonic tone can introduce a chromatic change. The insertion of an enharmonic situation provides opportunity for a small but beautiful prolongation: here one finds an allusion to what is to come.

[Exx. 8–10: Here, too, the effect of a direct chromatic succession is prevented by the insertion of enharmonic situations.]

Section 6: Cross-relation

§ 250. Examples

In contrast to strict counterpoint (see *Kpt. I*, II/2, § 28 and *Kpt. II*, III/1, § 25), free composition permits a succession of chromatic tones which have no actual relationship, using them merely as mixtures or for various other purposes.

Fig. 115

Ex. 1: a) Extremely profound voice-leading! The relationships in the middleground make clear that eb^1 (the original lies an octave lower) is only an embellishing chromatic passing tone leading to d^1. Therefore, the lesser value of this chromatic tone also lessens the tonicizing value of the chromatic tone $F\sharp$ in the bass; the bass tone $F\sharp$ is there only on account of the eb^1. Once eb^1 moves to d^1 the $F\sharp$ has no further purpose and $F\natural$ is again desired, especially since only this tone can prepare the ⌢7 in the next measure. That $F\sharp$ does not move back to $F\natural$ is, however, quite understandable. It is instead preferable, according to C. P. E. Bach, to retain the f in the inner voice—here in the left hand—so that one has, as he says, "the interval *(den Griff)* in the hand." No actual relationship exists between $F\sharp$ in the bass and $f\natural$ in the middle voice; hence these tones cannot be regarded as a true succession. They do not therefore represent a cross-relation. Each of the two tones has its own origin; they do not belong to each other. The sixteenth-note figure of the right hand (m. 23) seems to occupy the space of a third in the foreground, whereas the actual harmonic situation presents only a second: the space of a second would not have permitted a composing-out in terms of the previous motive.

b) In this example there are also no cross-relations. In measures 2–4, $c\sharp^2$ and $C\natural$, $f\sharp^1$ and $f\natural^2$ are without relationship to each other; the auxiliary cadences here *(A—D, C—F)* each start anew, that is, they have no connection to what has gone before (Fig. 110). In measure 5 there is a mixture.

c) The upper voice composes out a diminished fifth based upon IV—V. The consonant passing tone (at a in the bass) obviates any close relationship of g^1 in the inner voice and g in the bass to $g\sharp^1$ in the upper voice.

Ex.2: Occasionally the desire for a register transfer causes a chromatic succession to be distributed between two voices. Such a succession of chromatic tones cannot be considered a cross-relation (cf. *Jahrb. III*, p. 32).

Ex. 3: a) The fact that $g\sharp$ and $g\natural$ follow each other in rapid succession has to do with the necessity of avoiding the augmented second g—$a\sharp$.

b) Here the auxiliary cadence counters the effect of a cross-relation.

d) The 6 of the 5—6 exchange here calls forth the chromatic tone $e\natural^1$ in the lower voice. However, it would have been impossible to present this chromatic tone on the fourth eighth-note of the upper voice, since, as can be seen at N.B., eb^2 and f^2 are each to be retained for two full measures. In addition, an $e\natural^2$ already present on the fourth eighth-note of measure 2 would affect the $e\natural^2$ in measure 3 adversely. All of these considerations combine to make the eb^2 and the $e\natural^1$ in measure 2 unrelated. Therefore, one cannot speak of cross-relation in this instance either.

Section 7: Diminution *6

§ 251. Historical background; particulars concerning the concept of diminution

We have already mentioned *diminution*, in the true sense of the term, in many places in the present work, but we have not had occasion to discuss the concept historically.*7 This special chapter on diminution will supply such a discussion and should establish a secure foundation for the teaching and practice of diminution.

Though music was destined to reach its culmination in the likeness of itself, without having recourse to outside associations, it was at first dominated by the needs of the word, the march, the dance. The word alone was the generator of tone successions. This condition prevailed during the prehistoric era when music had no rationale; it continued even for a considerable time into the historical ages of counterpoint, of monody, and of the newly found vocal forms which, without modification, were transferred to instruments. The chief representatives and

*6. The term *diminution* as used by Schenker means embellishment in a general, broad sense. It has nothing to do with *diminution* meaning "repetition in smaller note values" (i.e., the opposite of augmentation). See the third paragraph of this section and what follows it. (Oster)

*7. See part I, chapter 1, section 4; also §§ 26, 30, 46, 49–52, 83, 85, 116. (Schenker)

creators of this music were the Italians, who with natural Latin logic viewed music through the lens of words, and so found it to be a carrier of outward reality.

Music yearned for greater length, further extension in time, greater expansion of content from within, as do all physical or spiritual beings that obey nature's law of growth. But the slower pace of the text hindered this. For a long time words and music were bounded by the same limits, even during the period when counterpoint achieved diatonicism and specific linear progressions and so established the basic prerequisites for music as an art. But then the Italians began to embellish a series of tones, and even individual tones. So they were able to meet the inner needs of music, at least as far as was then possible, and also to yield to their natural desire for beautiful singing. This process of embellishment they called diminution. No matter where and how embellishment was used, however, the word continued to generate music. Thus, the embellishments related only to the words, not to one another, with the result that the embellishments lacked logic, proportion, and all else which would have made them part of a true musical organism. These embellishments often sprang less from musical impulse than from the caprices of vanity, especially since no two singers sang the same piece in the same way.

Nor could the instrumental music of that time advance far from its vocal beginnings. The innate capabilities of the instruments, as well as the natural law of growth, called for an expansion of the musical material. And indeed the instrumental diminution tried to discover itself, as it were, in the fugue, the toccata, the ricercare, the cantata, the overture. But only diminution generated by the word was in the blood of the Italians and so they unconsciously gave it precedence.[*8] As a result

*8. Robert Haas, *Aufführungspraxis der Musik* (Wildpark-Potsdam, 1931) deals extensively with the early Italian diminutional practice as well as with later German diminution. The work contains a great number of musical examples. (Schenker)

See also Ernest T. Ferand, *Improvisation in Nine Centuries of Western Music* (Köln, 1961). (Oster)

they never made German instrumental diminution their own, despite the fact that this alone brought about a true art of music, self-generating, and developing from its own laws. Ultimately, however, the entire word-tone diminution of the Italian *opera seria*, and all of its later offshoots, collapsed. For the diminution did not mirror the text, and, more important, its lack of any organic inner relationship belied the truth of music—a fact which was not recognized at first. The art of absolute diminution in Germany has amply demonstrated the opposite. But the Italian musician could not follow the German example, and so he has had no choice—even to the present day—but to cling to the word-generated diminution of opera or, at best, to create program music, which deals, after all, with word, picture, and idea. Incidentally, even the Italian program music had finally to yield to the German; the Italian musicians lacked training in absolute diminution, which is the indispensable basis even for program music.

In only a single instance—that of Domenico Scarlatti—the Italian spirit revealed a superb capability for absolute diminution. Yet even he, a friend of Handel and a composer greatly revered by the last master of German tonal art, Johannes Brahms—even he had neither successors in his native country nor any real recognition of his unique worth. We must, however, give this Italian genius his rightful place with those Germans who mastered the art of absolute diminution.

The musical characteristics of the chorale—the achievement of Luther and the object of faithful Protestant cultivation—kept the German musician from slipping into a practice of ornamentation that was musically unfounded. In addition, the German climate was hardly conducive to the exercise of sheer vocal beauty. So the form and diminution of German organ music at first remained under the influence of the chorale. Gradually, insofar as the organ permitted, this music came to acquire the freedom of absolute diminution, at least in those cases in which the music did not serve the word. The Germans also tended to turn away from the word, overexplicit as it is; they did not usually allow it to generate the music. This tendency expressed itself in a stronger predilection for instrumental music. Left thus to itself, diminution had somehow to discover its own nature. So it did, thanks to those composers of incomparable genius who gave it consummate organic unity.[*9]

A choral setting by Hans Leo Hassler provides clarification:

Fig. 116

One can easily recognize that this example is a setting of a text. The prosody of the original madrigal poem is faithfully reflected, as one can see from the passages set off by breath-commas. These passages correspond to the individual lines of verse, including their respective upbeat syllables. The rhythmic ordering 2×3 in measures 1, 3, 9, and 11 is in accord with the notational conventions of the time. Since a detailed contrapuntally worked-out subdivision was lacking in the music, the notation itself implied, indeed required, a certain freedom in performance; the apparent ordering 3×2 in measures 2, 4, 8, and 10 derives from the inclusion of the upbeat.[*10]

Nevertheless the tonal structure is remarkably independent of the word. As we know, Hassler's moving melody was later to be used as a chorale; the spirit of J.S. Bach was soon to hover over this melody, in the several settings of it which this master made. So the melody served both secular and liturgical texts. The chorale became, so to speak, a musical article of the Protestant faith.

In the strictest sense of absolute music, Hassler's setting approaches perfection. In the foreground the upper voice pre-

sents a definite composing-out of the D-major harmony in the form of an octave transfer, $f\sharp^1 - f\sharp^2$,[*11] followed by a closure, $\hat{3} - \hat{2} - \hat{1}$. The conduct of the bass line is just as definite as it composes out the arpeggiation I—V—I. Thus, an unmistakable fundamental structure is present which supports the foreground. Other settings of Hassler's upper voice, such as those by J.S. Bach (in the edition of Erk-Smend nos. 122, 126, 127; in Breitkopf und Härtel—and Riemenschneider—nos. 21, 89, 345) offer only a superficial tribute to the lingering Phrygian system which musicians still believed in. In these settings, the Phrygian system was suggested, indeed almost required, by the final note. However, the latter is correctly understood as the third of the tonic chord in the major mode (as in Erk-Smend nos. 74, 123, 124; Breitkopf nos. 74, 98, 80). It is precisely the definiteness with which the major mode is achieved in the total span that allows Hassler to use an incomplete full close, in which the hidden $\hat{1}$ is understood.

Despite the sparseness of tonal material in Hassler's setting, several bold events in the composing-out do arrest the attention. Bold though they are, they are all musically cogent.

Measure 1: The a^1 normally required by the arpeggiation $f\sharp^1 - a^1 - d^2 - f\sharp^2$ is missing here. Yet it is understood from the opening chord, and thus can be absent in the motion to d^2. The diminution of the b^1, which replaces a^1, results from the composing-out of the third in ascending and descending directions:

$$b^1 - c\sharp^2 - d^2 - c\sharp^2 - b^1.$$

Measure 4: The setting of the passing tone $f\sharp^1$ over the bass $G(G^{8-7})$ at the first structural level is ingenious. The passing tone is made consonant by the bass tone B.

Measure 5: As the upper voice is composed out within the A-major harmony the bass follows it in parallel tenths.

Measures 6–8: The composing-out of the descending sixth $d^2 - f\sharp^1$.

[*9]. Passage (M), omitted here, is supplied in Appendix 4. (Rothgeb)

[*10]. Fig. 116 contains an engraver's error which it was impossible to correct. Measure 4 of the composition has a repeat sign after the B-major harmony. In the *prima volta*, which is omitted in the example, this chord appears as whole notes, but as half notes in the *seconda volta*. Thus the *prima volta*, together with the repetition of the upbeat to measure 1, comprises three half-notes. This is the reason why Schenker included measure 4 among those measures which show a 3×2 ordering. See §298 for further discussion of this metrical scheme. (Oster)

[*11]. Regarding the eventual transfer of $f\sharp^2$ to $f\sharp^1$, see below. (Jonas)

Measures 9–10: In the composing-out of the descending fifth e^2—a^1, $c\sharp^2$ replaces the a^1 in measure 10, thus avoiding the ill-sounding total interval of a seventh, e^2—$f\sharp^1$. In measure 10, in order to maintain the obligatory register, a descending register transfer finally occurs in which $f\sharp^2$ is replaced as $\hat{3}$ by $f\sharp^1$, which was already prepared by the $f\sharp^1$ in measure 8.

The fact that the contrapuntal practice of that time restricted itself to $\frac{5}{3}$ and $\frac{6}{3}$ chords throughout does not affect the above explanation (*Harm.*, note following § 88). Even in this early music, the fundamental structure has so much strength that we have no difficulty in recognizing the passing tones in the middleground. Those passing tones which the earlier level shows as dissonances remain passing tones, even though the foreground shows them as consonances.

Despite its origin in a text, this music, as art, is completely pure. It is clear and organically unified, as absolute music always is, in contrast to music generated by the word. During the composing-out, it can even forgo repetitions which ordinarily establish so-called motives. Of course, the brevity of the composition as well as the vocal element might also tend to oppose motivic patterns (§ 50).

Now to the most important consideration: it is obvious that a composition such as that given in Fig. 116 does not admit of embellishment in the Italian style. Moreover, when the chorale text was introduced, embellishment was out of the question because of the words. Extensive embellishment in such a case could only lead to a "chorale prelude." Yet the strong bond to canonic repetition, whose origin ultimately lay in the word, stood in opposition to such a form of free diminution—genuine diminution which is completely self-generated. Therefore, other paths to genuine diminution had to be sought: just those which the great masters found.

The setting by Hugo Riemann appended at N.B. below Fig. 116 illustrates the latter-day disastrous growth of chords in the exclusively vertical sense. These "chords" paralyze the contrapuntal flow of the bass as well as that of the inner voices—it matters not whether this flow occurs by means of a compositional technique such as that of Hassler or by means of the procedures of J.S. Bach, which are more elaborate melodically.

§ **252.**   Figurations and small notation

Indeed, all foreground is diminution. But even within the foreground, figurations frequently appear which are based on previous statements in the foreground. The occurrence of both statement and variant (figuration) at the foreground level—that is, the presence of two structural levels within the foreground—creates the illusion that the variant belongs only to the foreground statement, but in fact, through this statement it also relates to the background and middleground.

Nevertheless, in the masterworks it is often quite difficult to decipher such figurations, as the following examples illustrate:

Fig. 117

Ex. 1: Statement and variant are presented under a) and b). The derivation of both from the middleground is evident from the other illustrations. The first line shows a third-progression which departs from the $\hat{3}$. In the second, the $\overset{\frown}{6}$—5 suspension is added. The third line shows the diminution in eighth notes, and so the upbeat also becomes an eighth note. At a) the diminution appears in sixteenths, prepared by the subdivision of the ♪–upbeat into ♫, with b^1 appearing as a neighboring note. In the next line this b^1 appears at the beginning of the measure, so that the auxiliary harmony produces the effect of V^7. The composing-out continues within this harmony in the form of ♪ ♪ ♪, two-voiced, with fifths on the afterbeats. Finally, in the figuration at b), the two last thirty-second notes of the upbeat, $c\sharp^2$ and $b\sharp^1$, prepare the chromatically filled-in span from b^1 to $e\sharp^1$. Only by experiencing these relationships can a performance of the figuration shown at b) really succeed.

When statement and variant return, as for example in antecedent and consequent settings or in the parts of a song form, the figurations become ever more richly elaborated. In this way they evince a process of growth like that of an organism, which also adds to the unity of the whole ⟨cf. Chopin, Nocturne op. 15 no. 2, mm. 49 ff.⟩.

The foreground sometimes exhibits merely a simple figuration of the fundamental structure, as has already been pointed out in § 26.

In the strictest sense, variations as an art form belong here. They may be called Variations, Doubles, Agréments, Partita (Chorale Variations); they may be disguised as Chaconne, Passacaglia, or Rondo (C.P.E. Bach); or they may even appear, as they did later, in movements of sonatas or symphonies—not only in first movements by Haydn, Mozart, and Beethoven, but also in the slower movements, especially those in Haydn's works or in Beethoven's Ninth Symphony. In each case, statement and variant exhibit relatedness and coherence even at the foreground level. It must always be borne in mind, however, that the middleground and background present the ultimate, decisive relationships.

Occasionally the German masters faced problems of diminution similar to those encountered by the Italians. Such problems arose not only in the aria, the origin of which was Italian, but also in absolute music, in situations where it was essential to embellish in order to gain an expansion of content not easily obtainable by other means. They solved this problem with incomparable mastery, for while the Italian musicians lost themselves in extemporaneous diminutions which remained nonorganic and unrelated to each other, the Germans succeeded in achieving strong, organic relationships of all kinds. These relationships were, of course, favored by the organization of the pieces themselves, in which the bass was also fashioned in a contrapuntal-melodic manner, that is, displaying its own prolongations, linear progressions, couplings, and the like.

There follow examples of parallelism as the motivating force of such relationships:

Fig. 118

Compare Ex. 1 with *Five Graphic Analyses*. The creation of such diminutions reveals spiritual and intellectual powers which can scarcely be described in words. These diminutions can be appreciated only through the experience of struggling to decipher them! The profundity of this music is difficult to perceive even when, as in the Air of Handel's Suite III in *D* Minor, one has recourse to the master's first version, which is entirely without ornamentation. Another beautiful example by Handel is the Sarabande from his *B*♭-Major Suite; an earlier unembellished version of this is also preserved.[12]

The performer is confronted with enormous difficulties in such instances. To achieve an overall dynamic shading appropriate to the basic version while presenting the inner shadings of the ornamental details, such as chromatics, neighboring notes, and suspensions—all this in the proper light and shade—indeed transcends the powers of all but the most gifted performers.

It is clear that the thorough study of such art of embellishment must necessarily give insight into the art of improvisation.[13]

[12]. The early version of the Air is shown in the *Gesamtausgabe* by Breitkopf und Härtel, vol. 48, p. 156, and also in the Lea Pocket Scores, *Works for Clavier*, p. 124; the early version of the Sarabande in the *Gesamtausgabe* vol. 48, p. 147, and a slightly embellished version in *Hallische Händel-Ausgabe, Klavierwerke II*, p. 113. (Oster)

[13]. Compare Schenker's important essay "Die Kunst der Improvisation" in *Jahrbuch I*. (Oster)

Composers apparently were conscious of the difference between essential content and mere embellishment, for they sometimes wrote embellishments in small notes. This gave rise to the practice of using large and small notation. The most frequently recurring ornaments, the so-called *Manieren*, became fixed as signs, a sort of musical shorthand, and the large notation remained uncluttered. But C.P.E. Bach in his *Versuch über die wahre Art, das Klavier zu spielen*, chapter 2, section 1, § 6 contrasts such fixed embellishments with *Manieren* in a broader sense: those presented in large notation which he terms "Manieren of the second class."[*14] With this broader concept C.P.E. Bach touches upon the world of diminution in the deeper sense of its relationship with the middleground and background. Most of the so-called varied reprises belong to that world.[*15]

It is regrettable that the small notation in the first Adagio of Handel's Suite II in *F* Major and in the Air of his Suite III in *D* Minor are not available as such either in the *Gesamtausgabe* (Breitkopf und Härtel) or in any other edition.[*16] The small notation in such cases reveals the middleground elements, directing the reader or player more easily into the path which leads to the true sense of the music. Chopin very often made use of small notation in passage work, arpeggiations, and other figurations. Perhaps the most interesting example of its use is the notation of the bass in the Étude op. 25 no. 1, where at the first tonic *A*♭ he indicates, by distinguishing between large and small notation, the correct performance even of the bass.[*17]

*14. Compare my *Beitrag zur Ornamentik*, pp. 24 ff., 71. (Schenker)

*15. Compare C.P.E. Bach, *Klavierstücke mit veränderten Reprisen*, edited by Oswald Jonas, who has also provided a separate commentary (in German and English) on the significance of the diminutions in these compositions (Universal Edition 13311). (Schenker, Oster)

*16. The small notation is now reproduced in *Hallische Händel-Ausgabe (Klavierwerke I)* and in Lea Pocket Scores (*Works for Clavier*, p. 123). (Oster)

*17. In the manuscript of the first version of this étude, Chopin placed stems upon the quarter notes in the first ten measures before beginning to differentiate only by means of large and small noteheads. (Jonas)

§ 253. The achievement of organic relationship in genuine diminution (1) Through the whole

It would be impossible to make a complete listing of all the forms of organic relationship which occur in true diminution. Therefore, I shall present here only the most essential.

First, all diminution must be secured firmly to the total work by means which are precisely demonstrable and organically verified by the inner necessities of the voice-leading. The total work lives and moves in each diminution, even those of the lowest order. Not the smallest part exists without the whole. The establishment of an inner relationship to the whole is the principal problem not only in the creation of diminution out of background and middleground, but also even in its re-creation, where constant reference to middleground and background must be made.

The atmosphere of diminution is the whole.

True song is given to diminution. It is born with the movement in seconds of the fundamental line, and develops further life through the seconds of the lines which evolve from it. So it sings its way through all these seconds, the conveyors of the melodic, into the foreground and within it further and further. All the manifold experience of the lines—which are none other than our experiences—are transformed into song. Wherefore then words to generate music, to point up its meaning, when music itself organically lives, sings, and speaks? Its inner song elevates absolute diminution above word-generated diminution, which is eternally chained to "love," "hate," and "jealousy."

Performance, too, must sing from the whole, whether the piece moves slowly or quickly. Everything in the genuine masterwork is song-like, not only those passages which are obviously "cantabile." C.P.E. Bach, in whose path Haydn followed, deserves praise as the originator of this deeply songful, absolute diminution. And he was tireless in his zeal for a singing manner of performance. Indeed every line of his immortal masterwork, *Versuch über die wahre Art, das Klavier zu spielen*, expresses song! Alas, I fear that the day of this noble inner song is past, both in composition and performance.

§ 254. (2) Through repetition

An enormously long time was required before music incorporated the principle of repetition. As long as the word interpreted music and determined its dimensions, music was absolved from the obligation to interpret and develop itself. Thus it was in the epoch when music had no rationale. Even in the first melismas, those first embellishments of individual syllables in which the human voice reveled with delight, repetition was lacking. Consequently these embellishments remained illogical for centuries, until counterpoint, by clarifying both vertical and rhythmic aspects, succeeded also in defining the horizontal dimension: a tonal succession could achieve a specific inner relatedness, limited and meaningful, since it was based upon specific intervals and also specifically determined in the manifold time-values of the individual notes ⟨§§ 4, 21, 67⟩. Only a unity of this kind could have led, indeed it had to lead, to repetition. Repetition presented itself as a symbol of organic life in the world of tones, as though statement and variant were connected by bonds of blood. The ever stronger inner desire of music to follow its own course, to strive toward expansion of content, found its counterpart in the pleasure the ear derived from repetition— a joy in recognition itself. And thus for centuries music proceeded through the school of the canon, the fugue, and related imitative forms. Repetition lay always on the surface; it was immediately and constantly perceptible to eye and ear as inversions, augmentations, contractions. These early discoveries made by Western man have remained effectual throughout subsequent time. Even now we find that kind of music most accessible in which there is repetition that is immediately recognizable. The ease with which we recognize a tonal series adds to the pleasure we derive from that recognition—what is simpler than to recognize a repetition of the brief succession of tones customarily designated a "motive"?

However, the facility with which the tonal materials were enlarged and enjoyed ultimately decreased the interest in earlier imitative forms, especially since they became stereotyped and shop-worn in the hands of composers of little talent. New types of repetition then revealed themselves to composers of genius. Although these new types seem to lie just as clearly before eye and ear as the repetitions that occurred within the imitative forms, they remained less accessible because they did not offer creator and listener the same ease of perception. They were fully as effective as the simpler repetitions; they, too, sprang only from the blood relationship of statement and variant, almost beyond the composer's volition—but they remained concealed. Yet it was precisely these concealed repetitions which freed music from the narrowness of strict imitation and pointed the way to the widest spans and most distant goals; thus even very extended tonal structures could be based upon repetition!

In these concealed repetitions lie the seed and flowering of German creative genius. Therefore, the technique of "motive" repetition in the German music-drama, in program music, and in the sonata forms of the lesser talents signifies retrogression to the earlier stage, and thus a decline.

Of course, the early type of immediately recognizable repetition coexisted with the new type of repetition. Each is, in its place, beneficial and advantageous. The new type of repetition is recognizable, above all, by its derivation of tonal successions from the simplest element (§ 30). The magnificent heritage of the German chorale brought forth many boldly conceived compositions. These compositions show how such a simple derivation can suffice for the creation of a great work of art—even without recourse to repetition in the foreground.

The repetitions indicated in Fig. 118,1 and 2, which belong to the middleground, are not to be regarded as motive repetitions in the usual sense. They are, however, repetitions and they thus bring about relationship. And certainly the foreground here in no way suggests "motives."

Exx. 1–21 in Fig. 119 confirm the fact that concealed repetitions are not merely imagined by the ear, nor are they only the result of fantasy. They could, in fact, even be grasped visually, if in music the eye were able to see without being guided by the ear. Repetitions of this kind have nothing to do with "motive" repetitions; they are so simple and so minute that they often do not fall within the concept of a motive.

Fig. 119

Exx. 1, 2, 4–6, 8–10, 15: Repetitions by augmentation.
Exx. 3 and 11: Repetitions by contraction.

The following examples cannot be termed either augmentation or contraction:

Ex. 7: Here gb^2 and g^2 are engaged in a struggle with one another—only two single tones, certainly not a motive repetition in the usual sense. And yet the synthesis of the entire first movement circles around this conflict.

Ex. 13: The statement, a), shows an augmentation of a simple arpeggiation. Therefore, b) cannot be called an augmentation; it is rather an elaborate repetition of a). ⟨In contrast to a), b) is wholly contained within the I of Db major. Cf. Fig. 102,6 and § 303.⟩

Ex. 14: Here we have the repetition of a mere neighboring-note figure which maintains its pitch position while the harmonic degrees (V—I, IV—I) change; yet precisely this feature contributes greatly to the cohesiveness of the whole.

Exx. 16–18: These repetitions approach the very limits of what may be considered repetition; they are like the smallest cells of a diminution.

Ex. 19: In such diminutions of the upper voice, the repetition would ordinarily begin with the upbeat. In both these examples, however, the downbeat must be included in the repetition, creating a somewhat peculiar effect. Both analysis and performance must show full recognition of this feature. ⟨Compare the different situation in Fig. 147,4.⟩

Ex. 20: The repetition here plays a decisive role in creating the form—the f^1—eb^1 in b) opposes itself to the f^1—eb^1 in a) and leads to the III of f minor, to the so-called second theme ⟨cf. Fig. 154,4⟩.*18

Ex. 21: ⟨These repetitions take place in the middleground. Therefore,⟩ only awareness of the middleground makes it possible to recognize them.

Such repetitions, and similar ones, have a far-reaching effect in synthesis. They contrast strongly with the repetitions usually taught today, which tend only to restrict the scope of synthesis.

It is surely time that we learn to recognize such repetitions as the prime carriers of synthesis in order to be able to express them in performance also. In view of the fact that the masters based their syntheses mainly upon such relationships, there can be no doubt of the importance of projecting them—it remains only to find the specific means of achieving such projection. Once the musician has made the perception of such relationships an integral part of his musical thought, he will know how to restore them to the synthesis. Ex. 15c, for instance, makes an entirely different effect when it is performed as a repetition and when it is performed as a completely new event, which the new diminution in measures 8ff. easily tempts one to do [§ 303]. And how different the "well-known" Overture to *A Midsummer Night's Dream* would sound if the conductor brought the repetition shown in Ex. 9a–e to life! One cannot repeat too often that the way to a true understanding of this type of repetition leads through the middleground and background.

§ 255.   (3) Through preparation

Diminution at the foreground level is often open to misunderstanding, for it frequently makes use of concealed repetitions

---

*18. In *Der Tonwille 7*, p. 7 Schenker mentions that the chromatic step $e\natural^1$—eb^1 in measure 23 may have suggested fb^3—eb^3 in measures 26–27, and further on (mm. 30–31, 47–50, etc.). I believe that this is the case.   (Oster)

in the middleground rather than obvious repetitions in the foreground. When such foreground diminutions occur, they require additional relationships in order to obviate misunderstanding.

Fig. 120

These examples show how such relationships can also be established by preparing a diminution. Preparation makes the subsequent diminution organic. It is frequently so delicate that it hardly need penetrate into the artistic consciousness; one can almost assume a sort of self-generation. Here, strangely enough, the concealed process supports the organic element more strongly than literal repetition could.

Ex. 1: Beethoven avoids proceeding directly from the g^1 in measure 4, the final tone of the descending line, to g^1 in measure 8. Instead, in measures 5–8, he inserts the ascending semitone $f\sharp^1$—g^1 and thereby achieves a preparation for the chromatically ascending seconds which follow. In so doing, he also uses the third-arpeggiations in the bassoons to prepare the third-arpeggiation in measure 8, which later serves to eliminate consecutive fifths (Fig. 62,2).

Exx. 2–4: Here the change of direction of the diminution which follows is prepared in simplest fashion. This preparation is invaluable in the service of unity.

Ex. 5: With the change of octave in measures 1–2 the move into still higher registers is prepared. This move helps to bring about the unification of the measure group (cf. Fig. 62,4).

Ex. 6: In this example, the peak tones (*) of the diminution relate to one another in a different sense. Under no circumstances may we read them as a genuine linear progression, for example, as a sixth-progression at a) ⟨mm. 1–12, b^1— g^2⟩ or as a fourth-progression at b) ⟨mm. 8–10⟩. Were such linear progressions intended, they would have to be compositionally worked out, which does not happen here.

§ 256. (4) Through enharmonic restatement

Enharmonic restatement does not involve the contrast of major with minor third, sixth, or seventh, as it occurs within the concept of mixture, nor does it involve the chromatic passing tone. Only voice-leading events such as those in the following examples can be considered parallelisms which do involve enharmonic restatement:

Fig. 121

Ex. 1: The inner voice a^1 in measure 139 should progress to $a\sharp^1$ in the next measure; however, the $a\sharp^1$ appears as bb^1, whereupon the $C\sharp$ of the lower voice descends to C, thus achieving the effect of a C^7 chord. Accordingly, the diminution in measures 140–44 moves as if it were in the key of F major. But in measure 145 the enharmonic is withdrawn; $a\sharp^1$ assumes its rightful position replacing bb^1, and the principal tonality can continue. The play of the enharmonic restatement creates a delaying effect, a feeling of suspense, which strongly enhances the sense of diatonic unity.

Ex. 2: At b), a parallel passage to a) seems at first to be in progress. But the b^2, originally a passing tone, provides an opportunity for a dreamlike digression into E major, through which sounds the beginning of the Rondo. The contradiction of the initial tonality by this enharmonic interpolation creates a very special feeling of suspense. It is like an awakening when, in measure 161, the composer suddenly—at the ffp—transforms $g\sharp^1$ back into ab^1 (ab^2) and then ends in the main tonality.

Ex. 3: An enharmonic restatement can be effective even on a small scale: in a) the cb^3 in measure 11 gives rise to gb^1, whereas b^2 gives rise to g^2.

[Compare Fig. 149,6.]

§ 257.   Bass diminutions

Within the limits defined both by nature and by the arpeggiation of the fundamental structure, diminution in the bass employs the entire array of prolongational techniques (§§ 20, 185) [§ 210]. The bass participates in the formation of all unified configurations of the upper voice, of whatever nature they may be, and decisively determines their beginnings and endings. The value of a masterwork rests to no small degree upon a purposeful and ingenious construction of the bass.

No better introduction to the art of bass diminution can be found than the chorale settings of J.S. Bach. Short as a chorale is, it provides the bass with opportunity for the boldest diminutions; every impulse of the chorale text is mirrored in the bass ⟨cf. Fig. 22a and *Five Graphic Analyses;* also Fig. 83,3⟩. However, this profound art has not yet been really heard or appreciated, nor has it ever been equaled, much less surpassed, by any other master of the tonal art. Altogether, J.S. Bach remains the master teacher of a genuinely contrapuntal bass; even with the most extensive unfolding of diminutions he never exceeds the limits set for the bass. Therefore, a nonlegato performance of his basses is usually appropriate.

§ 258.   Descending diminution

The various concealing devices of foreground diminution have a particular musical attractiveness. We delight in them, and diminution has its greatest triumph in the fact that it can make us forget the bare outlines of a work. (So we also delight in the human form, whose shape is made more attractive in flesh and color.) Particularly the high and low registers, which contribute to the expressive and ecstatic quality of instruments—and so are indispensable—often disguise the actual path of the diminution.

In the case of descending foreground diminutions, the significance of the goal tone can be determined only if one considers the relationship to the middleground and background. Thus, a goal tone can be part of the fundamental line (Figs. 89,4; 91,4); it can be a neighboring note (Figs. 82,5c; 83,2); it can be a tone in an initial ascent (Fig. 120,6b), in a motion from an inner voice (Fig. 102,7) or in an arpeggiation (Fig. 110b,3).

Compare the examples in *Jahrbuch III* (Beethoven, Eb-Major Symphony). It is in the nature of such diminutions to be, as it were, closed off from the voice-leading which precedes their beginnings (§§ 244 ff.). Further examples follow:

Fig. 122

Ex. 1: The tones g^1 and a^1 of the initial ascent are reached simultaneously by descending diminutions in the upper voice and ascending fourth-skips in the inner voice. These tones therefore result from the contrary motion of two voices (octave to unison), which has great charm. This attractive feature also requires special treatment in performance.

Ex. 2: This example illustrates very clearly that the beginning of a descending diminution can be independent of the vertical element. This diminution begins at d^3 and descends to the goal-tone ab^2 on the fifth eighth. At the same time, the left hand has the $\widehat{4}$—3 suspension eb^1—d^1. Despite this suspension, Chopin was able to write the d^3, since it relates exclusively to the forthcoming ab^2; it does not relate at all to the suspended eb^1. The articulation, although it would seem to indicate otherwise, does not alter the situation.*19

Ex. 3: This example also illustrates independence of a descending diminution from the actual chord. There is no doubt

*19. In his personal copy of the nocturne, Schenker described the diminution as an "interpolation" and placed it in parentheses, thus putting into relief the main melodic progression bb^1—c^2—d^2—eb^2. With regard to the first slur bb^1—d^3, Schenker makes a suggestion for performance: "bb^1 to be sustained *(hält an)* to create the impression of a quarter note." (Oster) that the chord in the second measure is to be understood as a $\frac{6}{4}$. Ordinarily, the sixteenth (*) would have read d^2, not e^2, especially since with d^2 the initial octave-skip c^2—c^3 would find an answer. Nevertheless, C.P.E. Bach writes e^2 as if it were part of an independent chord, e^2—g^2—d^3, without, however, intending to allude to the E in the harmony which follows in measure 3. This subtlety brings to mind (see Ex. N.B.) the delicate way in which C.P.E. Bach, in another piece, avoids an augmented fourth in the diminution (cf. *Kpt. I*, Ex. 50).

§ 259. Ascending diminutions

Examples of ascending diminutions are presented in

Fig. 123

Ex. 1: a) The upper tones of the thirds are not to be regarded as goal tones with a consequent harmonic significance. They are only superposed as simple consonances. On the other hand, the lower primary tones form an ascending line. Thus there is no parallel-octave succession at the bar line [§ 162].

b) Similarly, $g\sharp^2$ must not be taken for a faulty doubling of the leading tone.

c) Only the initial tones are determinant; hence, the four-tone groups are not true linear progressions of a fourth.

Ex. 2: In the second measure, the fourth eighth note is a goal tone; the fifth eighth, in contrast, is a primary tone of the ascending diminution. This reading of the intervals is based upon the first measure, of which the second measure is the inversion.

Ex. 3: The primary tones of the diminutions ⟨b^1 and c^2 in mm. 3 and 5⟩ serve the tones of the initial ascent. The peak tones of the diminutions ⟨d^2 and e^2 in mm. 3 and 5⟩ are not to be considered goal tones, nor do they have a harmonic effect (Fig. 119,3 and Fig. 120,6).

Ex. 4: In connection with an unfolding, a diminution often shows a superposition of the inner voice (Fig. 106,2).

Ex. 5: This diminution, by ascending, produces an octave transfer of two tones from the inner voice, b^1 and $a\sharp^1$, and, through this octave transfer, arrives at e^2 at the reaching-over on the fourth quarter; this makes it possible to retain the position of e^2, the $\hat{8}$. It is interesting to note that $c\sharp^2$ progresses to b^2 through skips of thirds, without, however, implying a seventh chord.

§ 260. Balancing of directions; boundary-play

No matter whether a diminution ascends or descends, the composer may seek to regain the position occupied earlier or to reach tones lower or higher. The first motion is followed by others; the tone which begins the total motion and the tone which ends it become its boundary tones [§ 143]. The first tone sets out toward the goal, the last one brings us to it.

Fig. 124

Ex. 1: a) The boundary tones of the motion, which takes place over the I, represent a stationary tone (Fig. 109e,2 and 5).

b) Here again the motion ⟨8—♭7—6—♮7—8⟩ has a stationary tone at its boundaries. At N.B. other possibilities are shown, which, however, have the disadvantage that they involve skips. With respect to this, compare Mozart, Symphony in G Minor, Andante, measures 44–47 (*Jahrb. II*, p. 140):

$$\overset{\frown}{\flat 7}-\flat 6-5-\natural 6-\flat 7$$

$\flat IV^{\flat 3}$————————— $\natural IV$—V, a motion frequently used by Mozart; also Fig. 79,5, where the first 8 is missing in the succession $\flat\overset{\frown}{7}-6-\natural 7-8$. The beginning of the Allegro in Fig. 119,7 again reveals a stationary tone, attained by the motion of a descending and an ascending fifth.

Ex. 2: In a) and b) the boundary tones form a descending second. Although the final tone of a motion of seconds is most naturally reached through a play of opposing descending and ascending motions (Fig. 20,3; Fig. 64,1), the same effect can be achieved through two descending motions, as it is here (Fig. 42,2; Fig. 62,2).

Ex. 3: The boundary tones are again stationary. Compare also measures 4–5 in Fig. 20,2 and Fig. 54,13.

Ex. 4: The second, g^1—ab^1 (the neighboring note), is realized by means of a detour in which the highest tone, c^2 (c^3), is supported not, as usual, by the IV, but by the VI (cf. Fig. 46,2: c^2—d^2; Fig. 53,3, mm. 5–31: e^2—$d\sharp^2$).

Ex. 5: a) A third-arpeggiation is formed by the boundary tones of the diminution in measures 1–4. The high a^2 in measure 3 has been prepared by the g^2 in measure 1. The a^2 in measure 5 begins the descending motion to d^2 and ultimately evokes also the g^2 at the end of the example (see the asterisks).

b) The situation here is similar, but the richness of the rhythmically elaborate detour to the third, b^1, in measure 4, and of the following embellished descent from e^2 to a^1 gives the effect—despite the small number of measures—of symphonic breadth, of a true Andante [Fig. 148,1].

Fig. 119,15 shows descending thirds. The lower boundary tone in each instance is also the root: $\frac{e^1}{c^1}$ in 15a, $\frac{g\sharp^1}{e^1}$ in 15b, and $\frac{b^1}{g\sharp^1}$ in 15c.

Ex. 6: Here are digressions involving thirds, which, however, in no way alter the progression in seconds (cf. Fig. 45).

Ex. 7: The third-progressions, designated by the brackets as a), b), and c) (mm. 1–3), contain the germ of all subsequent tensions, not only those which serve the $\hat{3}$ in measures 1–63,[20] but also those in the development and recapitulation. The change of direction in the third-progressions has to do with the stepwise progression at the change of measure: c^2—bb^1 determines the descending motion of the second third, g^1—f^1 the ascending motion of the third group, since the a^1 at the boundary is to be regained. These changes create a constant flow, which would be lacking if the middle third-progression were to ascend g^1—a^1—bb^1. With the change of register of the first third-progression, in measure 5, there arises the necessity of inverting the second third-progression, which appears in its original register. The skip of a seventh, c^1—bb^1, would otherwise come about at the change of measure 5/6. Since a seventh would scarcely achieve the melodic quality which the step of a second at the change of bar 1/2 does, the more natural form of a fifth, c^1—g^1, was given preference. Thus bb^1 leads to a^1. At this point it became necessary to avoid the inversion of the third third-progression in measure 7, since it would lead down to f^1 and thus a^1—a^1 as boundaries of the total motion would be lost. Because the third third-progression had to be omitted, the second statement is incomplete when compared with the first, measures 1–3. It is precisely this incompleteness which creates the feeling of suspense and maintains the tension throughout the subsequent incomplete statements in measures 7–8 and 9–12 until the third third-progression makes its appearance in measures 28–29. Likewise in what follows, tension is main-

*20. The first movement of the symphony shows the interruption-form

$$\begin{array}{c|c} \hat{3}-\hat{2} & \hat{3}-\hat{2}-\hat{1} \\ a^1-g^1 & a^1-g^1-f^1 \end{array}$$ (Schenker)

tained only by means of the contrast between incomplete and complete statements. For measures 16–28, where the fourth measure of the group which begins with measure 13 is ingeniously expanded, see § 297, next-to-last paragraph; with reference to the development section, see § 314.

Attention should be drawn once more to thirds which are thrown above from the middle voice, as those shown in Figs. 90 and 95d,3. They maintain the register, which otherwise would be carried too low by the descending line.

In conclusion it must be emphasized that considerations of space do not permit a treatment of more extensive diminutions here.

§ 261.   Deceptive intervals arising from diminution

Diminution often produces deceptive intervals in the foreground instead of authentic ones, which are ascertainable only by reference to a previous level. Such an occurrence may create a considerable hindrance to the recognition of the meaning of the diminution. Even thoroughbass figures can deceive if they pertain to the foreground only, as they frequently do. One of the prime purposes of C.P.E. Bach's treatise on thoroughbass was to show the continuo player that in many instances the figures had extraordinary significance and hence required a different realization. He ordinarily placed instructions for such special situations in the second part of each chapter.

Examples of deceptive intervals follow:

Fig. 125

Ex. 1: The necessity of avoiding the direct juxtaposition of different rhythmic values—eighths, sixteenths, quarters—leads to an equalizing into eighths, which in turn produces an occasional inauthentic interval. (Compare Beethoven: Sonata op. 27 no. 2, 1st mvt., mm. 55–57) ⟨also p. IV of my facsimile edition of the sonata⟩ [§ 197 in regard to Fig. 76,10.]

Ex. 2: Here the deceptive intervals arise out of the necessity to change from quarter notes to eighth notes in order to increase the rhythmic movement ⟨of the bass⟩.

Ex. 3: By means of the sixteenth-note figure an unpleasant fourth is bypassed. Compare Fig. 83,3, measure 1, where at N.B. in place of 8—7 the intervals 6—10 appear. These, although inauthentic, are used to better effect.

Ex. 4: The deceptive intervals arise here out of a rhythmic shift.

Ex. 5: Keyboard writing in particular often leads to the use of deceptive intervals when certain tones must be omitted, lest, in the absence of orchestral color, they make the texture too thick. This art of keyboard economy should be learned from the great masters. Examples to the contrary are to be found, for instance, in Reger's transcriptions of Bach's Brandenburg Concerti, in the four-hand arrangements of Bruckner symphonies, and in the piano reductions of the orchestral part in many editions of piano concerti.

§ 262.   Rejection of so-called "wandering melodies"

It can only be regarded as a ridiculous attempt at debasement and disparagement of the diminutions of the masters when a certain literature busies itself with finding "wandering melodies" in the foreground, maintaining that similarities exist where they do not, with drawing lines of historical connection in every direction, where none in fact exist, or with pointing out plagiarisms where none are to be found. The employment of comparable superficial methods in language and literature would call forth general laughter and head-shaking over the deplorable intellectual state of any such writers and teachers. I would be ashamed to quote examples from this grotesque literature here.

§ 263.   The natural and artistic principles of diminution transcend "folk art"

In view of the current veneration of "the people," it is necessary to reemphasize that an unbridgeable chasm has always existed and will continue to exist between art and the people. To the genius, the people are not strangers. But the people are indeed strangers to art; there is an inherent contradiction in the expressions "popular art" and "folk art." Today an effort is even being made to trace Brahms's music back to folk elements. First, one cannot speak seriously of Brahms's effect upon the people. Second, Brahms, like every musical genius before him, derived great effect from observing natural principles in art—particularly through employment of the linear progressions of the octave, fifth, and third, the linear progressions derived from them, the organic relationships of diminution, and other artistic means. This effect has been confused with alleged popular elements. Though in the course of centuries certain linear progressions and organic relationships in a masterwork may finally have reached the ears of a considerable number of human beings, this first gleam of understanding cannot be considered a proof that art is based on folk elements. Rather it is Nature that has triumphed, in that Nature has finally made its way to their ears. In no respect does "the people" exert influence upon nature or upon the genius. Genius alone transmits nature to us through his art.

§ 264.   The relationship between diminution and form

My theory of diminution invalidates the statements of textbooks regarding form in music, all made without knowledge of these hidden elements. They discuss form in words which don't even hint at that self-contained imitation that pervades music. To be sure, even while they make such statements, they assert and extol the organic life of the forms. It will be shown in the last chapter that the concept of form must accordingly be made different [§ 308].

§ 265.   The performance of diminutions

How curiously the perceptive faculties fail when they are applied to music! If music exists as an organic creation, we should be able to perceive it. In tone, word, and writing, all the great composers advocated an eloquent and songful way of performing. Nevertheless their contemporaries failed to recognize what it was they were hearing. It was said of Beethoven that he played "quite decently," that Brahms's playing was "blurred," that he struck wrong notes, and the like. Greater acclaim was always given to performances which neither spoke nor sang as eloquently as those of the masters. It was the failure to comprehend diminution that made a proper communication and hearing impossible (cf. p. 8) [also §§ 253, 254].

§ 266.   The decline of diminution

German musical genius gave greater depth to diminution by creating an especial abundance in the middleground, which, in turn, made a still greater abundance of foreground relationship organic. Schubert, Mendelssohn, and Chopin still revealed a genius for diminution, each expressing it in his own personal way. But their followers and imitators could equal neither the older nor the younger masters. Wagner's attack was then directed against the imitators—a point of least resistance. Wagner's inability to achieve diminutions like those of the masters made it necessary for him to turn away from diminution, and, in the service of drama, to make expressiveness, indeed overexpressiveness, the guiding principle of music. His very helplessness with respect to purely musical diminution appealed to the musical world, which likewise prefers to stay clear of all hidden relationships. In the final hour Brahms appeared with a masterful capability for synthesis and with his own special mode of diminution. But in the meantime the musical community in Germany had been disrupted, and Brahms's diminution was unable to exercise the same extent of influence that was granted the older masters. Then came the World War—and since that time the German ear has been lost in chaos. Wagner's train of imitators were stillborn, as were the imitators of the great masters. Today there is neither ability for compositional synthesis nor even any art which has expressiveness as its central principle. There are no models—only imitators of misunderstood models.

Section 8:   Cover Tones

§ 267.   Cover tones

A cover tone is a tone of the inner voice which appears above the foreground diminution. It constantly attracts the attention of the ear, even though the essential voice-leading events take place beneath it.

Such a cover tone can remain suspended above an entire piece, as does, for example, the $c\sharp^2$ ⟨with its neighboring note $d\sharp^2$⟩ in Chopin's Nocturne op. 15 no. 2 (*Jahrb. II*, p. 41) or the b^1 in Beethoven's op. 90, second movement, which hovers above the actual progression $g\sharp^1—f\sharp^1—e^1$ and carries with it a neighboring note of its own ($c\sharp^2$). See also Fig. 75.

Occasionally a cover tone appears in a coda: for example, the c^2 in the first movement of Beethoven's op. 57, which harks back for the last time to the c^2 of the beginning [§§ 304, 315].

Section 9:   Obligatory Register

§ 268.   General remarks

No matter how far the composing-out may depart from its basic register in ascending or descending linear progressions, arpeggiations, or couplings, it nevertheless retains an urge to return to that register. Such departure and return creates content, displays the instrument, and lends coherence to the whole (§ 8).

The principle of obligatory register applies not only to the upper but also to the lower voice.

In the upper voice it is usually the register of the first tone of the fundamental line which is later confirmed as the true register: Figs. 7b (Coda $f^1—f^3$); 47,3; § 151 and Fig. 48,1 (Coda); Fig. 49,1 *21 and 2. Also note the return to the upper-register d^2 in J.S. Bach's Little Prelude in *D* Minor (BWV 940).

Nevertheless the final tone of the fundamental line sometimes appears an octave lower or an octave higher than the obligatory register would require (Fig. 46,1 and 2).

Fig. 49,3 and Fig. 108,2 show obligatory register in the bass.

§ 269.   Obligatory register as a prime element of the art of orchestration

In keeping with the principle of obligatory register, the instruments should be brought in or retracted according to their distance from the obligatory register (pp. 7–8).

§ 270.   Certain falsifications of obligatory register by editors

Anyone aware of obligatory register will take exception to those editors of the classics who print certain repetitions and parallel passages in conformity with their first statement, even in cases where this violates the obligatory register. Such editors rejoice in hearing, and making everyone else hear, perfectly obvious repetitions, but they underestimate the sensitivity of the masters to the obligatory register.

Obviously composers would have written parallel passages differently had they had in mind a register other than the obligatory one! Considerations of structure may sometimes be decisive, as in

Fig. 126

To remain in the register of e^3, as such editorial "paralleling" would have one do, is contrary to the structural idea which

*21. In the earlier versions—one of them contained in the *Klavierbüchlein vor Wilhelm Friedemann Bach*—Bach still closes in the lower register. (Jonas)

expresses the descent $e^3-e^2-e^1$, among other things. In my complete edition of the Beethoven sonatas, as well as in the *Erläuterungsausgabe* of op. 101, 109, 110, and 111, I often refer to such trespassing. See, for example, op. 14 no. 2, first movement, measures 43 and 102; op. 22, Rondo, measure 35.

Section 10: Articulation

§ 271. Speech as the origin of musical articulation

Musical articulation has its roots and its likeness in human speech. In speech, syllables combine to form words; words are set off against words and gathered into a succession. The breath carries speech quietly or in agitation, accented or unaccented, with pauses, caesuras—in short, linguistic formations of the most varied kinds come from the human mouth. All this entered into music as long as it still clung to the word.

In polyphonic vocal writing the counterpoints, differentiated as they were according to syllables, words, and tone-successions, led to articulation divided among various voices (*Harm.* § 88, Ex. 169).

§ 272. The legato slur as means of articulation in instrumental music

In instrumental music the legato slur fulfills the same function as does the human breath in the articulation of both speech and vocal music. These slurs define tone-successions and produce various contrapuntal effects. They also achieve connections between voices and formal divisions ⟨Fig. 128,10a⟩. (The question of the execution of such a legato belongs to the area of performance.*22)

Slurs are determined by the content of the diminutions and by the relative emphasis of any parallelisms they may form,

by the tempo and dynamics, by the character of the instrument, and, in the case of orchestral works, by the combination and interaction of instruments.

The difference between instrumental and vocal articulation is shown in

Fig. 127

Ex. 1: Note how the instrumental articulation here is altered when the passage is given to the chorus. Also compare the theme of the "Hymn to Joy" in the Ninth Symphony in its first appearance in the strings (Fig. 109e,3) with its *forte* setting for the brass instruments.

For this reason it has always been a difficult task to transcribe from one instrument to another, though a task essential to practical musical activity. Beethoven referred to this in the "public announcement" he made on October 20, 1802.*23

It should be added that the nature of vocal composition does not admit of the addition of slurs as "phrase marks" (§ 274).

§ 273. Various uses of articulation

Various uses of articulation are shown in

Fig. 128

Ex. 1: The slurs here correspond exactly to the diminutions around a^2 and g^2.
Ex. 2: Here the slur serves expressive purposes.
a) At a slow tempo the long slur creates an effect comparable to the tension produced by a single sustained breath. See also the long slurs in measures 3–4 of the Adagio of the Ninth Symphony.

*22. See the third footnote in the preface by Oswald Jonas. (Jonas)

*23. See also Beethoven's letter to Breitkopf und Härtel, dated July 13, 1802, in which he mentions his arrangement for string quartet of the *E*-Major Sonata op. 14 no. 1. (Oster)

b) Seventeen measures before the end, a whim overthrows the slurs which in measures 9 ff. fit the diminutions exactly. The new slurs function as syncopes in that they carry over into the subsequent diminution.

c) In measures 9–10 the slur appears as in measures 5–6, although the triplet is replaced by a trill (starting on the main note), which brings about an intensification. At measure 41, however, the slur is divided, and the new slur in conjunction with the decrescendo sign demands a still richer execution of the trill; this, of course, requires also a freer tempo.

d) A case of Italianate articulation, whose performance offers difficulties to the violinist. The break after b^1 must be quite unnoticeable, as though a slur extended over the entire measure. It is the conductor's responsibility to give the necessary direction for this.

Ex. 3: Occasionally slurs are adjusted to one another.

a) In the repetition of measures 10–12, nine measures before the end, the original long slur is broken up in order to prepare for the final slur which extends over eight measures.

b) Here two short slurs prepare a slur which extends over four measures (Fig. 119,12). Also see the careful placement of slurs in Beethoven's Fifth Symphony, measures 71–93, in Violin I.

Ex. 4: The slurs change with the change of register.

Ex. 5: A change in articulation leads to new diminutional formations.

a) The new form of articulation creates the diminution which dominates the development—compare this with the articulation in the first measures (Fig. 109e,2). At measure 140 the slur again appears as it did in measure 1 and thus prepares for the recapitulation.

b) The division of the slur gives rise to new formations.

c) The slur which occurs within the first measure of this example groups together tones which do not belong to each other; nevertheless, Chopin achieves in this way the separation of the tones e^1 and d^1 from f^1, to which they appear to belong as part of a third-progression. Two measures later, the two tones thus separated form a group which now plays a role familiar from the first measures of the composition.

Ex. 6: Sometimes the placement of the slurs helps to create an orchestral effect.

a) The slur is interrupted at the end of measure 1, as if to allow for the entrance of a new instrument in measure 2.

b) The alternation of the melodically leading instruments and the supporting ones is obvious.

Ex. 7: Articulation can assume the task of contradicting the actual relationships. In most cases the contradiction is easily recognizable.

a) Here it is as though grief had choked off the breath prematurely.

b) The slurs tend to obscure the relationship between main and secondary tones.[24]

c) The slurs obscure the octave relationships.

d) The separation of the a and f on the third and fourth quarters has a somewhat uncomfortable effect; this makes their joining in the coda (m. 78) all the more satisfying.

e) The two-measure grouping given in the example (cf. also N.B.) clearly shows the neighboring notes and their metrical placement. However, once the c^2 in measure 1 is expressed by a diminution of three quarter-notes, the tones of the succeeding four measures, since they have the dotted half-note in common, must be brought under a single slur. The abbreviated version in measures 58 ff. and measures 76 ff. corroborates this reading.

f) The slur in the first violins in measures 8–12 of the middle

---

[24] $a\sharp$—b at the turn of measures 1 and 2, then $e\sharp$—$f\sharp$, $d\sharp$—e, $c\sharp$—d (from an earlier note by Schenker). (Oster)

section contradicts the half-step parallelisms (indicated by the brackets) which eventually lead to the a_2 section. The slur in the flute part at measures 7–8 of the b section conceals the beginning of the slur under discussion.*[25]

g) *[26] Among articulation slurs, a special position is occupied by the slur which extends over four tones. Whether these constitute a genuine fourth-progression or only an illusory one (§ 207), the articulation goes its own way—which can often be quite confusing. Thus, in our example, the articulation is not in accord with the actual meaning (as, in mm. 1–3, third-progressions with a neighboring note), but is arranged according to the measure groupings 2—1 : 1—1, 2—1 : 2. The viola provides counterpoint to these slurs with an articulation that is in keeping with its own diminution ⟨cf. Fig. 138,3⟩.

Ex. 8: a) It would be wrong to employ only one slur rather than letting each diminution retain its own slur.

b) These slurs specifically contradict the actual relationships (compare the examples under 7 above). Therefore it would be wrong to nullify this purposeful effect with a single slur.

c) Because of the suspension in the second flute, the first slur is extended to the next downbeat, although the diminutional components are as shown at N.B.

d) Especially in suspensions and their resolution, a distinct separation of the resolution from the following diminution is always to be observed. The great composers have always held fast to this principle, making exceptions only in response to necessities of a higher order. The "phrase mark" is especially fond of tampering with suspensions—all edi-

tors of classical works disfigure the text by placing only a single slur over the suspension, its resolution, and the succeeding tones (*Jahrb. I*, p. 49, Fig. 5d) ⟨§ 274⟩.

Ex. 9: Exx. a) through e) illustrate slurs counterpointing against each other. The effect of such articulation is that of genuine polyphony.

Ex. 10: Sometimes a slur can even counteract a chromatic succession. In the case shown at b), the performers should strive to attain a similar effect (§ 249).

Ex. 11: Chopin, with his penchant for the melodic, employs the slur in his own special way. Thus the song of this upper voice, as if absorbed in itself, seeks to remain an indestructible unity and therefore basically resists articulation. Also, there are not enough contrapuntal devices here to balance the melody. To solve such problems by means of slurs counterpointing against each other (as at Ex. 9, c–e) is particularly characteristic of Chopin. Here he goes even further in that he binds different sections of the composition with a slur (at *).

§ 274.   Rejection of "phrase marks"

The true implications of the "phrase mark" are explained in my essay "Weg mit dem Phrasierungsbogen!" (*Jahrb. I*, pp. 43–60): "This slur is truly a reflection of the confusion with which editors approach the masterworks. Their hodgepodge of work plus clarification, of composition plus pedagogy is expressed with particular crudity in the 'phrase mark,' which falsifies not only the legato slur but the whole musical form as well." I should like to add here that the editors' predilection for phrase marks clearly indicates that even they, in the midst of the foreground, sense background relationships. But precisely in the foreground, diminution has to go its own way with its own articulation which diverges from that at earlier levels. (Also it is technically impossible to show in the foreground the slurs of all levels. A differentiation such as the small and large

*[25]. The autograph is somewhat ambiguous in these two measures. The *Neue Mozart-Ausgabe* presents a compromise reading.   (Oster)

*[26]. Through an oversight, g) is missing from the example volume. There can be little doubt that Schenker here refers to the fourth variation of Brahms's *Haydn* Variations, op. 56a.   (Oster)

notation mentioned in § 252, permitting middleground elements to be shown in the representation of the foreground, is out of the question for articulation, since there can be only one kind of slur.)

§ 275.   Articulation in the autographs of the masters

There can be little question that the autographs of the masters contain an occasional incorrect slur. Even the great composers, obsessed with the daemonic forces of the middleground and background, could confuse the articulation of the foreground:

Fig. 129

Ex. 1: The passage aims at an orchestral effect. Beethoven's articulation simulates the entrance of a new and enriching instrument ⟨ as at N.B.⟩.*27

Ex. 2: The masters have often let their way of playing be reflected in their notation. Thus, Beethoven probably reveals that, when he performed, he accented the passing seventh, gb. For this reason he begins his slur with the second sixteenth, despite the fact that the fourth-progression would call for one slur.

*27. In both these examples it would seem that errors in engraving have produced a certain confusion. In Ex. 1, Beethoven's autograph discloses a slur under the first three dotted quarters and a new one connecting the *sfp* to the downbeat of measure 62, which clarifies Schenker's comment. The slur at N.B. is like that in Beethoven's measures 62–63 (one octave lower). Schenker's explanation of Ex. 2 does not apply to measures 86 ff., but instead explains the similar passage in measures 83–84, where Beethoven's manuscript very clearly shows the slur beginning with gb, and where a fourth-progression may be read.—In his analysis of op. 57 (*Tw. 7*, p. 29), Schenker suggests that one play the sixteenth notes ab and gb in measure 83 "portamento." This is all the more noteworthy since at that time (1924) the autograph was still inaccessible to Schenker.   (Oster)

Section 11:   The Scale Degree

§ 276.   Historical background

In the beginning only the horizontal dimension existed, in accord with the first instrument, the human larynx. The discovery of counterpoint in the West was succeeded all too soon by its overuse—man always tends to use to excess what is newly discovered. The horizontal necessarily suffered because of the plethora of counterpoint.

The return to the horizontal, to monody, initiated the second great phase of music. Counterpoint, of course, could not be disregarded, yet it had to achieve an adjustment to the new monody. In the hands of the masters the horizontal, which always took precedence, combined with a vertical dimension. The vertical dimension fulfilled the fundamental arpeggiation through the fifth of the triad and, at the same time, was free to serve the many specific purposes of the horizontal dimension.

It is clear that there can be no new way, no third approach to the horizontal, no third kind of counterpoint—a suggestion to coming generations!

§ 277.   Differentiation of the scale-degrees according to levels

Scale-degrees are present even in the fundamental structure itself. These degrees are the strongest of all, since the fundamental structure assures the coherence of the work. Therefore, the scale-degrees of the fundamental structure have decisive control over the middleground and foreground. Throughout the prolongation-levels it is sometimes the horizontal which determines the particular course and meaning of the vertical, sometimes the vertical which by its own voice-leading dictates the horizontal. So, in one instance we can speak of the horizontalization of the vertical, in another instance of the verticalization of the horizontal ⟨§ 79⟩.

It would be erroneous, therefore, to read all degrees in the foreground without discriminating between them, as though they were all of equal significance and origin. Rather one must make the following distinction: between those harmonies that, in a particular way, serve particular diminutions close to the foreground, and those harmonies which, in their origins, express strong relationships in the levels close to the background.

The question of illusory keys at the foreground level is relevant here. The coherence of the whole, which is guaranteed by the fundamental structure, reveals the development of one single chord into a work of art. Thus, the tonality of this chord alone is present, and whatever else we may regard as a key at the foreground level can only be an illusory one. Since the bass arpeggiation of the fundamental structure is also transferred to the illusory keys, there chords, too, represent harmonic degrees within the newly emerged cadences. Nevertheless, since these degrees belong to a cadence which is merely transferred, they occupy a different rank from the degrees of the earlier levels. The error in the viewpoint of present-day theory consists in its mechanical reading of the degrees at their face value. This can only obstruct the perception of coherence.

An example: in Fig. 39,3 Haydn's "Kaiserhymne," the degrees at the various levels, as shown at a), b), and c), are to be clearly distinguished from one another.

a) These degrees control the entire song.
b) Here the degrees serve the initial ascent, g^1—d^2, in its entirety.
c) These serve a^1—d^2, that is, only a part of the initial ascent.

Accordingly, the key of D major at c) is only illusory. Also, the chords with which Haydn supports the diminutional structures (Fig. 120,6) in the foreground, even though they are unmistakably cadential degrees, are subordinate to the degrees shown in Fig. 39,3. Indeed, they are subordinate to the same extent as are those diminutions to the simple forms in Fig. 39,3.

§ 278.   Summary of previous conclusions

Previous discussions have provided clarification of the roles played by chords in the service of prolongations of the first level.[28] Either the chords belong to one of the cadences of the fundamental structure, with their characteristic involvement in contrapuntal-melodic motion (§ 79), or they stand (despite the effect of a IV or VI) apart from a cadence and, by their consonance, underscore what was originally a voice-leading event, such as a neighboring note (§ 108).

Frequently even a prolongation of the first level manifests such a strong desire to achieve its own unity as a diminution that it utilizes one of the cadences of the fundamental structure for this purpose. This can happen even when the prolongation ascends, in contrast to the fundamental line, which knows only the descending direction.

Now it should suffice to merely refer to further events in the foreground [29] in order to make one fact abundantly clear. Beyond their originally exclusive obligation to the descending fundamental line, the cadences of the fundamental structure can also serve all manner of diminutions. It is precisely this possibility that guarantees the unity of the diminutions and ultimately makes them organic. This insurance of the organic is the essence of musical art in its highest fulfillment. In it is expressed the precedence of the horizontal and the horizontalizing of counterpoint for the purposes of diminution. This is the highest achievement of the great composers!

§ 279.   The V

The V chord in the fundamental structure (Figs. 9–11) is dealt with in §§ 15, 31–34, and 41. V chords in middleground and

---

[28]. §§ 60, 73, 74, 79, 86, 89, 95, 103, 105, 108, 111, 117, 118, 120, 125, 131, 136, 140, 146, 150, 151, 153.   (Schenker)

[29]. Passing tones (§§ 168 ff.); sevenths (176 ff.); suspensions (180 ff.); prolongations at later levels (183–241); and particularly, transference of the forms of the fundamental structure (242 ff.); and auxiliary cadences (244 ff.). (Schenker)

foreground, as dominants of transferred cadences, are discussed in §§ 277 and 278.

The applied dividing dominant, the *applied divider*, takes a special place among V chords. The $\overset{\hat{2}}{V}$ which arises in the case of a division at the first level, with its characteristic interruption of the voice-leading (§§ 89 ff.), can also be used in an applied sense in the foreground, even when no such division is involved:

Fig. 130

Ex. 1: The transference of the divider is made possible by its fifth-relationship to the chord. It is to be understood as a projected fifth [Fig. 112,4].

Ex. 2: The characteristic feature of the interruption must always be present.

Ex. 3: The applied divider, too, makes the upper voice and inner voice move. The particular purpose of this stepwise motion within the diminution can only be determined from the earlier levels.

For an illustration of this see Fig. 85, where the step of a second, c^2—bb^1, is taken only for the purpose of allowing the subsequent parallelism bb^1—db^2 to begin with bb^1. The bb^1 is supported by a divider: it would have been impossible to place a IV beneath the initial tone bb^1, even though the earlier level shows c^2 (m. 4) progressing directly to the neighboring note db^2 (m. 5) above IV. What an ingenious solution to a difficult structural problem!

Ex. 4: Here is another remarkable use of the divider. Only by means of the two dividers in measures 24 and 47 was it possible to continue the fundamental tone A (VI) from measure 17 to measure 47. When A is sounded for the second time, in measure 25, it is in conjunction with g^2, which as ♮7 constitutes an appoggiatura to the neighboring note f^2. The expression of this appoggiatura is very moving, if one understands it correctly: the configuration $\overset{\frown}{e^2-g^2}-f^2$ has

the effect of an *Anschlag*, or a compound appoggiatura (see C.P.E. Bach's *Versuch*, part I, chapter 2, section 6).

In Fig. 35,2 (mm. 9–16) the skips of fifths are to be understood not as a succession of two dividers, but rather as substitutes for the progression in parallel tenths (see the inner voice c—b, a—$g\sharp$). Since, in accord with the interruption, the last tenth in measure 16 had to move to E as the fifth of the fundamental chord A, the second tenth was also transformed into a fifth, as a preparation ⟨§ 247, commentary to Fig. 112,4⟩.

The divider is particularly useful in the composition of fugues. Beethoven, in the huge fugue in op. 106, follows the entrance in the Db harmony (mm. 52 ff.) with the next entrance in Ab (mm. 65 ff.) in accord with the principle of the divider, that is, without returning to Db ⟨cf. Fig. 156,2⟩.

The divider proves to be indispensable in the service of the organic, yet its resemblance to the V degree has brought it into disrepute with those whose hearing is of short span. However, not all chords which resemble V are necessarily true dominants (*Jahrb. II*, pp. 23–24: "Vom Quintklang und der Dominante").

It is necessary to distinguish the divider from the auxiliary cadence (§ 244, Fig. 110). Both events have in common a "closing-off" of the voice-leading. The difference between them is that in the auxiliary cadence the "closing-off" occurs before the V, whereas in the divider it occurs after the V.

Finally, the *third-divider* should also be mentioned in this connection:

Fig. 131

As is to be seen in both examples, the dividing third also causes either an upper or an inner voice to move, depending on the position. The motion thus produced can have various purposes. In the second example, the first horizontal motion in the inner voice, which is the result of the third-divider in measures 1–8, is answered in a parallel manner by the motion of a second in the upper voice ⟨*Jahrb. I*, pp. 163–64⟩.

The third-divider differs from the arpeggiation through the third (illustrated in Fig. 113,3) in that an interruption occurs in connection with the third-divider as it does with a fifth-divider, whereas in the third-arpeggiation the third returns to the root.

§ 280.   The IV, II, and VI

The nature of the IV and the II is determined by their significance within the cadence of the prolonged fundamental structure (§§ 73, 74, 79). Several special cases are here added to the many examples of these degrees which have already been provided:

Fig. 132

Ex. 1: The tonicizing seventh within the I points to the IV; thus, in measure 57 the lower third e^1 must be understood as a part of the implied IV$^{(5)-6}$ (ellipsis).

Ex. 2: The omission of c^2 on the third quarter of the first measure ⟨in favor of tying over the bb^1⟩ (see N.B.) confirms d^2 on the second quarter as the seventh of a IV ⟨rather than a possible ⌒7—6 suspension over II⟩.

Ex. 3: An interpolated II$^8_{\sharp3}$ or II$^7_{\sharp3}$ either causes the upper voice to descend in the case of the octave position (Ex. a) or causes both uppermost voices to descend in the case of the position of the third (Ex. b). Relevant to Ex. 132,3a, see *Jahrbuch I*, p. 61; to Ex. 132,3b, see Fig. 76,2 and also Chopin, Étude op. 10 no. 8, measures 1–11–13, in *Five Graphic Analyses*.

Ex. 4: Here is an exceptionally beautiful use of the II, despite the semblance of IV. In essence, the bass shows a rhythmic displacement; in order to secure at V a parallelism to the octave-coupling at I, the statement of II had to be shifted to the first quarter of measure 2, the only beat available.

The bII, it should be added, appears less frequently in root position than as $^{b6}_{3}$ (the so-called Neapolitan sixth, see § 105). The root position is necessitated in Fig. 54,8 by the ⟨motivic⟩ parallelism ⟨*Harm.* § 50⟩; in Fig. 48,1 by the ascending linear progression of the bass.

It is not always easy to decide whether IV or II is present. The skip of a fourth suggests IV, in the sense of a descending fifth (I—IV), yet other characteristics may suggest II:

Ex. 5: a) The skip of a fourth and the $b7$ indicate a $\sharp IV^{b7}$.

b) Here, in contrast, the $^6_5$ suggests II. But, precisely because of the skip of a fourth, a voice-leading of this kind is more pliable than that shown at Ex. 3 (I—II$^{\sharp3}$—V).

Ex. 6: The I here does not include a $\natural7$; therefore, in contrast to Ex. 1, the lower thirds ⟨specifically the b^1⟩, despite the skip of a fourth, obviously indicate II. In Fig. 120,6 the diminution which descends from e^2 to a^1 points clearly to II.

These and similar examples clarify what I mean by the contrapuntal element in IV and II—the sense of harmonic relationship effected by the leap ⟨to IV or II^6⟩, in conjunction with the melodic progression of the bass ⟨on to V⟩.

A 5—6 exchange in particular often presents a problem. The horizontal and the vertical aspects balance each other; in most cases of $^{5—6}_{IV—II}$ it makes no difference whether one understands one harmonic degree or two (Fig. 37a and Fig. 76,2) [Fig. 82,5; also the commentary to Fig. 54,11a in § 164].

Ex. 7: Similarly ambiguous are cases involving linear progressions ⟨in the bass, which outline the IV⟩, unless a tone of the fundamental line, as in Fig. 76,6 $\left(\genfrac{}{}{0pt}{}{\hat{2}}{C—F}\right)$, or some other decisive tone in the upper voice, as in our example, comes to rest upon the fundamental tone of such a linear progression. For unequivocal examples, see Fig. 81,2 and Fig. 96,4.[*30]

Ex. 8: Here VI is to be understood as a VI that has a fifth-relationship within the context (Fig. 47,3; Fig. 65,1), in contrast to the similar chord which serves a neighboring note, I—VI—I ⟨as in Fig. 153,2⟩. A seventh appearing above VI causes the upper voice to descend (compare also Exx. 3 and 5).

Whether, in I^{5-6}—II, a VI is to be read at I^6 depends upon the context. In most instances the horizontal and vertical aspects balance each other, but sometimes important considerations may decide in favor of the VI.

§ 281. The relationship of suspensions to harmonic degrees

Examples of suspensions as they relate to harmonic degrees are found in

Fig. 133

Ex. 1: The suspension here marked ⌒4—3 suggests II. Even if we were to understand the first quarter-note $g\sharp^1$ as a seventh over the root $A\sharp$, the root of the II would have to follow on the second quarter. Were such the case, the arpoggiation $A\sharp$—$D\sharp$ (VI—II) would still roprosont only $D\sharp$, that is, II (§ 277) ⟨§ 245, Fig. 110a,4⟩.

Ex. 2: The $I^{\flat7}$ prepares for IV; the seventh over IV, in resolving to the sixth, brings in II.

Exx. 3 and 4: The examples show suspended ninths. The ninth in Ex. 3 certainly relates to the bass F; however, since the bass diminution primarily expresses a succession of tenths, the bass note on the third quarter cannot be considered a real harmonic degree. Similarly, in Ex. 4, the relationships shown at N.B. make it unnecessary to read the bass note of the suspended ninth as a harmonic degree.

§ 282. Fifth-relationships which lack the significance of harmonic degrees

Earlier, in connection with the presentation of prolongations at the various levels as well as other events in the foreground, examples were given in which the vertical was subordinate to the horizontal to the extent that its various fifth-relationships did not achieve the significance of actual harmonic degrees. For the purpose of special comment the following examples are added:

Fig. 134

Exx. 1 and 2: When the bass moves stepwise upward and the upper voice starts from the octave position, a skip results in the upper voice; if this is filled in by a passing tone, an ascending fifth can be interpolated, which makes the passing tone consonant (cf. Fig. 56).

Ex. 3: In measures 11–12, the passing tone a^1 in the inner voice, which fills in the skip b^1—g^1, is supported by the consonant $F\sharp$. The resulting $\frac{6}{3}$, however, is not to be equated with I (Fig. 119,5a).

Ex. 4: In connection with the syncopation of a dissonant passing tone there arises the possibility of interpolating fifths. However, these are not to be construed as harmonic degrees (*Kpt. II*, VI, Zweite Abteilung).

Ex. 5: Here interpolated fifths which do not qualify as harmonic degrees support a succession of four tones. However, the significance of these tones can be understood only in terms of far-reaching relationships which cannot be represented in this example (*Tw.* 8/9).

[*30]. The V in Fig. 132,7 pertains to the last g^1 in measure 2. See Schenker's complete analysis of the Fugue in *Jahrbuch II, Urlinie-Tafel* to p. 59. (Oster)

Exx. 6 and 7: Interpolated fifths support neighboring notes (cf. Figs. 42,2; 76,7; 102,2).

Ex. 8: The descending register transfer d^3—c^2 incorporates two descending fifths, III$^{\sharp3}$—VI—II—V. (It is not a true linear progression, for it represents only a second.) However, the interpolated bass tones supporting d^3—g^2 express merely a neighboring note (Fig. 82,2; also Fig. 82,1).

Fifth-interpolations of various kinds are to be found also in connection with authentic linear progressions, such as those shown in Figs. 123,5 and 124,6b, as well as with all other types of prolongation.

Ex. 9: Finally, here is the exceptionally bold example of a bass succession which through many interpolations expresses only a neighboring-note harmony, that is, VII.

§ **283.**   Additional fifth-interpolations as harmonic degrees

Frequently VI is preceded by III. The increased number of descending fifths thereby gained serves various purposes. In Fig. 40,10 they support an arpeggiation; in Fig. 42,1 a neighboring note with a motion from the inner voice; in Fig. 82,2 an illusory linear progression.

The VII rarely appears before III without being preceded by IV. When I—IV—VII occurs, I—IV ordinarily sets the upper voice in motion, upward or downward, depending on the position.

With —IV—VII—III— the chain of possible interpolated fifths ends; the prolonged cadence of the fundamental structure is now completely filled in by fifths.

Fig. 135

Ex. 1: Here I—V—I stands out clearly as the fundamental arpeggiation controlling the cadence. It would be a contradiction to place a fundamental line, $\hat{3}$—$\hat{1}$, $\hat{5}$—$\hat{1}$, or $\hat{8}$—$\hat{1}$, over a chain of fifths of this kind in the manner of Figs. 15–

17, for so long as the fundamental lines are unprolonged the bass can and indeed must concentrate only upon the contrapuntal-melodic filling-in of the ascending fifth I—V. At that ⟨background⟩ level such a filling-in does not admit of fifth-interpolations.

Ex. 2: Only a prolongation can clarify the particular purpose of fifth-interpolations as harmonic degrees. Naturally the evaluation of the particular prolongation can derive only from the general context, that is, from the progression of levels. Thus, we see here a transference to an individual harmony, as explained in §§ 242 ff.; the succession of fifths in the bass serves the second part of a linear progression of a fifth which departs from b^1. In terms of the middleground the passage has the same structure as that shown in Fig. 15,6: $\begin{array}{c} g\sharp^1-f\sharp^1-\ e^1 \\ \text{I} \ \ -\text{II}-\text{V}-\text{I} \end{array}$. In the foreground, however, the descending fifths interpolated between the I and the II support the parallelistic, superimposed third-progressions. The parallelistic significance of these linear progressions elevates the supporting fifths to the position of harmonic degrees.

Ex. 3: Here, in contrast, the lower voice moves in parallel tenths with the upper, leading, voice; the interpolated fourths (fifths) do not alter the situation (Figs. 54,10; 123,5).

The fifth between IV and VII is diminished, and so not a true fifth. From the contrapuntally prolonged forms of the bass arpeggiation shown in Fig. 15,2c and d, 3c and d, and 5 it is clear that within the contrapuntal-melodic filling-in no tone except F can occur in conjunction with d^2 as $\hat{2}$ ⟨aside from D as in Fig. 15,2d⟩. Thus, already at the first level, F*[31] has proved itself to be organically necessary by virtue of its service to the fundamental line; the IV may on occasion appropriately take part in a chain of descending fifths ⟨Fig. 135,1⟩. Indeed,

---

*31. In the original: the IV.   (Oster)

without IV—VII no such succession of fifths would be possible at all (*Harm.* §§ 17, 19).

Ex. 4: A chain of ascending fifths lacks V—I and thus ultimately contradicts the primary requisite of a cadence. Such a fifth-succession therefore can never express the unity of a prolongation or a diminution. To be sure, an ascending fifth-succession causes the upper voice to move, either by seconds or more extended diminutions; such diminutions, perhaps more than any other foreground occurrences, have led to the concept of sequence, which I have rejected.*32 Yet, whatever the resultant upper-voice motion means, it does not suffice for the establishment of an essential unity; therefore a reversal of the flow into the prolonged cadence form, with its descending fifths, becomes necessary if a unity is to be expressed. This is the meaning and purpose

*32. To illustrate, Schenker here refers to "Fig. 106,3, fourth example," which does not appear in the example volume. Possibly he meant Fig. 135,4a, which resembles measures 1–6 of Bach, Twelve Little Preludes, No. 1 in *C* Major (BWV 924). The bass in both the example and the Bach, however, displays an ascending linear progression with fifth-dividers rather than a chain of ascending fifths.   (Oster)

of "inversion," which I discussed in my *Harmony*, §§ 14–16.

To summarize: a chain of ascending fifths, in the absence of V—I, cannot produce unity of prolongation and diminution in art. At best it can furnish only fragments. Music as an art recognizes only the one ascending fifth I—V for the purpose of bringing a specific harmony into relief.

In contrast, a chain of descending fifths is a product of art alone, and not of Nature. Such a chain does serve the projection of the horizontal, which alone is the purpose and content of music—the projection of complete prolongations as well as the projection of parts (e.g., Fig. 135,2).

The IV does not appear in the series of ascending perfect fifths. Neither does it appear (in the specific sense of the descending fifth I—IV, which alone does not constitute the true harmonic relation of the descending fifth V—I) in the prolonged bass arpeggiation of the first level (Figs. 15–17). The descending I—IV is, however, used to introduce a chain of descending fifths which fill out the prolonged cadence ⟨Fig. 135,1 and 2⟩. In contrast, the descending fifth in Fig. 66,2a and b is merely an inversion of the ⟨ascending⟩ fourth which directly precedes V in the prolonged cadence (Ex. 5 in Figs. 15 and 16; Fig. 132,1 and 2; Fig. 133,2).

Chapter 4

Meter and Rhythm

Section 1: Meter and Rhythm in General

§ 284. Meter and rhythm in language and music

Meter and rhythm play the same role in music as in language. The basis of meter is the division of time itself; the basis of rhythm is the organization of specific word- and tone-successions which occur within time. Meter is absolute—the time-pattern itself; rhythm is relative—the particular play of successions of words or tones within this time-pattern.

Apart from this common ground, music and language of course preserve their own special characteristics. How, for instance, could a phenomenon such as the inner-voice prolongations shown in Fig. 102 find an analogy in the meter and rhythm of language?

Section 2: Meter in Music

§ 285. Repetition as prerequisite for a metric unit

The Biblical story of the creation tells us that the Spirit which moved upon the face of the waters was timeless. With creation, a process of division, came the first division of time also. Division, however, rests upon repetition, which is a biological law of life, physical life as well as spiritual (*Harm.* §§ 4 ff.), like the contrast and the repetition of day and night.*[1]

Repetition is also a prerequisite to meter and rhythm. Without repetition a metric scheme is inconceivable. But even repetitions ⟨that make up a metric scheme⟩, like all foreground repetitions, are clarified and confirmed only by the background and middleground.

Fig. 136

It is of little consequence that at Ex. 1 a linear progression is entirely lacking, that at 3 and 5 there is a third-progression and at 2 and 4 a fifth-progression: most important is the fact

---

*[1]. Passage (N), omitted here, is supplied in Appendix 4. (Rothgeb)

118

that the 3- , 4- , 5- , and 6-measure pieces lack repetitions. Their content is just enough for preludes, which, as their name implies, merely prepare for genuine compositions, that is, those founded on repetition. Nor does it make any difference that they have a metric scheme (2/4, 3/4, 4/4); the meter derives only from figurations whose repetitions are completely unessential and so can do nothing to alleviate the basic weakness.

In Ex. 6, a passage from Haydn's *C*-Major Fantasy, the previous duple ordering ⟨2-measure groups⟩ suddenly changes into a triple ordering ⟨3-measure groups⟩. Here ⟨in contrast to the ametric Clementi preludes⟩, the meter plays a most important role; in fact, the diminution adjusts itself to the new meter. In the parallel passage ⟨m. 324⟩, however, the 4-measure grouping is maintained and the figuration again is altered accordingly.

§ **286.** Metric ordering in 2- , 4- , 8- , and 16-measure groups (duple ordering)

Since the principle of systole and diastole is inherent in our very being, metric ordering based on two and its multiples is the most natural to us.

The metric unit of four measures does not necessarily require four tones as its content. A third-progression also can be the content of a 4-measure group, as in the first and second 4-measure groups of Fig. 124,6b. This example very quickly shows us the difference between the 4-measure unit, which has an absolute metric grouping, and this particular third-progression, whose rhythm is only relative. Several examples of duple ordering follow:

Fig. 137

Ex. 1: Auxiliary harmonies and those arising from neighboring notes or suspensions in no way disturb a metric ordering; in fact, they, too, can appear on the accented, strong measures (cf. Figs. 128,9d; 54,11b). One can only call this a triumph of absolute meter; in such cases the performer must also emphasize the metrical superiority of the auxiliary harmonies.[*2] Incidentally, the placement of the scale-degrees points up the inseparability of this 8-measure group. How would it be possible to assume two 4-measure groups when the descending arpeggiation, $C\sharp$—$F\sharp$ (I—II⁶), comes to an end only at measure 5?

Ex. 2: The entity of this 8-measure group derives from the unfolding of the sixth, g^1—eb^2—g^1, in which eb^2 is the neighboring note of d^2, the $\hat{5}$ (cf. Fig. 119,21).

Ex. 3: We should consider this a 16-measure group, despite the repetition of the first eight measures—this merely repeats the passage an octave higher. See also Fig. 124,6b, which, because it expresses only the third-progression e^2—$d\sharp^1$—$c\sharp^1$, must be considered one single 16-measure group.

§ **287.** 3 (3 × 2, 3 × 4)–measure and 5 (10)–measure groups

Measure orderings in odd numbers (such as 3 or 5) have their roots in a duple ordering in the background and middleground;

[*2]. Especially today, it is necessary to recall the principle of the *Abzug* (release), which was once generally taught. C.P.E. Bach, in his immortal work *Versuch über die wahre Art, das Clavier zu spielen (Essay on the True Art of Playing Keyboard Instruments)*, part I, chapter 2, section 2, "Von den Vorschlägen" ("The Appoggiatura"), § 7, expresses the rule thus: "With regard to execution we learn from this figure that appoggiaturas are louder than the following tone, including any additional embellishment, and that they are joined to it in the absence as well as the presence of a slur. Both of these points are in accord with the purpose of appoggiaturas, which is to connect notes. They must be held until released by the following tone so that both are smoothly joined. The undecorated, light tone which follows an appoggiatura is called the release." (tr. by W.J. Mitchell)

The sequence of strong and weak in the performance of appoggiaturas (suspensions) is practically identical with the sequence of downbeat and upbeat. Thus, the requirement of strict counterpoint *diss. cons.* is fulfilled even where, because of a prolongation, the foreground shows appoggiaturas on metrically unaccented parts of a measure. The principle of *Abzug* thus permits of no exception, no matter what the metrical position. (Schenker)

this brings into clear relief the fact that metric schemes involving the numbers 3 and 5 are man-made and not as natural as duple orderings [§ 318].

Fig. 138

Ex. 1: Levels a), b), and c) show a duple ordering of the content, in accord with the interruption $\hat{3}$—$\hat{2}$ ‖ $\hat{3}$—$\hat{2}$—$\hat{1}$. Even the neighboring-note diminution at b) and c) does not alter the pattern. The 3-measure grouping at d) arose from the fact that Bach, in order to arrive at the neighboring note bb^1, approached it from d^2. This engendered a fifth-progression; its need ⟨for confirmation by repetition and⟩ for further spacial expansion was fulfilled in the four 3-measure groups which comprise the second section (quoted in Fig. 82,5c). At e) the organic relationships of the diminution are indicated, revealing Bach's genius in the sharpest light (see §§ 253 ff.). The brackets show the relation of the first fifth-progression to the following augmentation. The succession d^2—e^2—f^2, marked by *, relates the high tones in a special way (cf. Fig. 120,6). What boldness in the connection established by the fifth-progressions leading to d^2, c^2, and bb^1, all parallelisms to the first fifth-progression! At the neighboring note bb^1, Bach not only brings his fifth-progression from f^2 to an end, but also continues the fifth-progression in augmentation, which starts from the d^2. Hence one must read here an interlocking of two fifth-progressions: f^2—bb^1 and d^2—g^1, but under no circumstances the octave f^2—f^1.

Ex. 2: As can be seen at a), a diminution with a neighboring note creates a duple ordering. The presentation of the foreground at b), however, shows three 2-measure groups. The triple ordering arises from the fact that the I chord fills a 2-measure group—which I have indicated in the sketch with a tie—and both subsequent 2-measure groups present parallelisms—which I indicate with slurs. Thus, this 6-measure group results from a purely organic growth.

A 12-measure group, comprising three 4-measure groups, is found in Chopin's Mazurka op. 24 no. 3 (Fig. 40,7). The triple ordering arises because, in the arpeggiation up to c^3, ab^2 has its own 4-measure group.

Ex. 3: Fig. 42,2 shows the duple ordering of the middleground, in accord with the interruption form. However, in our example, which depicts the foreground, the interpolation of the neighboring note in the first third-progression gives rise to a 3-measure group. Since the second third-progression, eb^2—d^2—c^2, retains its fundamental 2-measure group, a 5-measure group results, clearly divided, however, into $3 + 2$. Thus, this 5-measure ordering is based on a duple ordering, and the second third-progression in measures 4–5 has the effect of an acceleration.

Ex. 4: The third-progressions which in measures 1 and 2 descend from eb^2 and db^2 are followed by the third third-progression from c^2 in measures 3–4; it occupies three quarter-beats and by means of this expansion prepares the three beats of the extended bb^1 in measures 4–5. Hence c^2 and bb^1 divide the beats of measures 3–5 between themselves. This is the origin of the first 5-measure group. The second 5-measure group, showing two third-progressions inverted, is brought about by the augmentation of the third, d^2—f^2. The two 5-measure groups are then followed by 4-measure groups.

Ex. 5: Here the 5-measure group results from a rhythmic shift. Without the eighth-note acceleration in measure 4, answered in parallelistic fashion in measure 5, six measures would have been required.

However, a 10-measure group need not always mean 2×5. Fig. 61b, for example, shows a 10-measure group which, without subdivision, develops organically from the tonal progression outlined there. Compare Mozart's Symphony in C, K. 551 *(Jupiter)*, Andante Cantabile, measures 1–10, and Beethoven's

Sonata for Piano and Violin op. 24, first movement, measures 1–10.

§ 288. Meter and cadence

Unless there are rhythmic demands to the contrary (see § 296), every metric scheme is capable of enclosing the cadence within itself in such a way that the I appears in the final unaccented measure of the measure group:

Fig. 139

Compare in Fig. 138,3 the I in measure 10, which in this 5-measure group is an unaccented measure. Similar instructive examples are to be found in abundance in Schubert's waltzes and Ländler. It is evident that there are advantages for sonata movements, too, in placing a concluding I in an unaccented measure. I refer, for example, to Beethoven's Sonata op. 28, first movement:

The first 10-measure group (see end of § 287 and Fig. 61b) closes with the I in the unaccented measure 10, and, in the repetition, at measure 20. The succeeding 8-measure group ends with I in measure 28, again an unaccented bar. The repetition of this group begins in measure 29, but now it lasts only seven measures; for measure 36, which should have been the eighth measure, is interlocked with a 4-measure group, measures 36–39. Thus the final I appears in measure 39, again the unaccented measure of the 4-measure group. ⟨For mm. 40 62, see Fig. 110c,1 and Fig. 148,4.⟩

Bringing individual measure groups to a close with the I on an unaccented bar is advantageous for synthesis; it gives the groups the effect of a surface contiguity. Thus no reinterpretation of such metric values as the upbeat is necessary when one group moves on to another (§ 298). Sometimes it even becomes imperative to conclude with I on an unaccented bar. When

in Fig. 137,1, for instance, an auxiliary harmony occupies the first measure, it must in the repetition of the measure group again appear on an accented bar; this necessitates placing I on the weak bar 8. In addition, the example shows that it thereby became necessary to put V^{6-5}_{4-3} into measures 6 and 7 (weak–strong), contrary to the requirements of strict counterpoint, which allows a suspension to appear only on a downbeat, that is (in a prolongation of strict counterpoint), on an accented measure in a metric ordering.

§ 289. Subdivision of measures

The metric principle of the duple and triple orderings and their multiples affects even the subdivision of the measure and the beats themselves. Here, too, we differentiate between accented and unaccented beats, thesis and arsis. Again the metric pattern of the subdivision is absolute, in contrast to the relative and special nature of rhythm.

Fig. 140

However varied the rhythmic forms may be, as for example those in Fig. 140 a) 4, 6, 8, 10, 11 and b) 3 and 5, they nevertheless do not contradict the bar's metric pattern which governs them all unalterably. As long as there is an audible downbeat, the remainder of the measure until the next downbeat belongs entirely and unmistakably to the arsis. The arrows used in the illustrations merely show the impulse of the arsis toward the next emphasis.

a) 4: Compare Ex. 1; the impulse indicated by the arrow must be expressed in performance.
   6: Compare Exx. 2 and 3.
   7: Compare Fig. 141d.
   8: Compare Schubert's "Des Fischers Liebesglück."
   9: Compare Beethoven's Seventh Symphony, first movement (in the form of ♪. ♪ ♪   ♪. ♪ ♪).

10: Compare the Rondo of Beethoven's Sonata op. 49 no. 1.

11: Compare Brahms's First Symphony (Fig. 147,3).

b) 3: Compare the sarabandes in the suites of Bach and Handel.

In Ex. 4 of Fig. 140, the repetition from the fifth thirty-second onward is to be understood and executed as at a) 4. The bass in Ex. 5 unequivocally shows 4/4, that in Ex. 6, 3/4, despite the freer upper voices.

Section 3: Rhythm in Music

§ 290. The concept of rhythm in music

Since rhythm, like meter, is closely connected to specific contrapuntal situations, it changes from level to level ⟨Fig. 138,1⟩.

Fig. 141

This figure illustrates the origin, development, and meaning of a rhythmic motion (cf. Fig. 87,5 and its commentary in § 212; also, the different situation in Fig. 72,3). Were the subdivision of the fourth-progression into two third-progressions, as at a), developed by a diminution in broken thirds, six such thirds would be needed. But how are the two third-progressions to be fitted into a 4-measure ordering? The possible solution at b) would seem to suggest $\hat{3}$ as the primary tone; at c) the change in rhythm is too abrupt (see § 291). Both these dangers are overcome by the 6/8 rhythm at d). This version, too, shows three broken thirds in the service of the first third-progression; but a bridge to the second third-progression—whose second note is treated as a passing tone—is organically established here by the insertion of a·passing tone into the last broken third also.

§ 291. An abrupt change of rhythmic values is to be avoided

The fifth species of strict counterpoint (see *Kpt. I*, II/5, § 4) reveals that a succession of sharply defined groups of contrasting rhythmic values (four half-notes and four quarter-notes) creates a poor effect. Since the same holds true in free composition, the masters sought to avoid such abrupt changes by spreading out the different metric values into a more even pattern (cf. Fig. 125,1a and b):

Fig. 142

Section 4: Antimetric Rhythmic Situations

§ 292. The rhythmic shift as a means of evening out metric values

The way in which a rhythmic shift helps to avoid an abrupt change from one metric value to another is shown in

Fig. 143

The smaller values are kept apart by placing them at the beginning and end of the measure groups, as indicated by the interrupted beams.

§ 293. The hemiola

For the purpose of a ritardando, especially in an ending, two 3/4 or 3/2 bars in a triple meter are often combined in a way that produces within the two measures an extended triple-measure—the hemiola ⟨see also Fig. 132,4⟩:

Fig. 144

§ 294. The rhythmic shift as anticipation

What strongly distinguishes the rhythmic shift from the syncopation is the rhythmic shift's almost violent intrusion into the subdivision of the measure:

Fig. 145

Ex. 1: The expressiveness of the ab^2, which seems to be a last eighth note analogous to those in the preceding groups, is so much heightened by its treatment as an anticipation, as a rhythmic shift!

Ex. 2: No less boldly does the rhythmic shift in the bass carry out a parallelism to measures 3 and 4 of the Mazurka (see Fig. 128,9d).

§ 295.   The upbeat

Starting a diminution with an upbeat implies a certain contradiction to the metric scheme. Since it is in the nature of parallelism that the rhythmic pattern of the upbeat be repeated in what follows, the conflict with the metric scheme continues. To bring the rhythm sooner or later into agreement with the meter is a difficult problem, one which inexperienced composers are often unable to solve.

Examples of upbeat forms:

Fig. 146

In Exx. 1, 3, and 4 the upbeat, too, is supported harmonically, as if it were a downbeat.

Ex. 1: The adjustment of rhythm to meter occurs at measures 43–44.

Ex. 3: Here the adjustment occurs at measure 20. The section from measures 21 to 37, which conforms to the meter, is followed by a return of the former upbeat pattern. This pattern adjusts to the meter for the last time at measure 55, but even the two closing chords must be considered an augmentation of the upbeat form.

Ex. 4: The form of the opening is boldly maintained throughout the entire theme and even in the variations. Hence, performers and listeners alike tend to confuse the upbeats with downbeats.

Exx. 5 and 6: Here the upbeat is of unusual length, which has significant consequences for the further course of the work. It would be contrary to the meaning of the composition to perceive and perform it on the basis of the metric scheme alone. Compare Ex. 5 with my *Fünfte Sinfonie*, p. 48. Ex. 6 shows at a) the upbeat and at b) the forms which the adjustment takes.

Compare Fig. 91,5 and also the ingenious adjustment of the upbeat in Beethoven's Sonata op. 109, first movement, measure 15 (see *Erläuterungsausgabe*).[3]

§ 296.   Heightening of the conflict between rhythm and meter

The upbeat generally leads to the first measure that is metrically strong. However, the composer occasionally contradicts this function of the upbeat if he imbeds the upbeat within this first measure:

[3]. "Beethoven wanted the development section to start in the same manner as the first subject, that is, with a quarter-note upbeat. His further intention was to hide this upbeat in the 3/4 time of the 'adagio espressivo' so that its thematic significance would not become too grossly apparent. While still imbedded in the continuing flow of the 3/4 meter, the upbeat was to be sneaked in unnoticeably. The task was indeed a difficult one, considering the huge difference between 3/4 and 2/4 meter, between Adagio and Vivace! . . . . One must admire Beethoven's truly creative and honest approach as he took this problem in hand. Since he had used the low register in the cadence in measure 15, he felt he had the right to a free expansion of the ending: as if unintentionally, he continued the passage which emanated from the cadence. This continuation presented him with the fourth and fifth quarter-beats, and when he now added the upbeat, the sum total of six quarters was reached. Only in this manner could he achieve his goal: to give the 3/4 time complete measure units, and, while in 3/4 time, to simultaneously incorporate the upbeat of the development section." (Schenker)

Fig. 147

This heightens the conflict between rhythm and meter (cf. Fig. 119,19a and b).

Ex. 1: The broken intervals of the simple accompaniment in the metrically strong first measure take on parallelistic import and decisively affect the synthesis of the theme, as shown at N.B.

Ex. 2: Here the rhythm and the meter do not conflict, even though this may seem to be the case. The first measure is certainly a true upbeat, yet it subsequently takes its place within the metric scheme as a fourth measure. In the first three 4-measure groups, the third-progressions $f\sharp^1—e^1—d^1$, $f\sharp^3—e^3—d^3$, and $g^1—f\sharp^1—e^1$ follow one another directly with no connecting link; this feature probably influenced Brahms to use the neighboring-note figure in the fourth measure. In measure 9 he placed the neighboring-note figure on B, which is part of the necessary 5—6 exchange: $I—\overline{(IV)}\overset{5\quad6\quad5}{—II—}V$. I have indicated these relationships by means of broken beams. ⟨The interrupted brackets indicate the parallelism of the descending fifths $A—D$, $E—A$.⟩ Only a study of the score can provide insight into the further service which this seemingly insignificant neighboring-note figure renders for the synthesis.

Ex. 3: In contrast to Exx. 1 and 2, we find here a real conflict between rhythm and meter. There is no doubt that the first diminutional entity goes on to $c\sharp^3$ in measure 5 of the example; but the modified repetition, which ends in its fourth measure, does not follow the same metrical grouping. Thus the 5-measure group extends into the first measure of the next four measures. This, however, in no way involves a reinterpretation of the fifth bar as a first bar (§ 298).

Ex. 4: A still clearer example of heightened conflict between rhythm and meter. The rhythm of the upper voice seems to be part of a metric scheme different from that of the bass. It is as if two metric schemes were operating against one another. To bring such sharp contrasts into balance within a single meter requires special powers of synthesis ⟨compare the different situation in Fig. 119,19⟩.

§ **297.** Expansion

The concept of expansion does not include those 6- , 10- , and 12-measure groups which serve a diminution organically. Nor does it include the kind of measure-insertion which accompanies the repetition of upbeat forms. These phenomena, with their particular origins, belong in their own categories (§§ 287, 295). In contrast to these, an expansion follows from one or more measures of a metric prototype.*[4] There must be an organic relationship. Despite the fact that prototype and derivation follow one another in direct succession, their relationship can be recognized only from the middleground and background. Such recognitions are doubly difficult, for one must also be aware of the special laws which govern an expansion and mold it into a self-contained organism. All theories of meter err when they fail to recognize such expansions and simply trot along in the established metric scheme.

Fig. 148

Ex. 1: The approach to a^1 as the $\hat{2}$ of the movement (see Fig. 124,5b) takes up two 4-measure groups. The last measure of the second 4-measure group, which contains the a^1, is expanded by a play of neighboring notes. This is combined with an octave coupling that serves to bring the fifth-progression descending from the $\hat{2}$ into the higher octave (see $a^2—d^2$ in mm. 18–33). Concerning the organic relationships within the diminutions here, see §§ 253 ff.

*[4]. Exx. 2 and 3 of Fig. 148 show expansions that derive from metric prototypes appearing at an earlier structural level. (Oster)

Ex. 2: The expansions here take the form of embellished fermatas (cf. *Kpt. I*, Ex. 36).

Ex. 3: The middleground unfolding of four tones at a) takes place within a basic 4-measure group. Ex. b), however, shows a first prolongation in six measures. In the foreground realization at c), the third and fourth bars of this 6-measure group are expanded. Within this expansion the octave coupling ab^2—ab^1 employs two measures, which evokes three further 2-measure groups to serve the motion from the inner voice f^1—gb^1—ab^1, ultimately leading back to ab^1. Thus there are four 2-measure groups in place of the original third bar at Ex. b). These are followed by a 4-measure group, which includes the tying-over of the ab^1 and the resolution to g^1, as well as the two last tones $f\sharp^1$ and d^2. It is obvious that ab^1—g^1 really express only g^1— see bar 4 at b)—and that the further expansion made it necessary to compress the $f\sharp^1$ and d^2 into one measure, lest this 4-measure group should also produce an expansion. Such an expansion would destroy the value of the group as a bridge to the normal ordering which follows.

Ex. 4: Two expansions. First the third measure, and then the fourth measure, is extended.*5 ⟨For mm. 1–47, see § 288 and Fig. 110,e1.⟩

Ex. 5: Two 4-measure groups are actually followed by a third such group, which brings with it g^1 as the $\hat{2}$. However, before the real first measure of this third group Chopin inserts two bars in which he contrasts the $b\flat$ with the $b\natural$, the $\natural$ third which breaks up a 5—5 succession (see Fig. 54,1). The expansion gives the impression that Chopin is trying out the step from a^1 to g^1 before he actually takes it. (Compare *Five Graphic Analyses*.)

*5. This means that $d\sharp^2$ of measure 3 is expanded in measures 7 to 9, and e^2 of measure 4 in measures 10 to 11 (see the upper line of measure numbers added by Schenker). The lower line of measure numbers, in parentheses, pertains to the bass: measures 8 to 11 of the example constitute an expansion of measure 4 into a 4-measure group of its own. (Oster)

Ex. 6: In contrast, this example shows no expansion, but instead a 6-measure entity which evolves organically out of a progression of the harmonic degrees I—VI—$\natural$II, with each harmony filling two measures.

Compare Fig. 124,7: measures 9–12 form the prototype, measures 13–29 the expanded repetition, which grows specifically from the fourth measure (bar 16 corresponding to bar 12). The purpose of the expansion is to give the second third-progression so much momentum through sheer repetition that it can run up into the higher octave and there prepare for and yield to the third third-progression, f^2—a^2 in measures 28–29! And the inner organization of the expansion is particularly ingenious. Measures 16–24 are so divided that the fifth bar, with its special entrance of the bassoon, marks the midpoint of the 9-measure group. Then follows a 4-bar group in which the rising repetition simultaneously presents an augmentation of the third-progression. An error on Beethoven's part has been suspected at the bassoon interpolation in measure 20, but my clarification should put any objection to rest.

In Fig. 138,3 the fifth bar of the last 5-measure group is expanded to a 7-measure group by means of a neighboring-note motion in the inner voice. Compare also Fig. 146,5.

§ 298.   Reinterpretation of metric values

In order to fit meter to the needs of rhythm, a reinterpretation of metric values is occasionally necessary.

Fig. 149

Ex. 1: The first group, an 8-measure unit, is followed by a group which consists of only seven measures. Therefore one should not regard the first measure of the third measure-grouping as a possible eighth bar of the second group and reinterpret it metrically.

Ex. 2: Here, however, the fourth bar of the second 4-measure group is reinterpreted as a first bar. Incidentally, music is the only art in which an ending can also be a beginning; this situation is clearest when one single tone is involved. In this phenomenon lies the root of any possible reinterpretation of metric values (cf. Fig. 150, m. 12).

Ex. 3: Since the first 6-measure group ends on a^2 and the second 6-measure group begins on $c\sharp^3$, a juxtaposition of two first measures is unavoidable. An actual reinterpretation occurs only after the close of the third 6-measure group.

Ex. 4: Here also two first measures appear in direct succession: first, the ending and beginning tones, e^1 and $g\natural^1$, are different; second, and equally important, the fifth-progression E—$A\sharp$ (m. 12) in the bass begins under the $g\natural^1$. N.B. reveals the reason why the upbeat is metrically incorporated into the first measure of the second group.*⁶ This differentiates the example from the one in Fig. 147,1, which is outwardly similar.

Ex. 5: Twice in the same theme, two first bars clash with one another.

Ex. 6: Here we see how a change in diminution can bring with it a change in meter. Note also the contrasting play of $c\sharp^2$—d^2 and $d\flat^2$—$c\natural^2$ (cf. § 256).

Ex. 7: This manner of impelling the content forward through reinterpretation is one of the most important compositional devices of the masters.

Ex. 8: As long as musical content moved principally in imitations of canonic and fugal forms, it was somehow illogical to presuppose a specific metric scheme. Each of the numerous imitations, after all, involved reinterpretation. Where would we find ourselves if we were to pursue the idea of rein-

terpretation in the manner indicated at a) ? We can, at b), clearly see that subject or answer can appear in such contradiction to the original metric scheme that the new ordering amounts to a complete change of that scheme. This is of special significance for fugue writing!

In this connection we should recall Fig. 116 (§ 251), in which a metric scheme, 3×4 measures, is ascertainable but whose exact subdivision cannot be determined—is it $2 \times 3, 3 \times 2, 2 \times 2$? The composition reveals a rhythm based merely on words; as yet the rhythm has no purely musical basis. Only the freeing of music from too much imitation allowed rhythm and meter to interact in a way that might serve absolute diminution.

Even the freest sort of rhythmic play, as in the works of Schumann and Brahms, finds its basis and clarification in the fundamental principles we have now discussed.

§ 299. Transcending the meter in performance

It is the responsibility of the performer primarily to express the special rhythmic characteristics of a composition, as they sometimes coincide with the meter, sometimes oppose it. Today, not only the failure to recognize rhythmic relationships but also sheer indolence creates a preference for the metric scheme alone—a dismaying evidence of decline [§§ 286 and 295, footnote].

§ 300. Rejection of prosody as the basis of rhythm in music *⁷

⟨Schenker here speculates at some length on the nature of prosody in the Greek and German languages, and poetic feet in general. Since Schenker appears to doubt his own hypotheses in this matter, the editor here includes only the portion which pertains to music. (Oster)⟩

---

*6. Since the upper-voice diminution of measures 5–9 repeats that of measure 1–5 (first beat), one has to understand measures 5–6 as representing two measures $g\sharp^1$, in analogy to the two full measures e^1 at the beginning. The $g\natural^1$ at the start of the "second group" then likewise extends over two measures. (Oster)

*7. Passage (O), omitted here, is supplied in Appendix 4. (Rothgeb)

It is impossible to apply poetic feet to music, since it lacks words, the bearers of such metric feet. Music can have only a series of tones, and these attain identity through parallelisms alone.

The unsuitability of applying principles of prosody to music is shown in

Fig. 150

We might regard measures 1–2 as $-\smile$, since c^3 is emphasized as $\hat{5}$ of the fifth-progression and appears in the first bar. Next, measures 3–4 would probably have to be considered $\smile -$ to correspond with the position of bb^2 as $\hat{4}$ of the progression and as the goal of an upward arpeggiation. The following 4-measure group would seem to be $-\smile$, or possibly $--$, in contrast to the next 4-bar unit, which would have to be regarded as $-\smile\smile$. To which patterns would we adhere if we attempt to establish the sense of the musical rhythm on this basis?

Chapter 5

Form

A. FORM IN GENERAL

§ 301.   Historical background

In the music of the early contrapuntal epoch, including even Palestrina, the basic voice-leading events, such as passing tones or neighboring notes, had not yet come to fruition, like flowers in bud. Who would have suspected, at that time, that these phenomena, through the process of diminution, were to become form-generative and would give rise to entire sections and large forms! Although the art of prolongation and diminution ultimately expanded and enriched the form, it was the force of the first passing tone, the first neighboring note, the power of the first structural division which bound form to take on organic unity; and the composer had to make these inner necessities of the background his own. Only when the ear deteriorated did musicians take refuge in the program as the provider of form. This meant a flight from musical conscience and from musical coherence, ⟨which is⟩ the fruit of background alone.*1

The great masters took the background as their source of memory. Improvisation certainly gave their memory greater strength, but the ability to improvise depends, to a great extent, upon memory. In very extended works, only the greatest composers have been able to envision the form as a totality [§§ 29, 93]. They are as much at home in intervals, linear progressions, and diminutions as fish are in water. Even though they may have been unable to describe precisely the element in which they flourished, nevertheless they occasionally gave out a few words which shed light upon their nature and their work. Here are a few such remarks:

C.P.E. Bach: "One must have a vision of the whole piece." *2

Haydn: ". . . a composition should have a songful flow, coherent ideas. . . ." "I sat down, began to improvise. . . . Once I got hold of an idea, I directed my efforts toward working it

---

*1. Passage (P), omitted here, is supplied in Appendix 4. (Rothgeb)

*2. *Versuch*, "Vom Vortrage," § 31. (Oster)

out and sustaining it according to the principles of art. Thus I sought to help myself. And it is this which so many of our new composers lack; they simply tack one little piece on to another, and then break off when they have scarcely begun. When one has listened to their music, nothing whatsoever remains in one's heart."

Mozart (to van Swieten): ". . . and the work is really almost completed in my mind, even if it is very long, so that afterward I can see it in my mind's eye with a single glance, like a beautiful picture or a lovely person. And not all in succession, as it must come later, do I hear it in my imagination, but somehow all at once. That is a real feast! All the finding and doing happens in me just as in a powerful, beautiful dream. But this hearing it all, all at once, is still the best. . . ." *3

Beethoven: "Also in my instrumental music I always have the whole before my eyes."

Brahms: "More from the whole!" *4

§ 302.   The repeat sign

The fundamental structure and the first level know no repeat sign. Therefore, a repeat sign in the foreground must not lead us to misjudge the form. Such repetitions may consist not only of first sections based on the division $\hat{3}$—$\hat{2}$:‖ or $\hat{5}$—$\hat{2}$:‖ but also of sections which express only $\hat{3}$:‖ or $\hat{5}$:‖. Compare Figs. 26; 35; 40,1 and 9; 46,2; 48,1; 49,2 (110,b1); 68.

The actual performance of repeats is indispensable for establishing correct balance within the form. Hence it is not merely up to the performer whether or not he wants to play them. Nor should they be considered as an external matter which, at best, may serve to impress a section more strongly on the

hearer's memory. The omission of repeats which is so widespread today must be viewed as a violation of form.

§ 303.   Deceptive beginnings

Many pieces show deceptive beginnings which lead to a false conception of their form; in such cases only the middleground and background can give the true picture (Figs. 13; 89,4; 110,b3 and e3; 119,15).

A particularly striking example is shown in

Fig. 151

Every return to the first theme of this Rondo, which seems to begin in C major, had to be prepared through G major I♯7 (G: I♯7—IV = C major: V7—I). Despite the difficulties posed by the deceptive beginning, Beethoven boldly met this requirement of the rondo form, specifically by expansive embellishments of the fermatas which lead back to the initial tone.

Chopin, in his Scherzo in $D\flat$ Major op. 31, perhaps faced an even greater difficulty in this respect.*5 How ingeniously he finds his way, in measures 460–584, back to the $b\flat$-minor harmony, and so is able to begin with the initial arpeggiation! (Figs. 13 and 102,6)

§ 304.   The definitive close of a composition

The middleground and background also determine the definitive close of a composition. With the arrival of $\hat{1}$ the work is at an end. Whatever follows this can only be a reinforcement of the close—a coda—no matter what its extent or purpose may be (§ 24; Figs. 73,4; 109c).*6

*3. This letter is generally thought to be a forgery by Rochlitz. However, the content and the manner of expression point toward the possibility that it may record words spoken by Mozart.   (Jonas)

*4. G. Jenner, *Johannes Brahms*.   (Oster)

*5. See footnote to § 47.   (Oster)

*6. If recent musical products have almost no end or seem to find no end, it is because they do not derive from a fundamental structure and hence do not arrive at a genuine $\hat{1}$; without this $\hat{1}$ a work is bound to give the effect of incompleteness.   (Schenker)

Therefore, those closing sections which, for reasons of obligatory register, hark back to the third or fifth, must also fall into the category of coda. See Beethoven, op. 57, first movement [§§ 267, 315].

§ 305.   The background also clarifies some forms found in older music

Only a consideration of the background makes it possible to recognize a form such as that of Handel's Suite No. 2 in *F* Major. This suite does not consist of four movements, but only two, each preceded by an introduction. Thus, the main movements are the Allegro and the Fugue, since the two introductory pieces exhibit no true fundamental line. Although the short Allegro would seem almost too brief to constitute a main movement, the density of its voice-leading gives musical ears so much to hear that much time seems to elapse in the listening. Regarded as a merely mechanical finger exercise, the piece would of course be too slight; if one truly understands it, one can speak here of a Handelian "heavenly brevity," to alter Schumann's remark about the "heavenly length" of Schubert's *C*-Major Symphony.*7

§ 306.   Innovational aspect of this explanation of form

All forms appear in the ultimate foreground; but all of them have their origin in, and derive from, the background. This is the innovational aspect of my explanation of forms, which is to follow in the next sections. Previously in this book I have repeatedly referred to form as the ultimate manifestation of that structural coherence which grows out of background, middleground, and foreground; *8 but I here reiterate in order to stress the difference between this new theory and all previous

*7. Schenker planned to publish the entire suite in another set of graphic analyses.   (Oster)

*8. See §§ 25, 26, 29, 33, 40, 94, 99, 101, 103, 111, etc.   (Schenker)

theories of form. I very much hope that this explanation will be regarded as the true interpretation of the words of the masters quoted in § 301. May it also be absorbed by every creative mind and ear!

However, within the confines of a book which for the first time seeks to present the concept of organic coherence, the theory of form as a manifestation of the fundamental design must not claim as much space as it would ordinarily find in a separate treatise on form, complete with entire works as illustrations. It is precisely because I derive the forms from the background and middleground that I have the advantage of brevity in presentation. However briefly I express myself, I am happy to offer, at least in this manner, the "Essay on a New Theory of Form" ("Versuch einer neuen Formenlehre") which I have promised for decades. I have no doubt that the new theory of form will eventually triumph, just as will the concept of organic coherence itself.

B.   FORM IN PARTICULAR

Section 1:   Undivided Form

§ 307.   Undivided form

The undivided progression of the fundamental line generates undivided form. Repetitions indicated by :‖, or those written out in full, constitute neither an interruption of the fundamental line nor, consequently, a division of the form [§ 33].

Fig. 152

Ex. 1: All the rhythmic, prosodic events brought about by the setting of the text, as well as all the characteristic features of the piano part, fall within the undivided progression $\hat{3}$—$\hat{1}$ (cf. Fig. 40,2).

Ex. 2: The undivided form $\hat{3}$—$\hat{1}$ serves as the setting for each four-line stanza. The song has four stanzas; in spite of the alteration in the fourth stanza it must be considered a strophic song. Particularly beautiful is the fourth-progression in the inner voice.

Ex. 3: This is, despite the repetition, an undivided form (cf. Fig. 49,2).

Ex. 4: Although the four measures expressing the $\hat{5}$ are repeated, the form must be understood as undivided, as $\hat{5}$—$\hat{1}$; the motion of the inner voice is noteworthy in this respect. Similarly in Fig. 39,3 a three-part form is not to be understood: not a—b—c (*Harm.* § 5). Compare Figs. 40,8 and 9; 103,6.

Ex. 5: Despite the altered third stanza and a mixture in the fourth stanza, this song is written in strophic form. Here text and music are ingeniously bound together by means of the octave-progression, $\hat{8}$—$\hat{1}$. The poetic meter is delightfully treated within the 3/8 time, especially the first syllables in measures 6 and 12, and the syllable "Lenz" on the fourth sixteenth in measure 13.[9]

Obviously, preludes are the main province of the undivided form: Figs. 40,3; 43, example to b); 64,1; 73,2; 76,6; 136,2–5.

Ex. 6: In the absence of a fundamental line and a completed arpeggiation I—V—I, the example does not manifest a self-contained, undivided form. This composed-out I—V can only be understood as a prelude, in the strictest sense, to a piece in c minor.

Ex. 7: A fundamental line and V$^{\sharp 3}$—I in the bass are also lacking here; the uncertainty which rises about the tonality (see N.B.) almost prevents us from calling this Mazurka a completed composition. (This peculiarity was pointed out by Schumann.)

---

[9]. The singer's failure to perceive the unity of text and music too often results in an incorrect rendition of the first line—as if a self-contained thought were completed at the end of it. (Schenker)

Exx. 1–5 present independent pieces in undivided form. But undivided forms also occur as parts of larger entities. For instance, the example shown in Fig. 40,7 is undivided, due to the large arpeggiation which leads to $\hat{3}$—$\hat{2}$—$\hat{1}$; but it represents only the first part of a three-part song form. Similarly, the second movement of Beethoven's Sonata op. 110 (*Jahrb. I*, pp. 181–82) presents in its entirety a three-part form:

$$\hat{5}—(\text{Nbn})—\hat{5}$$
$$f \text{ minor: } \text{I}— \quad \text{VI} \quad —\text{I}.$$

Within the first part, however, there is an undivided fifth-progression, c^2—f^1, akin to that in Fig. 152,4 (one must disregard the repetition signs).

Section 2: The Song Forms

§ 308. General

Coherence in language does not arise from a single syllable, a single word, or even from a single sentence; despite the correspondence of words and things, every coherent relationship in language depends upon a meaning hidden in a background. Such meaning achieves no fulfillment with mere beginnings. Similarly, music finds no coherence in a "motive" in the usual sense ⟨§ 50⟩. Thus, I reject those definitions of song form which take the motive as their starting point and emphasize manipulation of the motive by means of repetition, variation, extension, fragmentation, or dissolution. I also reject those explanations which are based upon phrases, phrase-groups, periods, double periods, themes, antecedents, and consequents. My theory replaces all of these with specific concepts of form which, from the outset, are based upon the content of the whole and of the individual parts; that is, the differences in prolongations lead to differences in form.

These prolongations in no way determine the actual length of compositions; consequently, the customary distinction between large and small song forms must be discarded [§ 318]. Of course, the prolongations are fulfilled by diminution, as I have shown in my earlier explanations. Obviously, we do meet repetitions, but, in contrast to the motivic repetitions in the conventional theory of form, those which I describe are usually hidden. Such repetitions make possible far-reaching extensions and the organic connections of distant points. An expansion of content is also furthered by the play between registers of a particular instrument or of the orchestra. But the fundamental significance of the particular prolongation is always of paramount importance; at the outset, the prolongation assigns to each part its task with great exactness. The composer is thus spared the anguish of aimlessness, of happenstance, and of a continual search for the means to go on [§§ 83, 254, and 264].

§ 309. Two-part song form

Two-part form evolves most naturally from the division $\hat{3}$—$\hat{2} \| \hat{3}$—$\hat{2}$—$\hat{1}$, $\hat{5}$—$\hat{2} \| \hat{5}$—$\hat{1}$, or $\hat{8}$—$\hat{5} \| \hat{5}$—$\hat{1}$. This has nothing to do with the extent of the piece, which may be short, as in Figs. 22a and 76,2; or, as the result of more elaborate repetition, more extended, as in Fig. 12.

Even within larger forms which derive from the first or second level, a two-part form may appear at a later level.

Fig. 40,6: Although a three-part form is here established by the mixture $\flat\hat{3}$—$\natural\hat{3}$(Trio)—$\flat\hat{3}$, the first part itself, with its interruption $\hat{3}$—$\hat{2} \| \hat{3}$—$\hat{2}$—$\hat{1}$, displays two-part form.

Fig. 110,b3: This example also belongs to a larger three-part form, A$_1$—B(Trio)—A$_2$. However, this A$_1$ section is based upon an interruption that gives it two-part form, a fact which the daring ascending arpeggiation to $\hat{3}$ does not alter.

Fig. 137,1: This example is taken from a waltz whose three-part form is based upon a mixture ($C\sharp^{\natural 3}$—$D\flat^{\natural 3}$—$C\sharp^{\natural 3}$). Its first part is a combination of two two-part forms: $\underset{\quad a_1 \ : \quad a_2}{\hat{3}\text{—}\hat{2} \| \hat{3}\text{—}\hat{2}\text{—}\hat{1}}$ (mm. 1–32) and $\underset{\quad a_1 \ : \quad a_2}{\hat{3}\text{—}\hat{2}\text{—}\hat{1} \| \hat{3}\text{—}\hat{2}\text{—}\hat{1}}$ (mm. 33–48).

§ 310. Three-part song form

Many paths lead to the three-part form A$_1$—B—A$_2$.

(a) Occasionally the bass arpeggiation I—V—I alone suffices to establish a ternary form, even when an undivided fundamental line is repeated, as in Fig. 75. The fifth-progression b^1—e^1 descends twice without division, in both the first and third parts; in the middle section the single broad prolongation of V provides a counterbalance to these linear progressions.

(b) Division plays the most important role in three-part form also, even though at the first level it brings binary characteristics to the fore, as a consequence of $\hat{3}$—$\hat{2} \| \hat{3}$—$\hat{2}$—$\hat{1}$ or $\hat{5}$—$\hat{2} \| \hat{5}$—$\hat{1}$.

1. A simple expansion of V$^{\sharp 3}$, as, for example, in Fig. 7a, can constitute the middle section. Here the content of the expansion is the ingenious parallelism e^2—$d\sharp^2$, which is like an echo of the e^2—$d\sharp^2$ forming the $\hat{3}$—$\hat{2}$ of the first part. [This parallelism extends even to the descending third-progression $d\sharp$—$c\sharp$—$B\sharp$ in mm. 38–39.] Beethoven's indication "Sonata quasi una Fantasia" is very fitting, since the three-part song form of the first movement is unusual, whereas the last movement, in sonata-allegro form (Fig. 40,4), reasserts the character of a "sonata."

2. A thoroughgoing amplification of $\dfrac{\hat{2}}{\text{V}}$ even more effectively produces a three-part form, as in Figs. 22b; 76,3; 109e,3. In the illustration for a) of Fig. 43, two waltzes are combined to make a three-part form.

3. The process of "securing" a seventh whose purpose is to cancel the leading tone to the dominant can give rise to a three-part form, as in Fig. 46,1.

4. A retransition necessary because of an unusual beginning, such as the II—V—I in Fig. 53,3, can bring about a three-part form. ⟨The B section aims at the IV, $F\sharp$, which has the task of reintroducing the II, $D\sharp$.⟩

(c) Mixture also may produce a three-part form, as can be seen in Figs. 30a and b; 40,6.

(d) A neighboring note can also give rise to three-part form, as in Figs. 7b; 40,1; 42,1 and 2; 85. The outward appearance is of no consequence: the individual parts may be connected with one another; they may be set off by :‖, as often occurs in longer works, or the middle section may be given the special designation "Trio."

Further examples:

Fig. 153

Ex. 1: Here we see a very extended three-part form, boldly derived from a neighboring note, yet unfolding in a single broad sweep.

Ex. 2: In contrast to the neighboring-note settings at the first level (Fig. 32,3 and 5), the neighboring note here does not appear in the fundamental line. Instead, the I—VI—I succession of the bass creates the effect of a neighboring note and sets an actual neighboring note in the inner voice into motion [Fig. 130,4]. See also Figs. 39,1 and 88a.

Also within the larger forms themselves, three-part forms can be created by subdivision at later levels, as in Fig. 20,4 within a B section ⟨Trio⟩; in Fig. 30a, within A_1, B, and A_2 sections; in Fig. 35,1 and 2, within A_1 sections; further in Figs. 40,1; 73,3; and 82,2. In all these cases we find the same prolongations that lead to ternary form on a large scale.

Ex. 3: Within this exceptionally beautiful and bold example of a large ternary form achieved through a neighboring note, small three-part song forms are built. Like the large ternary form of the composition, the small three-part forms also utilize a neighboring note in order to attain their ternary form. Here, instead of the usual repeat required by :‖, the A_1 section includes a written-out repetition of b and a_2, an expanded composing-out of these sections. The reaching-over in the B part is amazing in its breadth and power. How imaginatively the neighboring-note harmony $II_{\sharp 3}^{7}$ is expanded in measures 22–41, how striking the figurations in measures 41–53! In the A_2 section the first small three-part form returns in an abbreviated version. The abundance of neighboring notes in all sections is almost bewildering; but they have different roles to play in the formal structure, and only with an awareness of these differences can we relate the parts to the whole with definition and clarity.

Section 3: Sonata Form

§ 311. Preliminary

Here, as in the presentation of the song forms, it is necessary to discard the concepts and terminology of conventional theory. These all involve the "motive" and are therefore most imprecise ⟨§ 50⟩. It does not matter that so many designations are offered for the prolongation of the primary tone of the fundamental line ("first theme," "main theme," "first theme-group," and such); what matters is that none of these designations answers the essential question, not one explains why the first prolongation takes just this particular course and no other. Conventional theory simply does not know how to read diminutions; it assumes erroneous entities, splitting up those actually present and creating new ones where none exist.

In such deplorable circumstances, hermeneutics can provide no possible assistance, regardless of the means to which it may resort: whether it inserts poetry into the score *[10] or employs the concept of "pathos" to bring us closer to the form of the sonata movements of the masters. How cheering it is to behold the purveyor of hermeneutics patting Beethoven on the back and praising him for his "complete regularity of formal design"!

---

*[10]. This was actually done by Arnold Schering, who provided the melodic lines, for example, of Beethoven's Sonata op. 106 with verses from Schiller's *Die Jungfrau von Orléans*. (Oster)

§ 312.   General observations on sonata form

Only the prolongation of a division (interruption) gives rise to sonata form. Herein lies the difference between sonata form and song form: the latter can also result from a mixture or a neighboring note.

Relevant to the forms of the division which are pertinent here, I refer to §§ 87–99 (also Figs. 23–26) and to the illustrations in Figs. 39,2; 40,4; 47,1. In addition I refer the reader to the presentation of Beethoven's Sonata op. 57 and his Fifth Symphony in the issues of *Der Tonwille* and that of his Third Symphony in *Jahrbuch III*. [Further, "Vom Organischen der Sonatenform" in *Jahrb. II*].*[11]

§ 313.   First part: the main section (exposition)

We begin the discussion of part I (the exposition) with some general observations.

The primary tone $\hat{3}$ can be prolonged by means of a third-progression, as in Figs. 81,2 (mm. 1–19); 122,1 (mm. 6–8); Beethoven, op. 90, first movement (mm. 1–24). However, a third-progression of this kind must not be confused with the first third-progression in an a_1 section of a song form: in sonata form it is imperative that the third-progression be followed by $\frac{\hat{2}}{V}$. Compare Beethoven, Sonata op. 14 no. 2: a^2 as $\frac{\hat{2}}{V}$ (Fig. 47,2), and Brahms, Fourth Symphony: $f\sharp^2$ as $\frac{\hat{2}}{V}$ (m. 95).

Since the prolongation of $\frac{\hat{2}}{V}$ (in accord with the principle of transference of the forms of the fundamental structure to individual harmonies) will naturally involve chromatics, their preparation by means of auxiliary harmonies on the way to $\hat{2}$ is not

*11. English translation in *Journal of Music Theory* 12:2 (1968).   (Oster)

absolutely necessary. A direct succession $\frac{\hat{3}—\hat{2}}{I—V}$ is also perfectly possible. It remains for the development section to eliminate the chromatics. So, the great masters are not to be criticized when they allow the $\hat{3}$ to move directly to the $\hat{2}$; for this procedure is very much in accord with the sonata form, that is, with the division that is basic to it. In Fig. 47,1 the d^2 which appears above the first V is not yet the $\hat{2}$, since it carries no chromatics with it and belongs merely to the divider. But the d^3 which follows immediately expresses itself in a fifth-progression carrying chromatics which seem to belong to the key of G major.

Fig. 154,1–4

Ex. 1: This example differs from Fig. 47,1 in that, with the entrance of $\hat{2}$ at measure 17, auxiliary harmonies (VI$^\sharp$—II—V—I) appear which prepare for the bass tone G. However, there is no doubt that the $\hat{2}$ is in force from the entrance of this d^2; therefore measures 17–20 cannot be considered merely a transition.

Ex. 2: This case is more difficult. The events shown in measures 27–43 may under no circumstances be taken for a prolongation of the $\hat{2}$, but must be regarded merely as an extension of the d^2 which appeared over the dividing dominant in measure 25. The contents of these measures serve only to effect the ascending register transfer $d^2—d^3$ for the sake of the obligatory register—see e^3 in measure 15 (§ 268). This is carried out by means of reachings-over and the diminution $d^{(3)}—c^2—(b\flat^2)—c\sharp^3—d^3$.

Most often, as in this case, the $\frac{\hat{2}}{V}$ is preceded by a tonicizing II which has the effect of V—I in the key of the dominant (Figs. 40,4; 47,2; 115,2).

It has been shown previously that the $\hat{3}$ can be reached through various diminutions—for instance, by an initial ascent (Fig. 39,2), or by the arpeggiation of a third (Fig. 124,5a and b) or of a sixth (Fig. 40,4).

Ex. 3: A linear progression can also depart from $\hat{5}$, as does the fifth-progression in this instance; but only a continuation to $\frac{\hat{3}}{\text{III}}$ or $\frac{\hat{2}}{\text{V}}$ fulfills the basic requirement of a first section of a sonata form. Specifically, if in *minor* the motion takes place according to Fig. 26a, as in our example, $\hat{5}$—$\hat{4}$—$\hat{3}$ then constitutes that third-progression which leads to the key of $\frac{\hat{3}}{\text{III}}$. This provides for the path that the development will take until it reaches $\frac{\hat{2}}{\text{V}^{\sharp 3}}$. If, however, the motion has already advanced to $\frac{\hat{2}}{\text{V}^{\sharp 3}}$ in the first section, as in Fig. 26b, opportunity is again provided for chromatics (of course, different ones) relating to the seeming key $\text{V}^{\natural 3}$ ($=\text{I}^{\natural 3}$). Here, such a procedure also creates the necessity of moving on to the development. ⟨As noted above, it is then the task of the development to eliminate the chromatics. Compare Fig. 40,4.⟩

Ex. 4: This example follows the same procedure as does Ex. 3, except that in the preceding example auxiliary harmonies appear and the primary tone is prolonged by a fifth-progression (mm. 1–30), whereas here it is prolonged by neighboring notes. In the previous example it is immaterial that the line $\hat{5}$—$\hat{4}$—$\hat{3}$ is followed by a repeat sign; here the development follows the exposition directly. In addition, the $\hat{5}$ (c^2) is lowered subsequently (mixture), so that the third-progression reads $\frac{cb^2—bb^1—ab^1}{\text{III}_____}$.

When, in *major*, $\hat{5}$ is the primary tone, a progression to $\frac{\hat{3}}{\text{III}^{\sharp 3}}$ creates difficulties; such a progression also requires

a raising of the primary tone, and it must be approached logically through auxiliary harmonies, as in Beethoven's op. 53, first movement, measures 35–42:

$$\hat{5}_____\sharp\hat{5}\_\_\_\sharp\hat{4}\_\_\_\hat{3}$$
$$g^2—(a^2)—g\sharp^2—f\sharp^2—e^2$$
$$\text{I}\ —(\ \ )—\text{III}_____$$

[cf. § 315]. Measures 74 ff., of course, supply $g\natural^2$, $d\natural^2$, $c\natural^2$.[*12] Compare this raising of $\hat{5}$ ⟨in major⟩ with the lowering of $\hat{5}$ ⟨in minor⟩ in the preceding Ex. 4.

The composing-out of $\frac{\hat{2}}{\text{V}}$ or $\frac{\hat{5}—\hat{3}}{\text{I}—\text{III}}$ is designated by conventional theory as the second theme, the subordinate theme, the lyrical theme, or the like; occasionally there is reference to two subordinate themes, to a new section, a dissolution of the subordinate theme, to one or even two closing themes. Once more I must emphasize that these are in every respect inadequate terms and concepts which afford no insight into sonata form.

A fifth-progression in itself suffices for the prolongation of $\frac{\hat{2}}{\text{V}}$ without necessarily involving a "lyrical" or "contrasting" theme. The chromatics brought about by the linear progression clearly point up the significance of such a prolongation for the sonata form. For this reason the masters felt no qualms about restating some part of the diminution of the primary tone with the $\hat{2}$. (Examples are to be found particularly in Haydn's compositions written in sonata form.)

*12. In the German editions (which are full of misprints in this section): "$g^2—db^2—c^2$." Assuming that dcs^2 is a misprint for d^2 (db^2 for $d\natural^2$), the sentence probably means that $g\sharp$, $d\sharp$, and $c\sharp$ of III$^{\sharp 3}$ now yield to $g\natural$, $d\natural$, and $c\natural$ of the overall tonality, C major (*Harm.* §§ 14, 18); in other words, the foreground key of E major becomes e minor. Beethoven proceeded in the same way in two other sonata movements that are based on I—III—V: the Piano Sonata op. 31 no. 1 in G Major ($d^2—d\sharp^2—d\natural^2$) and the Third *Leonore* Overture ($g^3—g\sharp^3—g\natural^1$ in mm. 38–70, 120–68, 188). Concerning I—III—V in major and in minor, see also the editorial comments following § 316.   (Oster)

This emphasis upon a linear progression which prolongs $\frac{\hat{2}}{V}$ or upon the third-progression $\frac{\hat{5}-\hat{4}-\hat{3}}{I\text{——}III}$ should remove all the unfortunate misunderstandings so often associated with the so-called subordinate theme. It cannot be denied that a lyrical quality makes the perception of the section which evolves from the $\hat{2}$ easier, but despite the convenience of this lyricism for composer and listener, structural division is the principle which is basic to sonata form. Furthermore, in the sonata movements of the masters, this songfulness is never found in the manner in which it is generally understood and taught. Even the most cantabile utterance tends to give way to diminutions which, as they emanate from the middleground levels, also contribute to the prolongation of the $\hat{2}$. Really, in the organic development of such a prolongation all the diminutions sing; therein lies the true singing quality of every $\frac{\hat{2}}{V}$ section—indeed, of the whole composition (§ 50). It is therefore dangerous if the composer, following conventional theory, sets out to achieve a "songful" theme—this can only lead to a mechanical, rubriclike filling-in of the form. Once again it must be emphasized that insight into all these matters can be gained only from the middleground.

So, in the first movement of Mozart's *Haffner* Symphony (K. 385) the fifth-progressions

$$
\begin{array}{lll}
 & & \hat{2} \\
 & & e^2\!-\!a^1 \\
D \text{ major} & V & \text{——} \\
(A \text{ major} & I & \text{——)}
\end{array}
$$

are entirely sufficient for the fulfillment of $\hat{2}$ as a so-called subordinate group. Similarly in Beethoven's op. 28, first movement, one can speak of a subordinate theme only because there is a motion from e^2 to a^1, a fifth-progression prolonging the $\hat{2}$.

Moreover, the number of linear progressions is not limited. There may be two fifth-progressions, as in Fig. 47,2 or, as in Beethoven's Third Symphony, no less than four linear progressions, from $f^{2(3)}$ as the $\hat{2}$ *(Jahrb. III)*. To designate the last of these progressions as "closing theme" ⟨ in the Third Symphony, mm. 109–44⟩ would seem to be beside the point.

The masters were blessed with the ability constantly to live and move within the realm of prolongation of the formal division. Thus they were able to traverse the path of the exposition with giant strides, as if improvising, creating thereby the effect of a dramatic course of action. The preparation and working-out of motives as such was not the issue ["Vom Organischen der Sonatenform," *Jahrb. II*].*13

§ 314.   Second part: the middle section (development)

Conventional theory calls the middle section of the sonata form the development, assigning to it the task of manipulating, or "working out," the "motivic" material, of changing keys and of avoiding any self-contained ideas—all of this in a section about two-thirds the length of the first part. None of these assignments, rooted as they are in the "motivic" concept, are pertinent for the development section. Its only obligation, according to the structural division, is to complete the motion to $\frac{\hat{2}}{V^{\sharp3}}$ ⟨or in some way to expand that point⟩. In minor it is usually necessary to achieve a leading tone over the V (Figs. 39,2; 40,4). In major the seventh may be transferred upward, in accord with Fig. 23 (Figs. 47,1 and 2; 154,5 and 6), or the V^7 may be composed out in various ways (Figs. 62,1, 3, 4, 11; 100,5; 154,7).

Fig. 154,5–7

Ex. 5: Here we have a seventh transferred upward, analogous to that in Fig. 23a. This seventh bb is prepared, appearing

*13. See the footnote at the end of § 312.   (Oster)

first as the octave of Bb, the lower neighboring note of C, the V—see at a). At b) the upward transfer bb^1—bb^2 is shown. Although the bb^2 in measure 272 and the g^2 in measure 282 do not appear simultaneously over the V, they must be understood as V_5^7, as at a) (cf. Fig. 43).

Ex. 6: As in the previous example, a seventh is transferred upward (V^{8-7})—here, however, in a different way ⟨Fig. 23b⟩.

Ex. 7: This follows the pattern of Fig. 26a.

The use of new diminutions is entirely permissible in the development: Beethoven, Sonata op. 7, first movement, measures 173 ff.; op. 10 no. 1, first movement, measures 118 ff.; Third Symphony, first movement, measures 285 ff.

It is understood that the composer may use diminutions taken from the exposition. But no matter how the diminutions are employed and manipulated, this new use is not the basic idea or the main purpose of the development, but only a means of reaching the goal set for this section by the basic division. The goal is everything; therefore, such new utilization of diminutions from the exposition merits no special concept or designation, such as "the working-out of the material," even when the diminutions are taken up in the same order in which they appeared in the exposition. For instance, in Beethoven's Sonata op. 2 no. 2, first movement, measures 122 ff. and 161 ff. correspond to measures 1 ff. and 9 ff. In Beethoven's Sixth Symphony the development section of the first movement follows the succession a—b—c (mm. 1–3) shown in Fig. 124,7: a in measures 135 ff. and 143 ff., b in measures 151 ff., and finally a-b-c in measures 237 ff. The high points of the register transfer in the development, as shown in Fig. 154,5 (mm. 243 ff.), follow the pattern of the inversions of a and b in measures 9–12. Nonetheless, even this employment of the germinal a—b—c material must not be designated a "working-out," for greater than these hidden relationships is the significance of the register transfer bb^1—bb^2 and the task given it in prolonging V^7.

§ 315.   Third part: the repetition (recapitulation)

Since the principle of division necessitates the closure of the fundamental line and the bass arpeggiation, a return to the main key is understood for the recapitulation.[*14] When the main tonality is thus secured, it is also possible to take some liberty in restating the content of the exposition. For example, in Beethoven's op. 10 no. 2, first movement, the primary tone $\hat{3}$ (a^1) enters first at measure 118 over the VI[#3] (= I in D major). But once VI—II—V has proceeded to I (mm. 131–36), this primary a^1, heard for the second time, is understood in the main tonality. The appearance in D major of a^1 ⟨and with it, of the "first theme"⟩ might seem to be an irregular feature. This a^1, however, has meaning merely as a "resemblance" ⟨Anklang⟩.

More frequently the liberties are associated with $\dfrac{\hat{2}}{V}$ or $\dfrac{\hat{5}-\hat{4}-\hat{3}}{\text{III}}$. In the first movement of Beethoven's op. 53, for instance, the third-progression $\dfrac{g\#^2-f\#^2-e^1}{\text{III}^{\#3}}$ in the exposition (mm. 35–42) is answered in the recapitulation first by $\dfrac{c\#^3-b^2}{A-E}$ in measures 196–99 (as though it were to be $c\#^3-b^2-a^2$), then by $\dfrac{c^2}{A}$ in measures 200–201 (as though it were to be $c^2-b^1-a^1$). Only in measures 204 ff. does the appropriate third-progression $e^3-d^3-c^2$ appear [§ 313] (Fig. 154,4).

*14. In discussing the *Leonore* Overture no. 3, Wagner objected to the recapitulation because such a repetition does not bear out the events of the drama ⟨in contrast to the Overture no. 2, which contains no recapitulation⟩. His error is obvious. In music, the drama of the fundamental structure is the main event. Even though the story of Leonore provides opportunity for a music-drama, the prime concern of the music must be, not her experience, but first and foremost that purely musical motion whose ultimate aim is the unfolding of one chord by means of the fundamental line and the bass arpeggiation through the fifth.   (Schenker)

Even a reordering of the original sequence of the material is possible in the recapitulation, since the fundamental line and the bass arpeggiation ultimately restore the balance.[*15] In the case of $\hat{3}$—$\hat{2}$ ‖ $\hat{3}$—$\hat{2}$—$\hat{1}$, a fifth-progression is frequently superimposed on the final third-progression. There is no doubt that the primary tone remains the $\hat{3}$; the fifth-progression is merely a final reinforcement.[*16]

Once the $\hat{1}$ has been reached, a coda section may follow, and there may be a harking-back to the position of the primary tone in the exposition, as in Beethoven's op. 57, first movement, the final c^2 [§§ 267 and 304].

Only the middleground and background can determine the meaning of slow introductions such as those in Beethoven's op. 13 and op. 81a. For the most part the diminutions of such introductions are organically related to those of the main sections (Fig. 119,7).

Changes of tempo like those in Beethoven's op. 31 no. 2 or op. 109, first movements, do not affect the true course of the division and the composition. In op. 31 no. 2, despite all change of tempo, a^1 moves to c^2, and c^2—d^2—e^2—f^2 (mm. 2, 8, 9–12) to f^3 as the primary tone $\hat{3}$ (m. 13). In spite of the tempo change in op. 109, the primary tone $g\sharp^1$ ($\hat{3}$) continues as $g\sharp^2$ and then proceeds to $f\sharp^2$, the $\hat{2}$, in measure 11. This connection would be destroyed were an entirely new section to be understood as a result of the tempo change.

*15. Mozart, Sonatas in D Major (K. 311 and 576), first movements, and some of Mozart's later concertos. (Oster)

*16. The superposition reads: $\hat{3}$ $(5\,4\,3)$ $\hat{2}$ $\hat{1}$. Its purpose is to restate in the main key the diminution which appeared at the first $\frac{\hat{2}}{V}$. A few examples from first movements by Beethoven: Piano Sonatas op. 109 (see end of § 315), op. 2 no. 3 (cf. Fig. 154,2), op. 14 no. 2 (Figs. 47,2 and 132); Violin Sonata op. 24; Sixth Symphony. Compare also a similar situation in Fig. 35,1, where, although the fifth-progression appears at the $\hat{1}$, measures 41–48 are analogous to measures 11–18. (Oster)

§ 316. Critique of teaching methods

Admittedly it is both necessary and expedient to adjust the instruction of young students according to their ability to understand. They cannot be led to the loftiest heights and the profoundest depths immediately, even if the teacher were capable of such a task. Hence, one should not expect the impossible. Yet, if true knowledge is disseminated neither by the schools nor by the textbooks, where, one may well ask, is it to be presented? [See also the Introduction, as well as *Harm.* §§ 90–92, 181.]

In academic circles the opinion is very widespread that a masterwork which is in contradiction to the textbook represents an exception, a liberty not to be allowed to young music students. On the contrary, the instruction and practice in schools should be recognized as a departure from the teachings of the masterworks, a departure which is perhaps necessary but, at best, worthy of no more than toleration.

Instead of dealing with the organic nature of the sonata form as it prevails in a masterwork, the textbooks present rubrics, which are like a set of children's building blocks.

The quality of improvisation evident in the works of the great masters makes it impossible to conceive of an intellectual and chronological separation between a so-called first and second theme. All the examples I have shown clearly demonstrate the organic process and the breadth of scope inherent in the initial concept.

Also, for the great composers the development section is primarily a purposeful motion (in the sense established above) and not merely an area in which "motives" drawn from the exposition are "developed." The very concept of "development" can only be a hindrance to the aspiring musician in arriving at the true significance of this section. Certainly it is undesirable and unnatural continually to place new diminutions in this path, ignoring the familiar ones from the exposition; after all, the constant employment of new elements would be contrary to the concept of diminution. It must, however, remain a firm principle that the development section is above all a path, determined by the structural division, which must be traversed.

⟨In § 306 Schenker explains why he kept the discussion of form rather brief: he mainly intended to show in broad outlines how the forms, as they appear in the foreground, derive from background and middleground. If one bears in mind that it was Schenker's main purpose to clarify this most important fact, one might consider his discussion of the undivided form and the song forms sufficiently detailed.

When dealing with the sonata, this highly developed and most varied form, Schenker of course goes into greater detail. Even so, his presentation is sketchy and in a number of ways incomplete: above all, he leaves unmentioned various procedures which Beethoven employed for the first time in sonata form, and which later composers adopted. In what follows I shall describe some of the most important of these procedures, especially since their existence is barely mentioned in the literature and surely their true meaning is never explained. The readings given are my own, except where specially noted.

Schenker does show one unusual sonata-form procedure in this work, and therefore I will mention it first. It is set forth in one of the examples, although it is not really discussed by Schenker as an example of sonata form. In Fig. 100,5 he presents a background picture which basically departs from that given in Figs. 23–26 and § 312. Strangely, he does not comment on the formal aspect either in § 230 nor in the chapter on sonata form. The first part of the piece (the exposition) moves to V as usual; but this V, instead of being prolonged through the development section, is treated as an applied divider (§ 279) within the large-scale progression I—III—V. Thus the III appears at the beginning of the development section and not in the exposition where it would ordinarily appear (Fig. 26a). Even though one may have some doubt about Schenker's reading (but after all, it is an early work by Beethoven which may be composed in a strange, perhaps experimental way), the example shows in any case that Schenker himself was flexible in his views; he did not rigidly adhere to his own concepts and formulations whenever an unusual musical situation made it necessary to digress from them. And there is at least one other instance where one probably has to understand the V of the exposition as an applied divider: in the first movement of Beethoven's *G*-Major Sonata (Sonatina) op. 79. Here the overall bass motion is I (V): ‖ VI♯3—IV♯5—V—I, with the VI appearing at the beginning of the development section. This remarkable progression contributes greatly to the conciseness of the movement, which has genuine sonatina character.

Quite frequently found, yet never mentioned by Schenker, is the following: in a sonata movement that starts on $\hat{5}$, the upper voice does not descend via $\hat{4}$ and $\hat{3}$ to the $\hat{2}$ at the interruption point, as it normally would (Figs. 24–26). This means that the composition is not based on the interruption principle in the strictest sense. The background of the exposition rather resembles the voice-leading of Fig. 152,4, measures 1–4: the tone that would be the $\hat{2}$ of the fundamental line (b^1 in m. 4) comes here from the chordal third of the tonic harmony, and it must therefore be considered an inner-voice tone. In such a sonata exposition this tone is then composed out in the usual way, by means of a fifth-progression. In the meantime the $\hat{5}$ is extended till the end of the exposition and from there to the beginning of the recapitulation; it only descends to $\hat{1}$ as late as the end of this section. Examples of this way of writing are the first movement of Beethoven's Seventh Symphony (where there cannot be any doubt that e^3 at the beginning of the Vivace is the primary tone, the $\hat{5}$), or the first movement of Mozart's *D*-Major String Quartet, K. 575. Neither in the symphony nor in the quartet do the fundamental-line tones $\hat{4}$ and $\hat{3}$ follow the initial $\hat{5}$ in the exposition. The situation is quite similar in the first movement of Beethoven's *E*-Major Sonata op. 14 no. 1, except that, before the main V appears in measure 23, the composition makes an "attempt" to describe the fourth-progression b^2—f♯^{1} in measures 5–10.

In § 313, Schenker mentions only briefly that Beethoven's *Waldstein* Sonata op. 53 shows the bass progression I—III—V—I. This progression, so common in minor, was rather infrequently used in major before Beethoven's time. The reason is probably that in minor, the diminished fifth is located on the II; and the II, once it occurs, has a tendency to continue to III. Thus the minor mode has an inherent tendency to move to III (*Harm.* § 50, fn. 11 by Oswald Jonas). In contrast, the major mode lacks this "built-in" tendency; it is not really in its nature to move from I to III. As a consequence, the III in major has to be approached through auxiliary harmonies which carry with them further chromatics (see Schenker's comment on op. 53 in § 313). For these reasons we rarely find I—III—V in major, particularly not in earlier composers. Probably the only composer of early sonatas who used this progression on a larger scale was Domenico Scarlatti; Beethoven was the first to apply it to the fully developed sonata form. He first presented it, quite conspicuously, in the first sonata of op. 31, this striking opus in which he displayed three new ways of writing in sonata form. One year after the *Waldstein* Sonata he used I—III—V again in the Second and Third *Leonore* Overtures. Other examples are the Finale of the Piano Trio op. 70 no. 2 and the last movement of the Quartet op. 135. (The Scherzo of the Seventh Symphony—quoted in Figs. 37b and 146,6—which is not strictly speaking in sonata form, is perhaps better understood as showing the progression I—IV—V—I, as in Fig. 14,3d.)

Later composers, notably Brahms, made frequent use of I—III—V in major: see, for example, I—III♯—V in the first and the last movements of the String Quintet in *F* Major op. 88, or I—III♮—V in the Cello Sonata op. 99 in the same key (Fig. 100d,2). It is important to understand that the III is not just a "mediant" as it is usually described; its true significance is as a third-divider, a tone of arpeggiation on the way from I to V. In this connection, I cannot help mentioning the extraordinary case of the first movement of Brahms' Third Symphony, also in *F* major. Here, after I—III♯—♮ of the exposition, the composer *avoids* in the development section the expected V, which would ordinarily be followed by I of the recapitulation. Instead, he brings about the I by moving, in the most ingenious way, to an augmented-sixth chord on *G*♭ (at the end of m. 119), which acts as a neighboring-note harmony of the forthcoming I. The deeper reason for avoiding the V is that by writing I—III—I, *F—A—F*, Brahms presents the symphony's, and his own personal, motto in gigantic enlargement: *frei aber froh* ("free but glad"). The V finally appears, with great emphasis, in the Coda.

Beethoven would not have been the innovator that he was if he had not explored further possibilities of dealing with sonata form. In his String Quintet op. 29, he made I—(VI)—IV—V the basis for exposition and development section: the IV opens the development, while the VI, which ends the exposition, acts as a third-divider within the descending fifth I—IV. The IV then proceeds to V at the end of the development. (For the same bass progression, on a smaller scale, see Fig. 37a and Fig. 30b, mm. 10–16.) One advantage of this progression is that it provides as many as four stable points in exposition and development, as compared to three in I—III—V and only two in I—V. Strangely, Beethoven seems not to have used I—VI—IV—V again until much later—in the first movements of the Piano Trio in *B*♭ Major op. 97, and the Piano Sonatas op. 106 and 111. (According to an unpublished analysis of op. 106 by Schenker, which is in my possession, the V in the first movement appears in m. 226. In the Adagio, which is also in sonata form and likewise shows I—(VI)—IV—V, the IV occurs in m. 84, together with the background neighboring note d^3.) Other instances in which the exposition moves to VI are the first movement of the Triple Concerto, the Ninth Symphony, and the Quartets op. 95, 130, and 132. In the Triple Concerto and op. 95, the VI probably has to be understood as a neighboring note of the eventual V, and not as a third-divider as in the works mentioned before. It would lead too far astray, however, to discuss the specific function of the VI in the other three, late compositions.

Again it ought to be noted that Domenico Scarlatti employed I—VI—IV—V—I in at least one instance (Sonata in *B*♭ Major, Longo 500, K. 545). Both Schubert and Brahms used the progression occasionally: Schubert in his *Unfinished* Symphony, Brahms in the Piano Quintet in *F* Minor: measures 1, 34, 122, 150 (this reading is based on unpublished notes by Schenker; see also *Harm.* § 131). A curious instance of this progression is Schubert's early Sonata op. 164 in *A* Minor. Here I—VI—IV—V—I spans all three parts of the first movement, in such a way that the recapitulation begins on IV. (Discussion of further irregularities in Schubert's sonata movements is not pertinent here.)

Beethoven used still another bass progression in the Scherzo of his Ninth Symphony: $\begin{smallmatrix} D—C:\| —B♮—A—(B♭)—A \\ \text{I}\underline{}\text{V}\underline{} \end{smallmatrix}$. Here *C*, at the end of the exposition, is the first passing tone in the fourth-progression that leads from I to V.

Finally, one might describe as borderline cases of sonata form the first movement of Brahms's Violin Sonata in *G* Major and that of his Fourth Symphony, where the development sections begin on I. (A forerunner of these compositions is Haydn's late Piano Sonata in *D* Major, Hob. 51.) It is obvious that the background of such sonata movements differs greatly from what is shown in Figs. 23 to 26. In contrast, the last movements of the First, Second, and Third Symphonies by Brahms, occasionally called "modified sonata forms," are essentially rondos. (Oster)⟩

Section 4: Four-part Form

§ 317. Four-part form

Four-part form is given too little attention in theory. It is most often considered to be a sort of sonata form, in some way altered or mutilated. In actuality, the four-part form is just as independent as the two- or three-part forms. It is found especially in the slow movements of sonatas, chamber works, or symphonies, and its content reads: A_1—B_1 : A_2—B_2.

The unity of this form, too, is guaranteed only by the fundamental line and the bass arpeggiation. B_1 rests upon V, or is at least moving toward it, whereas B_2 is based on the I.

The slow movements of the following piano sonatas by Beethoven exemplify this form:

In op. 2 no. 1, A_1 has the structure of a small song form, B_1 shows the fifth-progression g^2—c^1 over V, and B_2 shows the same fifth-progression over I.

		A_1 —B_1		: A_2—B_2
op. 2 no. 3	: E I	$I^{\natural 3}$—$\natural III$—IV—$\sharp IV$—V	: I	—I *17
op. 7	: C I	—$\flat VI$—IV—V		: I —I
op. 10 no. 1	: $A\flat$ I	—($II^{\natural 3}$)—V		: I —I
op. 22	: $E\flat$ I	—$V^{5-\flat 7}$		: I —I
op. 31 no. 2	: $B\flat$ I	—V		: I —I

See also the Andante in the Fourth Symphony of Brahms.

Like the two-part form, the four-part form has two major sections with similar content. However, the four-part form brings more emphasis to the B_1 part in that it more strongly works out the motion to V, as well as the V itself. Thus in the second part the I—the main tonality—receives a still greater reinforcement, for here B_2 with its additional voice-leading events also appears on I.

Section 5: Rondo Form

§ 318. The concept of rondo form

When two three-part song forms are so combined that the last part of the first three-part form simultaneously becomes the first part of the second three-part form, a five-part form arises: A_1—B—A_2—C—A_3, which, after an old dance, is called "rondo." Thus, this five-part ordering derives from a duple ordering in the background (cf. § 287 and Fig. 138).

This principle, the combining of three-part forms, also makes it possible to connect more than two such forms; for instance, the combining of three three-part forms gives rise to a seven-part rondo. The form can appear in both slow and fast movements; it can be brief or extended without necessitating the differentiation "small" or "large" (§ 308).

§ 319. The individual parts

Some commentary on the individual parts:

A_1: If A_1 is to return several times (not only remaining in motion but also having the ability to counterbalance sections of strong contrast), it must in itself not be overburdened with too much inner tension—whether at a slow or fast tempo. Apart from this consideration, any type of composing-out is possible; the two- or three-part song form lends itself most suitably. The very nature of the three-part song forms on which the rondo is based (§ 318) causes the A_2 and A_3 to appear always in the main tonality.

B_1: Since the contrasting sections B_1, B_2, C, and D are basically middle sections of three-part song forms, they are to be composed in the ways set forth in § 310.

---

*17. Corrected in accord with earlier notes by Schenker. (Oster)

Fig. 155

As in these examples, B_1 usually begins after A_1 has come to a full close. Such a clear-cut beginning of B_1 does not always supply the V immediately: often the V is reached by way of auxiliary cadences, as in Fig. 155, 1. Thus B_1 encompasses the motion both to and from V, including the illusory key which V expresses in the foreground. There can, however, also be a transition from A_1 to B_1, as for example in the Rondo of Beethoven's op. 2 no. 3.

C: Frequently this part also begins independently, after a complete close of A_2. It makes no difference whether it is based upon III or upon IV, as in the Rondo from Beethoven's op. 2 no. 3 [or makes use of a mixture as in Fig. 155,1].*18

§ **320.** Liberties in the rondo form

The dance in which the rondo form has its origin consisted of the actual *rondeau* (refrain) as the main section and interpolated *couplets*, contrasting sections which signalled the entrance of new pairs of dancers. When the rondo became an art form, it held for a long time to its basic principle, as though it were still to be used for dancing. Hence the refrain always appeared in the same tonality. With the progressive development of the art of prolongation, and particularly the art of improvisation, it became possible for C. P. E. Bach, for example, to vary the key of the A section in his rondos so that not only the keys of the contrasting sections but also those of the A_2

*18. In the first edition of this book, Fig. 155,2 appeared as Fig. 155,3. The original Fig. 152,2 showed a broad analysis of the Largo from Beethoven's Sonata op. 2 no. 2, which Schenker interpreted as being written in a nine-part rondo form, plus coda (mm. 1, 9, 13, 21, 32, 40, 44, 50, 68). This interpretation is so obviously misconceived that the editor of the second German edition omitted the example; and I did not feel that it should be reinstated. It can be assumed from Schenker's earlier notes on this movement that this analysis might well not have been his final thought about the matter. (Oster)

and A_3 differed from the main tonality. Later composers, more concerned with the organic coherence of the whole, tended to base their rondos on the three-part song form and hence maintained the A section in the main tonality. Only within a larger passing motion did they occasionally allow an A section to appear in a different (illusory) key. This liberty creates the effect of a developmental section, but such a passage, strictly speaking, belongs to a particular contrasting section, to a C or D. Thus in Beethoven's Rondo op. 129 (Fig. 102,2), the illusory keys are subordinate to the higher concept of a motion-from-the-inner-voice, which leads to the neighboring note, the background tone that gives rise to the contrasting section. In Fig. 155,3 a rather astonishing example of such a liberty is seen. The bass reveals two cadences; this precludes a return to the main tonality at the points designated by the asterisks. The form here approaches that of the freest rondos of C. P. E. Bach.

Occasionally the repetition of the contrasting section B_2 follows immediately upon C; that is, A_3 is omitted between C and B_2. Such a free treatment is sometimes confused with a development section as it would be found in sonata form (cf. Mozart, Piano Quartet in *G* Minor).

Possible abbreviations of the A_2 or A_3 sections, or their appearances in embellished form, in no way negate the rondo form.

§ **321.** Distinction between the rondo and other forms

The significant difference between the rondo and the sonata form lies in the fact that the latter involves a forward thrust to $\dfrac{\hat{2}}{V}$ ⟨where an interruption in the sense of the structural division occurs—§ 312⟩; this motion is not present in the rondo. The consequence and effect of this thrust was discussed in § 313.

Frequently, in a three-part form, the b section belonging to A_1 is read as a B_1 section, and the real form, A_1 (a_1—b—a_2)—B—A_2, is thought to be a rondo. Such a misunderstanding is due to a confusion of levels. This also accounts for the fact that so many larger pieces such as nocturnes, novellettes, and intermezzi are sometimes considered to be "small" rondos, when they really are three-part forms into whose A_1 section a small three-part form has been built.

A simple juxtaposition of B_1 or C has a better effect than a well-intentioned but obviously contrived bridge from A_1 to B_1 or from A_2 to B_2, as, for example, in the Rondo in $E\flat$ Major by Hummel. Here the desire to go beyond his means forces the composer to accentuate the very sectionalization which he clearly wished to avoid—and the bridges remain very superficial. How gratifying it is, in contrast, to find the parts so frankly set off from one another in Mozart's a-minor Rondo! Even Mozart, the same master who was capable of handling the rondo form with the most abundant freedom, was content to use such a simple form. [See also the rondos in Beethoven's op. 7 and 22.]

Section 6:   Fugue

§ 322.   The content of the fugue

Growing out of imitation, the fugue became the first unified form of larger dimensions. The fifth-relation between the first three entries (subject, answer, subject) provided the form with direction and stability. Once it had gained some power, this principle penetrated the other parts of the fugue and helped to make it possible for the fugue to come under the control of the fundamental structure, of fundamental line and bass arpeggiation. Just this relationship to middleground and background enabled the master composers to treat the entrances and imitative content of the foreground in very free fashion. I refer the reader to the examples of fugue in *Der Tonwille* and in the *Jahrbücher* ["Das Organische der Fuge," *Jahrb. II*].

Fig. 156

Ex. 1: One can hear this fugue correctly only if one keeps in mind the indicated relationships which the fundamental line and the bass arpeggiation establish. Let us compare this with Riemann's explanation in his *Katechismus der Fugen-komposition*. Riemann calls so many events "complete and incomplete forms of the inversion," or answers of the subject "with various modifications" (e.g., in mm. 8–9, 13–15, 17–19, 18–20, 21–23). But in the light of the relationships mentioned above, all of these events have a far different intention than merely to provide "answers" to the theme. The various specific goals of the composition have such an obvious prominence that any existing relationships to the "subject" must become less conspicuous. In no fugue can such relationships be defined by rule.

Only this type of fugal writing belongs to the realm of art; in contrast to it stands the fugal composition which follows a rigid plan of entries. Often it is just such mechanically assembled fugues which the unschooled ear finds easiest to assimilate, since they indulge in orgies of readily recognizable repetition, with their entrances almost rattling in the ear [§ 254].

Despite the fact that each one exhibits a different design, the fugues of J.S. Bach are genuine fugues in the strictest sense; they are always determined by the subject, by its dimensions and harmonic content, and are controlled by a fundamental structure.

Handel followed perhaps even more hidden fugal paths than did Bach. Although his fugues are monuments to a freedom which seems to scorn all organic bonds, each one nevertheless fulfills a fundamental structure. I am reserving an example of Handel's fugal technique—the Fugue of the Suite no. 2 in F Major—for a new series of graphic analyses *(Urlinie-Tafeln)*; it can only be presented in a detailed picture [see § 218, Fig. 92, 1].

Haydn and Mozart were unable to maintain the high state of fugal art reached in the works of Bach and Handel. Neither did Beethoven achieve it, despite the Fugue in op. 106, whose bass progression is briefly indicated in Ex. 2 of Fig. 156, and despite the Fugue in op. 110, which is bound up with an Adagio movement. Mendelssohn comprehended very well how freely Bach and Handel treated the fugue, and consequently he decondensed, as it were, and demechanized the entrances in his fugues. On the other hand, he distributed the entrances too lavishly, which made them lose significance. Only Brahms again comes closer to Bach.

An applied fugal technique, consisting of a play of the first entries only, is to be found in various situations. In older forms it is often encountered in suites, at the beginning of a gigue, and also at the beginning of shorter preludes. In classical music there are examples in Beethoven's Quartet op. 59 no. 3, last movement, in the Trio of his Fifth Symphony, and even in a transitional passage in the last movement of Mozart's *Jupiter* Symphony.

Without improvisational gift, that is, without the ability to connect the composition to the middleground and background, no good fugue can ever be written.

Section 7: Variations

§ 323. Variations

The theme of a set of variations can have an undivided form—as in Fig. 152,4—a two-part form, or a three-part form as in

Fig. 157

A set of variations can be unified most naturally by means of a gradual increase in the motion, that is, progressing from larger to ever smaller note values. This technique, although

used for centuries, was employed by Beethoven even in his op. 111 and op. 127.

An ordering into groups, usually coupled with an increase of motion and an alternation of major and minor, was also familiar to the older masters. For example, in Handel's Chaconne in *G* Major, variations 1–8 show an increase of motion, 9–16 are in minor with an increase in motion, 17–21 are in major, with variation 17 repeating variation 7. See also Mozart's *A*-Major Sonata.*[19]

Brahms devised a new way of connecting one variation to another by means of hidden organic relationships between the diminutions. This I have pointed out in my discussion of the *Handel* Variations, op. 24, in *Der Tonwille* 8/9. ⟨Compare also the *Haydn* Variations, op. 56.⟩

The use of a more extended song form as a variation-theme often made it possible for the masters to create a piece of considerable length by embellishing the theme only two or three times. Such a piece might be an independent composition—for example, Haydn's Andante in *F* Minor ⟨Fig. 48,1⟩—or a part of a sonata or symphony—for example, the Adagio of Beethoven's Ninth Symphony. Young composers would be well advised to continue to use this form.

In addition to variations on a theme in undivided form (as in Bach's "Aria variata" ⟨Fig. 152,4⟩ or the *Goldberg* Variations) there are the earlier forms, the passacaglia and the chaconne. In the passacaglia (Fig. 20,1), the bass usually begins alone, as if it were a fugue subject. Variations follow over this same bass, which, however, does not exclude the possibility that the bass theme can also appear in the upper parts, as it does in the Bach *c*-minor Passacaglia or in the Finale of Brahms's *Haydn* Variations, op. 56. The fact that the bass begins alone distinguishes the passacaglia from the so-called basso ostinato, exemplified in Handel's *Saul* and some of his organ concertos; the "Crucifixus" in Bach's *b*-minor Mass; the "Zum

*[19]. Passage (Q), omitted here, is supplied in Appendix 4. (Rothgeb)

Schluss" of Brahms's *Neue Liebeslieder*, op. 65. To a certain extent the basso ostinato is an applied passacaglia technique, just as there is an applied fugal technique.

Conversely, in the chaconne a short theme, designed to support a large number of variations, is usually given to the soprano. In the brevity of its theme and the profusion of its variations the chaconne is related to the passacaglia, which accounts for the frequent confusion of these two forms in the older literature. The difference between them lies in the role played by bass and soprano. Nevertheless, in the Finale of Brahms's Fourth Symphony, the stating of the theme first in the upper register should not deceive us with regard to its inherent bass character—hence the passacaglia form. Indeed, the theme begins its journey toward the bass with the very first variation (Violin I), continuing in the second variation (Violas) until in variation 4 it is anchored in the bass. Similarly, the last movement of Handel's Suite No. 7 in *G* Minor rightly bears the title "Passacaille," despite the appearance of the theme in the soprano. The difference between passacaglia and chaconne perhaps lies in the fact that the chaconne tends toward songlike diminutions, while the passacaglia tends to emphasize a prolonged bass arpeggiation.

§ 324. Epilogue

It should be the task of music history to trace the paths along which form, as I have presented it here, has developed. The key to form lies, in some hidden way, in the number of parts. Just as 2, 3, 4, and 5 differ from one another, so do the forms derived from these numbers differ in their inner nature and significance. Strangely, in agreement with the principle of the number 5 which I mentioned in my *Harmony* (§ 11), the number five also represents the limit in the world of form. The above-mentioned seven-part rondo (§ 318) is only an extension of the five-part form, which leaves the essential nature of the rondo untouched.

Individual movements within older forms such as the suite or the concerto frequently offer more difficulties to the understanding than, for example, a sonata movement by Beethoven. The principles of voice-leading and especially those of linear progressions are, of course, the same in both; but in older music the foreground diminutions, which conform more closely to strict counterpoint, render insight more difficult ⟨§ 230⟩. Also, despite the unparalleled mastery of their voice-leading, the linear progressions themselves are not as sweeping or determinative of form as those in the works of the later masters. This, too, is related to the continuous strictness of the diminutions. Although the dances are, of course, written in two- or three-part song form, doubts may occasionally arise as to the exact identity of their form. For example: is the Allemande in the *E*-Major *French* Suite of Bach (Fig. 76,4), which shows $\hat{8}$—$\hat{1}$ with a neighboring note to $\hat{5}$, a three-part or a two-part form? The sparse tonal material does not permit a three-part form to evolve in any definitive way.

In most cases the older masters organize longer movements according to the arpeggiation I—V—I, with an extended prolongation of V. This, however, does not give rise to a three-part form; much rather the effect is of illusory keys spread out around a neighboring note of V:

Fig. 158

⟨cf. Fig. 76,9 and § 197⟩.

Similarly, in the sonatas of C.P.E. Bach, the forward thrust from $\hat{3}$ to $\hat{2}$, or from $\hat{5}$ to $\hat{2}$, is so brief that no inner need arises for the kind of development that characterizes the sonatas of a later period.

Appendixes

Appendix 1

Contents of Figures (Works Arranged by Composer)

CONTENTS OF FIGURES (WORKS ARRANGED BY COMPOSER)

Appendix 2

List of References to Figures

Appendix 3

Works of Heinrich Schenker[1]

The following is a list of Schenker's major publications, both in the original German as well as in English editions and translations. The German publications marked with an asterisk are in print.

Ein Beitrag zur Ornamentik. Vienna: Universal Edition, 1904.
    * New and enlarged edition, 1908. (See also under English translations.)
Neue musikalische Theorien und Phantasien.
    Vol. I: *Harmonielehre.* Stuttgart: Cotta, 1906. (See also under English translations.)
    Vol. II, Part I: *Kontrapunkt I.* Vienna: Universal Edition, 1910.
            Part II: *Kontrapunkt II.* Vienna: Universal Edition, 1922.
    Vol. III: *Der freie Satz.* Vienna: Universal Edition, 1935. * Second edition, edited and revised by Oswald Jonas. Vienna: Universal Edition, 1956.

---

*1. A complete, comprehensive, carefully annotated list of Schenker's writings is to be found in David Beach, "A Schenker Bibliography" (*Journal of Music Theory* 3, no. 1 [1969]: 2–26; a revised edition has been published in *Readings in Schenker Analysis,* ed. Maury Yeston [New Haven: Yale University Press, 1977]). This bibliography also includes the most important books, monographs, and articles by other authors.

J.S. Bach. *Chromatische Phantasie und Fuge, Erläuterungsausgabe.* Vienna: Universal Edition, 1909. * Newly revised edition by Oswald Jonas. Vienna: Universal Edition, 1970.
* *Beethovens neunte Sinfonie.* Vienna: Universal Edition, 1912.
Erläuterungsausgabe der letzten fünf Sonaten Beethovens. Vienna: Universal Edition.
    Op. 109, published 1913.
    Op. 110, published 1914.
    Op. 111, published 1915.
    Op. 101, published 1920.
    (Op. 106 was never published.)
    * New edition of Op. 101, 109, 110, 111, revised by Oswald Jonas. Vienna: Universal Edition, 1970–71.
Der Tonwille, 10 issues. Vienna: A. Gutmann Verlag, 1921–24.
* *Beethovens fünfte Sinfonie* (reprinted from *Der Tonwille*). Vienna: Universal Edition. (See also under English translations.)
Das Meisterwerk in der Musik. München: Drei Masken Verlag.
    Jahrbuch I, published 1925.
    Jahrbuch II, published 1926.
    Jahrbuch III, published 1930.
    * Photographic reprint in one volume. Hildesheim: Georg Olms Verlag, 1974. (See also under English translations.)

Fünf Urlinie-Tafeln. New York: David Mannes School, and Vienna: Universal Edition, 1932. (See also under English editions.)

* *Brahms, Oktaven und Quinten.* Vienna: Universal Edition, 1934. (See also under English editions.)

Editions of Music

* *Ph. Em. Bach, Klavierwerke* (selections). Vienna: Universal Edition, 1902.

Beethoven, Klaviersonaten: Nach den Autographen und Erstdrucken rekonstruiert eon Heinrich Schenker. Vienna: Universal Edition, 1921–23.

   * New edition, revised by Edwin Ratz. Vienna: Universal Edition, 1947. (See also under English editions.)

Beethoven, Sonata Op. 27 No. 2. Facsimile, with an introduction by Schenker. Vienna: Universal Edition, 1921.

English Editions and Translations

"J.S. Bach, The Largo from Sonata No. 3 for Unaccompanied Violin" (from *Das Meisterwerk in der Musik,* vol. 1). Translated by John Rothgeb. In *The Music Forum,* vol. 4. New York: Columbia University Press, 1976.

"J.S. Bach, The Sarabande of Suite No. 3 for Unaccompanied Violoncello" (from *Das Meisterwerk in der Musik,* vol. 2). Translated by Hedi Siegel. In *The Music Forum,* vol. 2. New York: Columbia University Press, 1970.

Beethoven, Complete Piano Sonatas. Reprint of the edition of 1921–23, with an introduction by Carl Schachter. New York: Dover, 1975.

"Beethoven, Fifth Symphony, First Movement." Translated by Elliott Forbes. In *Beethoven, Fifth Symphony* (Norton Critical Scores). New York: Norton, 1971.

"Brahms, Octaves and Fifths." Translated and annotated by Thomas Mast. In *The Music Forum,* vol. 5. New York: Columbia University Press, 1979.

"A Contribution to the Study of Ornamentation." Translated by Hedi Siegel. In *The Music Forum,* vol. 4. New York: Columbia University Press, 1976.

Five Graphic Music Analyses. Photographic reprint of *Fünf Urlinie-Tafeln,* with an introduction by Felix Salzer. New York: Dover, 1969.

Harmony. Edited and annotated by Oswald Jonas. Translated by Elisabeth Mann Borgese. Chicago: University of Chicago Press, 1954; (paperback edition) Boston: M.I.T. Press, 1973.

"Organic Structure in Sonata Form" (from *Das Meisterwerk in der Musik,* vol. 2). Translated by Orin Grossman. *Journal of Music Theory* (1968). Reprinted in *Readings in Schenker Analysis,* ed. Maury Yeston. New Haven: Yale University Press, 1977.

Appendix 4

Omissions from the Original German Edition

Translated by John Rothgeb

A large portion of the text translated here was already omitted from the second German edition. A few additional passages included here were excised by Ernst Oster in his translation.

These excerpts exhibit all of the difficulties of language alluded to by Oster in his preface. And one particular source of difficulty, the use of metaphor, causes unusually severe problems for translation. Moreover, certain words such as *Wurzel* (root) and *Zusammenhang* (coherence, inner connection) are used repeatedly with subtle changes in meaning or emphasis; in such cases, different English words are used to render a single German word, and there is necessarily some loss of meaning. This is partially compensated by the inclusion in parentheses, where appropriate, of the original German expression. Some especially elliptical passages required a few words of explanation; footnotes have been added for this purpose.

Special thanks are due to Professor Juergen Thym for his careful reading of the manuscript and for his valuable suggestions concerning some unusually problematical passages.

A

Only an artist in language invents words in a way that truly reflects their roots.*[1] The masses then transmute the artist's words in countless dialects that vary with landscape, mountain, valley, town, and village. Their ear does not reach down to the root; their memory seldom extends past grandfather. It is the same in music: a mode of thinking based on the roots of tone *(ein Tonwurzelhaftes Denken)* is given only to the genius. The others write fugues, sonatas, symphonies, and so forth, as though in careless dialects whose degenerate condition *(Abfall von der Wurzel)* is plain to see.

Nebular spirals solidify and become stars. Music, born from the original irrational state as if from a nebular spiral, and made ever more dense with diminution, grew into a star in the heavens of the spirit. But how strange it is: mankind is more interested in the most distant star in the firmament than in music, the star of the spirit's heaven! May the light of that noble star shine on! It surely is captured and protected in my eyes, but what will happen when my eyes have closed for good?

For the adherent of my doctrines an endless field of study opens up. He sees the ostensibly old creation of our masters anew, as if at the moment of its birth; he feels as the author of the Bible must have felt on being allowed to hail God's creation with the first words of the most blessed wonderment, the most ecstatic tremor.

Although favored by God, the genius is nevertheless removed ⟨from pure art⟩ by the material in which he works. The non-genius, however, is twice removed—by the material, and also by genius itself. The non-genius misses the complexity of genius; the genius appears too simple to him. The non-genius feels himself obliged to transcend the genius.

*[1]. *Nur ein Sprachschöpfer erfindet Worte wirklich wurzelhaft. Wurzel* (root) and its derivative *wurzelhaft* (rootlike; of or pertaining to a root) are used in various metaphorical senses in this passage and elsewhere.

Only the genius is connected with God, not the people. For this reason it is necessary to strip the masses of their halo.*²

The geniuses of art are its saints, so to speak. Of course in art, as in the church, the number of saints is very small.

The leveling force to which average people are subject is never imposed upon them by political or, in a broader sense, spiritual dictators; it is, rather, like an infection which passes from one average person to another.

Imitation is no substitute for evolution.

In epochs deprived of genius there is much lamenting of the "irretrievably lost" gift of genius. But did the people ever truly possess this gift? The possession was only illusory, and so is the loss. A history of mankind that tells this truth has yet to be written.

It is said that each generation understands the works of the genius in a different way. I say: *no* generation understands them; but each generation *mis*understands them in a different way.

Those who come and go without having understood the world or themselves revolt mechanically against their forbears in order to gain space for living. They condemn their fathers as reactionary, and consider only themselves the true progressives. It is futile, however, to try to escape from the genius with such a cheap device!*³

B

If I am dedicated in heart and mind to the greatest masters of my art, how can I be considered eccentric or reactionary?

Concerning the law of large numbers: two, four, or eight people can easily be brought together by games, if necessary also by intellectual entertainment. Art can bring together as many as two or three thousand people. But to assemble and entertain 50,000 people—this can be accomplished only by bullfights, cock fights, massacres, pogroms: in short, a brutal ranting and raving, a demented and chaotic outcry. Art is incapable of uniting such large numbers.

It is the same in art as in politics. Just as "freedom" for all is no longer true freedom—it is merely a utopian dream to "reconcile the ideal form of the liberalism, which really wanted only a new selection

*². *Entgottung der Masse tut daher Not.*
*³. . . . *mit solchem billigen Kniff auch dem Genie entlaufen zu wollen!* To invoke "progress" does not compensate for the absence of genius.

of elite in place of the obsolete feudal order, with the great experience of society and its great metamorphoses" (Coudenhove-Kalergi)—so "art for everyone is not art" (E.J. Schindler, the painter, in his diary).

High art cannot be attained if it strives to fulfill common ends. But it is not the declining human species that has chosen to allow art to die: on the contrary, art, because misunderstood and unattained, has left the human species behind. But those who have been thus left behind by art call themselves *modern*!

Culture, tradition, the discipline of genius—these terms are all synonymous; they all have to do with the phenomenon of genius. Civilization, however, relinquishes the support of the genius in every respect. When a generation begins to want a new culture, when it attacks tradition and the discipline of genius, it contradicts the true essence of culture.

Just as there are economics conferences which are intended to combat the decline of the world economy, there should be also world conferences for the economics of the spirit, whose duty would be to combat decline in the spiritual domain. In consideration of the petty jealousy which would inevitably arise, it would be advisable to follow the practice of politics—to have, behind the official politicians of the spiritual, unofficial operatives who understand how to conduct affairs of the spirit securely.

C

Here we shall be concerned only with the way this principle manifests itself in art. Thus, for example, it is not only the historical drama whose special environment must come across to the audience: *every* drama presents a content whose meaning truly reveals itself to the audience only if they perceive the fundamental *(Wurzelhaft)* significance of the inner connections which find expression in it according to background, middleground, and foreground. Whenever we lose even the background of a drama, we possess the drama no more, as is the case, for example, with Greek drama.

The background in painting is visible; it requires neither justification nor explanation.

D

Whenever and wherever such heroes are lacking, the masses can never become a true nation *(Volk)*. It is only through individuals, and according to the law of origin, development, and present, that the masses can be forged into a nation.

Technological creativity is chiefly concerned with the expansion of man's habitat and spatial existence, or with establishing surface connections between distant points. All such creation yields only surface, only foreground.

E

Included in the elevation of the spirit to the fundamental structure is an uplifting, of an almost religious character, to God and to the geniuses through whom he works—an uplifting, in the literal sense, to the kind of coherence which is found only in God and the geniuses.

Between fundamental structure and foreground there is manifested a rapport much like that ever-present, interactional rapport which connects God to creation and creation to God. Fundamental structure and foreground represent, in terms of this rapport, the celestial and the terrestrial in music.

F

Just as life is an uninterrupted process of energy transformation, so the voice-leading strata represent an energy transformation in the life which originates in the fundamental structure.

G

With limited spiritual vision, composition is no more possible than speech. Certainly both can be undertaken with just such a handicap, but the results will show it.

The most basic necessities of life by themselves foster a certain expansion of the power of thinking. Men must learn how to communicate with each other so that with a joint effort they can wrest from nature, society, and state such benefits as are necessary to survival. This common effort necessarily must be infused with coherence (Zusammenhang), even with love; and as a result, a modicum of coherence and a certain degree of love enter into men's spirit and their language.

By contrast, music, as art, has no practical benefit to offer. Thus there is no external stimulus for expansion of the powers of musical creativity and music's artistic means. The expansion of creative vision, then, must spring from within itself, only from the special form of coherence that is proper to it, and the special love intrinsic to it.

Therefore, the person whose tonal sense is not sufficiently mature to bind tones together into linear progressions and to derive from them further linear progressions, clearly lacks musical vision and the love that procreates. Only living love composes, makes possible linear progressions and coherence—not metaphysics, so often invoked in the present time, or the much touted "objectivity"; these, in particular, have neither creativity nor breeding warmth.

H

Just this passion for flying over *4 drives people to revolt against nature. Nature hews to landscapes as rubrics according to which she arranges and attunes her creations. But modern man thinks he can ignore the differentiations of landscapes simply because he is able to fly over them. There is no doubt, however, that nature, like art, will win out. Just as nature will always place elephants and crocodiles, for example, where she can provide their life's necessities, so she will place a Beethoven—if indeed ever again—among the German people!

There is but one grammar of the linear progressions—the one described here in connection with the theory of coherence in music. It sufficed for the masters; therefore those without knowledge or capabilities felt it necessary to seek newer forms of coherence. But I repeat here what I have often said before: the fact that all of the masterworks manifest identical laws of coherence in no way precludes a diversity in essential nature among the masters.*5

I

Today this is recognized even by the most noted conductors.

J

Until now, all theory had to founder on the foreground, because theory selected and read only from the foreground, using it as the only source of phenomena to be considered.*6 The sorry state of theory,

*4. *Die Leidenschaft des Ueber-fliegens.*

*5. That is, the masters achieved variety and newness without seeking fundamentally new principles of coherence.

*6. The verb *scheitern* (founder) also means to fail, and it is used in both senses here: first, a theory that looks only at the foreground will not be able to see past it; and secondly, such a theory will be unable even to interpret the foreground correctly.

whose arrogance and pretentiousness match its erroneous content, is most accurately characterized by the fact that it labels a true musical hearing process as "musical research" *(Musikforschung)*; what is commonly called musical research, however, has nothing to do with music. How sad that such a perverse way of thinking finds a place even in Germany, where the greatest music-geniuses practiced their art!

If the Italians object that German music is "philosophical"—perhaps they will also describe by way of thinking as philosophy—we need not pay it any heed; for they use music only for texts and for the folk song, opera, and so forth. Music from the sidestreets and for the sidestreets, so to speak. To be sure, the sun shines on their streets; but if the streets beneath other skies enjoy less sunshine, the music of genius is as sun to those who dwell in them—a sun which illuminates and warms their souls, bathes their chambers in golden light, and even makes the landscape sunny!

Theory today has sunk so low that it hearkens to the mouths of children, accepting their utterances as artistically valid revelations, instead of passing on to children the lessons and principles that have been derived from the masterworks. It even attempts to teach a kind of collective art, and approaches musical creativity, which was, is, and will remain truly the gift of the few, with a purely mechanical way of thinking. Theory courses today have become literally hobby courses for unmusical children.

K

Our era was the first to try to manufacture national musical languages—a political hunger—somewhat in the way that industries are founded on the basis of so-called autarky.

L

At best, the course of culture moves in curves, something like this: ⟨original Fig. 13 follows⟩.

M

I am aware that with the present discussion I am the first to have recognized and demonstrated in artistic terms the profound difference between Italian and German diminution—that is, between Italian and German music. This difference, however, is not to be interpreted as if the Italian and German types were of equal significance within musi-

cal art. On the contrary, one thing should be made explicit: Italian music, always bound to words, must be appraised as merely a preliminary step toward the German, just as in previous epochs the period of irrationality, the first contrapuntal attempts, and the first paths of Italian diminution, etc., signified preliminary stages of development, never equally valid states. (May the writers of music history at last recognize this distinction and put it to use in their treatises!) This is in no way negated by the simultaneous existence of such various stages of artistic advancement, of a preliminary stage alongside the most advanced. In nature, different stages of evolution are found not only in succession but also contemporaneously. Isn't the simultaneous existence of the genius and the average person exactly such a contemporaneity? (See Fig. 13.) However, in the last analysis, the standard for judging evolutionary plateaux derives from art as pure idea. Whoever has once perceived the essence of a pure idea—whoever has fathomed its secrets—knows that such an idea remains ever the same, ever indestructible, as an element of an eternal order. Even if, after millenia, such an idea should finally desert mankind and vanish from the foreground of life—that foreground which we like to call chaos—it still partakes of God's cosmos, the background of all creation whence it originated.

Therefore let all men, be they philosophers or not, cease to ruminate on the meaning of life, to lament life's ostensible meaninglessness. How can men hope to stumble upon the true meaning of life when, constrained by mortal organs, they must see immediately the end for each beginning, the fulfillment of each promise, the reward for each good deed, and the punishment for each crime in order to comprehend or even form a notion of the concepts of beginning and end. The "chaos" of the foreground belongs with the universal order of the background; it is one with it. All of the brief time spans of the foreground's chaos fall into the endless time continuum of the universe; let us finally learn humbly to love and honor the chaos for the sake of the cosmos, which is God's own. To partake of the cosmos and its eternal ideas— this alone signifies a life of beauty, true immortality in God.

N

Even the life of pure ideas moves in repetitions, for each of the individual manifestations of such ideas represents a repetition. In the history of humanity we see epochs in which ideas are disseminated and stamp mankind with the mark of evolution; but we also see epochs which, lacking any such working-out of an idea, are destined to be periods of decline.

O

I doubt that the Greeks attained complete clarity regarding the nature of their prosody. If, as I have demonstrated, all systems and scale formations which have been and are taught in the music and theories of various peoples were and are merely self-deceptions, why should I take seriously the Greeks' belief in the correctness of their prosody? Surely an understanding of their poetic meter would have involved first of all the discovery of the natural metric foot, and then how it fitted into a binary or ternary metric scheme. The poetic verse is thus illuminated, so to speak, from two sources at once: the metric foot, whose birthplace is the word, and the schematic meter which runs its course independently. It is this dual illumination which secures the special charm of verse, but at the same time creates an uncertain quality and also leads to insecure theoretical interpretation. Thus in Greek poetic theory it may have been only misunderstandings which led to the establishment of a multiplicity of poetic meters, whose explanation evidently would lie in the aforementioned duality. It is possible that the Greek words were based exclusively on binary and ternary patterns—the binary being the trochee,— ∨, and the ternary the dactyl,— ∨ ∨. It is questionable whether the Greek language really made use of an iambus, ∨ —, or of ternary schemes such as ∨∨—, or ∨— ∨.

The German language, too, appears to be based on trochaic and dactylic patterns. The illusion of iambuses and other words having metrically weak beginnings evidently has its origin in the use of prefixes; for example, *Geduld = dulden, Gewalt = walten*, etc. Therefore in German, too, the natural poetic foot of the words often conflicts with a predetermined metric schema. But in any case a mechanical application of the many Greek meters to the German language is not permissible (cf. Marpurg, *Anleitung zur Singe-Composition*, 1758).

P

The phenomenon of form in the foreground can be described in an almost physical-mechanical sense as an energy transformation—a transformation of the forces which flow from the background to the foreground through the structural levels.

Q

In the variation movement of Mozart's A-Major Piano Sonata, K. 331 ⟨300i according to Koechel-Einstein⟩, the increase of motion from sixteenth-notes to sixteenth-note triplets from Variation 1 to Variation 2 is interrupted by Variations 3 (minor) and 4 (major, with the left hand crossing over); Variation 5 brings thirty-second notes (Adagio), and Variation 6, Allegro, concludes the movement.

Appendix 5

List of Terms

This list of terms is given in two parts—German-English and English-German—primarily to afford the reader some access to other works of Schenker, most of which have not appeared yet in translation. I have not attempted to give definitions, for the book itself supplies them in the text or sometimes, more accessibly, in the musical examples. Except in the case of more generally used terms which occur throughout the book, I have provided references to sections in the text and to particular examples that will help to elucidate these terms.

German-English

(Alternative translations which the reader may find in other publications are shown in square brackets.)

Anstieg: (initial) ascent
Ausfaltung: unfolding
Auskomponierung: composing-out; (sometimes:) prolongation
Brechung: arpeggiation
Deckton: cover tone
Dehnung: expansion
Diminution: diminution

Gliederung: (structural) division
Hintergrund: background
Höherlegung: ascending octave transfer, [ascending register transfer, higher-placement]
Kopfton: primary melodic tone
Koppelung, Oktav-Koppelung: (octave) coupling
Lagenwechsel: change of register
Leerlauf: unsupported stretch
Mischung: mixture
Mittelgrund: middleground
Nebennote: neighboring note, neighbor, [auxiliary note, adjacent note]
obligate Lage: obligatory register
Schicht, Stimmführungs-Schicht: (structural) level, [stratum]
springender Durchgang: leaping passing tone
Stufe: (harmonic) degree, [step, (scale) degree]
Teiler, Oberquint-Teiler: divider, dividing dominant
Terzteiler: third-divider
Tieferlegung: descending octave transfer, [descending register transfer, lower-placement]
Uebergreifen: reaching-over, [overlapping, upper-shift]

Unterbrechung: interruption

Untergreifen, Untergreifszug: motion from an inner voice, [reaching up from an inner voice, underlapping]

Urlinie: fundamental line, [primordial line]

Ursatz: fundamental structure, [primordial structure]

Verwandlungen, Verwandlungs-Schichten: transformations, transformation levels

Vordergrund: foreground

Wechselnote: accented passing tone

Zug: linear progression; (short form:) progression; [line, span]

   Terzzug: linear progression of a third; (short form:) third-progression

   Quartzug: linear progression of a fourth; (short form:) fourth-progression

   similarly: *Quintzug, Sextzug, Septzug, Oktavzug*

English-German

arpeggiation: Brechung. §§ 125 ff., Fig. 40; § 230, Fig. 100

   bass arpeggiation in the sense of I—V—I of the fundamental structure: §§ 2, 15 ff.

ascent (initial ascent): Anstieg. §§ 120 ff., Figs. 37–39

background: Hintergrund

composing-out: Auskomponierung

coupling (octave coupling): Koppelung, Oktav-Koppelung. §§ 152–54, Fig. 49; §§ 240 ff., Fig. 108

cover tone: Deckton. § 267, Fig. 75

degree (scale degree, harmonic degree): Stufe. §§ 276 ff.

diminution: Diminution. §§ 251–66, Figs. 117–25

division (structural division): Gliederung. §§ 87–100, Figs. 21–27

divider (dividing dominant): Teiler, Oberquint-Teiler. § 89, Figs. 21 a; 42, 2

   third-divider: Terzteiler. § 279, Fig. 131

expansion: Dehnung. § 297

foreground: Vordergrund

fundamental line: Urlinie. §§ 2–6

fundamental structure: Ursatz. Fig. 1, §§ 1–4, 20–21

interruption: Unterbrechung. §§ 87, 90, Figs. 21–27

leaping passing tone: springender Durchgang. § 172

level (structural level): Schicht, Stimmführungs-Schicht, Verwandlungs-Schicht. See *transformation levels.*

middleground: Mittelgrund.

mixture: Mischung. § 102, Figs. 28–29; § 193, Fig. 73

motion from an inner voice: Untergreifen, Untergreifzug. §§ 135–36, Fig. 42; § 233, Fig. 102

obligatory register: obligate Lage. § 260

octave transfer, ascending: Höherlegung. §§ 147–50, Fig. 47; § 238

octave transfer, descending: Tieferlegung. § 151, Fig. 48; § 239

primary melodic tone: Kopfton. §§ 113, 115, 121

progression (linear progression): Zug (Stimmführungszug). §§ 113–24, Figs. 33 ff.; § 203 with examples mentioned

reaching-over: Uebergreifen. §§ 129–33, Fig. 41; §§ 231–32. See also editorial comments following § 134

transformation levels, transformations: Verwandlungs-Schichten, Verwandlungen. §§ 30, 46–49. See also § 45. (Several levels are shown in Fig. 22 b.)

unfolding: Ausfaltung. §§ 140–42, Fig. 43; § 234, Fig. 103

About the Translator

ERNST OSTER, 1908–1977

Ernst Oster was born in Mannheim, Germany on January 26, 1908. When he was still very young, his family moved to Hamburg, where he began his musical education. He showed a remarkable gift for the piano, and his early musical education was more a practical than a theoretical one. Indeed, it was through his activities as a performer that he first became interested in the work of Heinrich Schenker. He had come upon Schenker's annotated editions *(Erläuterungsausgaben)* of the last Beethoven sonatas and immediately realized that Schenker offered incalculably more to the serious musician than did any other theorist. That Oster first approached Schenker's work as a performer is, in a way, emblematic of his own later development as a musician and theorist. For, despite his formidable intellectual gifts and immense factual knowledge, he was convinced that musical analysis must be more than an intellectual activity, that the analyst—like the performer—must attempt an artistic recreation of the work. And he believed that Schenker's approach has as much to offer the practical musician—composer or performer—as the theorist or musicologist.

Oster was able to deepen his understanding of Schenker's work when, in his early twenties, he moved to Berlin, for there he had the opportunity to study with Oswald Jonas, Schenker's distinguished pupil and follower. Later, political conditions made it necessary for Oster to leave Germany. He first moved to Vienna, where he contributed to several issues of *Der Drei-klang*, a short-lived but important periodical, edited by Jonas and by Felix Salzer, and devoted to the Schenker approach.

The *Anschluss* of 1938 made another move necessary, and Oster emigrated to the United States. At that time, Schenker's widow entrusted to him a most valuable collection of Schenker's papers, fearing that the Nazis might destroy them. Oster devoted years to the study of this collection, which contains an enormous amount of unpublished material, including Schenker's preliminary work on *Der freie Satz*. Through this painstaking study, Oster was able to gain an insight into Schenker's way of thinking and of expressing himself that was unavailable to anyone else and that, together with his musical and intellectual gifts, made him uniquely well qualified to translate Schenker's difficult and often obscure writing.

During his later years, Oster led a quiet life, devoting himself to his music, his teaching (at the New England Conservatory and The Mannes College of Music), his friends, and—whenever time and weather permitted—to country walks and mountaineering. It was while on a hike in the hills of Orange County, New York, that he died suddenly on June 30, 1977.